THE LADY

BY MELLY MEL RICO

THE

LADY

BY
MELLY MEL RICO

Copyright©2018Melly Mel Rico. All rights reserved. Cover design by Melly Mel Rico and Elmondo Rico.
This book or parts thereof may not be reproduced in any form, stored in any retrieval system, or transmitted in any form by any means—electronic, mechanical, photocopy, recording, or otherwise—without prior written permission of the author, except as provided by United States of America copyright law.

For permission requests, email the author at mellyricorico@gmail.com

This work depicts actual events in the life of the author as truthfully as recollection permits and/or can be verified by research. Occasionally, dialogue consistent with the character or nature of the person speaking has been supplemented. All persons within are actual individuals. There are no composite characters. The names of individuals have been changed to respect their privacy.

Foreword

We all have a memory we never forget— a heartbreak, losing someone, betrayal, or something beautiful. Our memories shape our future. It is because of these memories that I am the person I am today. In regards to rejection or losing someone, it is human nature to grasp onto whatever we have left. As humans, we hold onto pain and nurture it because we feel like that's all we have left. Soon, this pain becomes our identity. I am hoping that my work in this book will give someone strength somewhere. If this person is you, I know how it feels. I was there once. I have been there done that, and now I make the t-shirts. Find your strength inside and focus on what you need to do. You're not alone.

As there are disturbing events in this work, my purpose is not to create any harm. My sole purpose is to express what I have experienced in my life. I want to show others that may have had similar experiences that you can keep going. You can do what you have always wanted to do even if people try to do anything they can to tear you down. Don't allow people to make you believe that you can't do it. You are strong. I promise.

I would like to thank the real-life members of the family portrayed in this book. I recognize that their memories of the events described in this book are different than my own. The book was not intended to hurt the family. I am sure that this book cannot do anymore harm that has already been done. Me, as the author do not regret any unintentional harm resulting from the publishing and marketing of "The Lady" because life happens and sometimes life happens more to others.

I am dedicating this book to my late Cheíí, Frank Nez.
March 17, 1930-July 16, 2016.
In third grade, I told you I'd write a book someday.
You smiled, hugged me, and said, "I know you will, Lady. You are a
great writer. It's your passion so, do it. Aww! My Lady!"
I always felt special growing up. You always called me, "The Lady." I
love you and miss you everyday, Cheíí. I hope you're proud of me.

For my Grandma, Rose Alice Nez. Thank you for being so loving. Your
food, especially your bread, is the best food I ever had in my entire life. You
always made sure there was bread on the table growing up.

For Tyler Denetdale, Nathaniel Denetdale, Daniel Denetdale, Nayeli
Rico, Nora Denetdale, and Kaliko Rico. You bring pure joy to my life and are very
special to me.

For my husband, my best friend, Elmondo Rico. Thank you for helping
me bringing it all together with coffee runs and support. I love you to the Moon
and back!

Sincerely,
"The Lady"

"We have to fight the injustices of our people (Diné) with education."
-Chief Manuelito

Contents

Chapter 1. Deer Caught in Headlights

Chapter 2. Challenger Deep

Chapter 3. Preparation

Chapter 4. Ceremony

Chapter 5. For the Money

Chapter 6. One Way Ticket

Chapter 7. Hey Arizona

Chapter 8. All Systems Down

Chapter 9. WTF

Chapter 10. Beauty in Chaos

Chapter 11. Morphine Memory

Chapter 12. Fuck-it

Chapter 13. Chop Chop

Chapter 14. Blast From the Past

Chapter 15. A New Destination

Chapter 1. Deer Caught in Headlights

"You have strength when you least expect it, my Lady. Hang on.
You're okay."

-Frank Nez

It's 2010. It's the era of social media supporting the deep narcissism of daily self-indulgence and alas the never-ending "selfies". Except, she wasn't into that. She has more important shit to deal with. As far as she knows, she doesn't want to be found. She doesn't want people to know what she's up to. She just wants to move on with her life.

It's been an irrational six months famished of normalcy. She just wants her modest life back.

She grabs the silver-colored, aluminum, door handle. She squeezes it releasing the latch and slides the double-glass sliding door to the right. She takes a few steps that lead her outside on the balcony. She smoothly slides the glass balcony door behind her.

Her silky, black hair is so long it goes down her back. She pulls her hoodie up over her long, black, shiny hair tied into a high ponytail. She reaches into her middle kangaroo pocket with her left hand.

She feels with her hand for the small hard box and pulls it out of her pocket. She takes a crisp, stiff, white cigarette out of the green cigarette box.

Her lips are dry, cracked, and stuck together. She presses the light brown filter side of the cigarette against her dry lips. She takes her sky blue BIC lighter out of her left pant pocket. She feels the bone cracking cold of the brisk air against her face, cheeks, and hands. She feels thousands of tiny pin needles stabbing her skin simultaneously. The unforgiving frozen air creates goose bumps on her delicate and soft skin. Her body stiffens up making her arm and leg muscles flex uncontrollably.

Her legs, arms, and hands are slightly shaking. The teeth chattering bitter cold claims the youthfulness and warmth of her skin making her skin crisp like the outside of a potato chip bag. The resentful cold burn of the frosty air stings her skin from pore to pore. Her body endures the pain of winter's cold blanket as she is now covered head to toe. As she moves her arms up and down from her side to her mouth to light her cigarette, she holds in her breath and squeezes her neck muscles. The bitter cold reminds her of home growing up.

She leans up against the wooden balcony. Her hands slightly tremble as she flicks her lighter to the end of her cigarette. Her dry, cracked lips suck the cigarette as the flame clings onto the white paper making it crackle. The flame grows bigger for a few seconds as it sets the cigarette on fire.

The bitter taste of tobacco hits the back of her throat as she inhales and holds her breath. As she inhales, she feels the arousing inferno burn of the tobacco smoke inside her lungs. She exhales with her mouth closed and feels the sensation of the smoke scorching through her lungs, up her throat, and out her nose.

The first exhale always makes her lightheaded and dizzy. She exhales the smoke once more through her nose. Three more sucks and puffs later, she looks down on the other apartment buildings.

For a few minutes she listens to the sound of cars driving by and car horns blare off in the distance. She sees a few people walking back and forth from the parking lot to their apartment. A few minutes turn into twenty minutes. She feels the calmness of her body and her breathing.

Cigarettes are the only things that help her forget. She doesn't want to think about what the fuck she is going to do next. She doesn't want to go anywhere knowing that he could be there looking for her. No matter where she went, she knew he would be there. She isn't scared. She just doesn't want to deal with the drama anymore. She just wants her life back. He already put her through six months of hell and back. All the pointless police reports she had reported on him were useless. She lost count of how many times she dealt with people yelling and fighting. She's never been personally exposed to any of it and to her it was all bullshit. A waste of time. Time that she knew she wouldn't get back and she was tired of it. Not only was she dealing with this white people world bullshit, the bullshit was knocking her off her ass spiritually, mentally, and emotionally, and even physically. She's Navajo and these elements in her life had a certain balance. It was almost like an earthquake ripping up every element in her life. She just wanted to move on. She didn't want to deal with any more of it. Any of it. What else could he add to it? She sure as hell doesn't want to find out.

Dakota, her friend, opens the sliding patio door and comes outside.

"What's up, girl? Whatcha doin'?" Dakota asks.

Melissa takes a puff of her cigarette and replies, "Nada. What's up?"

"Come on, girl. Let's go." Dakota says excitingly.

"Nah, I'm good." Melissa replies taking another puff of her cigarette looking off into the distance.

"Come on, girl!" Dakota says as she intertwines her right arm with Melissa's left arm.

Dakota whispers, "Come on. Some fresh air will do you good."

Melissa takes another puff, exhales smoke, and replies with a stoic face, "I *am* getting fresh air."

Melissa really doesn't want to go anywhere.

She thinks, "Man, why the fuck can't I just be left alone? Haven't I been through enough fucked up shit already?"

Melissa pauses for a moment and says under her breath.

"Fuck it," she says. "What else could happen?"

Melissa puts her cigarette out in the green decaf coffee tin can on the wooden balcony floor.

She replies with a stoic tone, "Fine, let's go."

Dakota jumps up and down happily with a grin on her face screaming with excitement. Dakota goes inside and grabs her purse on the couch. She follows Dakota. They go out the door. Dakota walks down the stairs of the second story apartment. Melissa follows Dakota down the stairs. In front of the stairs about twenty feet is apartment 132. Dakota's sister, Ruth, is sitting on the porch of the apartment texting on her phone.

Ruth looks up.

"What's up?" she says. "Where are you guys going? I was just about to smoke a cig."

Dakota replies with a smile, "To the movies, wanna come?"

Ruth answers, "Yeah, sure. Let me grab my purse."

Melissa and Dakota walk to Ruth's car. Ruth comes out to her car a few minutes later.

Dakota puts out her hand palm up and says to Ruth, "Keys. I'm driving."

Ruth gets the keys out of her pants pocket and throws it to Dakota. The car doors are unlocked. They open the doors and get in the car. Dakota sits in the driver's seat. Ruth sits next to Dakota in the passenger front seat. Melissa sits in the back seat behind Ruth. Dakota and Ruth buckle their seat belts following each other with their 'clicks'. Melissa pulls the seat belt away from the seat and slides her right hand down to the buckle. She holds the buckle with her right hand. Before she can feel where to buckle it into,

Dakota says, "Oh, my bad girl. The buckle is broken and doesn't work".

Dakota starts driving.

Dakota drives, looks in the rear view mirror, and asks Melissa, "So, what do you wanna see?"

Melissa softly sighs, "Whatever, bro. Doesn't matter."

Like an annoyed waitress working a double shift whipping out her small notepad and pen chewing her gum in a smacking manner rolling her eyes not wanting to take her assigned table's order, Melissa takes her android phone out of her left back pocket. Her phone is dark purple and very heavy. She swipes past the waterfall home screen on her touchscreen phone. Her right pointer finger 'taps' onto the only game on her phone, Angry Birds.

A local car dealership commercial plays faintly on the car radio as Dakota and Ruth are talking about what movie they want to see.

Ruth looks over at Dakota and asks Dakota, "Wanna see the second part to 'Hangover'?

Melissa takes a glance towards the front seat looking at Dakota. She sees Dakota turn the steering wheel clockwise with both hands a few times then counterclockwise three more times.

Dakota replies, "Nah, not really."

Melissa slightly bounces up and down as the car hits the potholes in the road. She continues to play Angry Birds on her phone as Dakota and Ruth talk.

Dakota asks, "Hey, what about Thor? Mel, wanna see Thor? Thor's cute. Meeellll? Melly Mel?"

Ruth interrupts Dakota and says, "Okay, yeah. I saw the previews. It looks good. Let's see that."

They pull up to the movie theatre parking lot a few moments later. Three car doors slam shut behind them. They walk towards the movie theatre. Melissa presses the side button of her phone to turn off the screen and slides her phone into her left back pants pocket.

They approach the front of the theatre and walk pass tall movie posters bordered with small yellow single light bulbs flashing. They approach the box office. They look at the listing of all the movies behind the movie theatre attendant.

Dakota looks up behind the movie theatre attendant, throws her hands up into the air, and exclaims. "Ah, fuck! We missed the movie!!"

Ruth replies, "Are you serious? That's okay we can come back. What should we do now?"

Dakota says, "Let's go get some ice cream. There's a spot I wanna try and it's on the way back home."

Ruth says, "Alright, yeah."

Melissa can feel both of the girls look at her.

Melissa shrugs her shoulders and replies calmly, "Yeah, sure, whatever. Let's go."

They get back into the car. Melissa sits behind the front passenger seat. She hears the seat belts 'click' in the front seat. She leans to her right and lifts her left butt cheek off the seat and slides her phone out of her left back pant pocket.

She presses the 'home' button to turn on her phone screen and continue her Angry Birds game.

She turns up the volume of the Angry Birds game. She 'clicks' on the 'resume' button. Melissa looks out her right side window and sees several businesses bunched up in small plazas. She sees plaza after plaza pass by as Dakota drives.

Dakota drives down a one-way street with two lanes. Melissa sees it's getting dark now. Five minutes ago, the sunset filled the sky with bright colors blasting of red and orange. That beautiful sunset is gone and the sky is now a dark dusty-brown quickly turning darker. They drive past traffic light after traffic light; green light after green light, then Dakota finally stops at a red light.

Dakota says happily. "Yayy! We are almost there."

As the traffic light turns green, Dakota takes a CD from the visor above her head and puts it in the car's CD player. She presses the button for it to play.

Dakota looks in the rearview mirror, "Mel, Meelllly Mel, I got this CD just for you. Come on, Mel. It's your favorite band of all time."

Melissa annoyingly looks up from her phone as Dakota and Ruth scream. "WHHHOOOOOOOO, YEAH!"

Dakota turns the volume up even louder. The song, "Changes" by Black Sabbath starts to play. Melissa looks up and gives a faint smile at the girls in the front seat and looks back down at her phone. In her peripheral vision, she sees Dakota and Ruth's ponytails flipping back and forth screaming with the lyrics.

With the song blasting in the car down the one-way street, Dakota passes two more green traffic lights. From the backseat, Melissa looks up and sees a six-way intersection ahead in the distance. Melissa continues to 'slide' and 'tap' her fingers on her phone screen in the backseat. Dakota begins to turn the steering wheel gradually to the left.

As the music blasts, the girls in the front seat are dancing and singing to the music. As the light remains green at the six-way intersection, Dakota drives through making a slight left turn. As Dakota drives through the six-way intersection, Melissa sees a bright light in her peripheral vision on her right. She turns her head to the right. She looks out the car window and sees a bright white light. It's a piercing, bright, spotlight pointing at her face. Ruth lets out a sharp scream. Dakota joins Ruth and screams even louder.

At that moment, a second turns into a minute. The blasting music slows down into a blur. Melissa hears the sharp blare of the car horn piercing in her ear. Her heart slowly beats just once, "buh....boom". At the end of her heartbeat, the car window shatters in her face on her right side. With the phone still in her hands, she feels a strong jolt of force that rams into her right shoulder, right hip, and right leg. The broken glass continues to shatter across her body from the right side to the left side. Her body is thrown across the back seat to the other side of the car. She is like a rag doll being thrown around in a dryer helpless with no control.

The left side of her head, shoulder, and hip hit the opposite door of where she was sitting. In less than a second, her body is slammed into the opposite door panel. She feels the force of a powerful energy so strong it pulls her phone out of her hands as if it is coated with melted butter.

The music stops. The time goes back into real time where a second is back to being a second. She faintly hears the sound of a car horn. She can't tell if it's Ruth's car or another car. Everything comes to a stop. The car stops moving and so does Melissa. She can't feel her body much less her thoughts.

Seconds later, she feels pain run from her neck to her head and down her back. It's a slow throbbing pain, then a sharp, piercing, stabbing pain. She realizes she can't breathe.

The single thought in her mind said calmly and very regretfully. "FFFFFuck."

Her breath is gone.

She feels her eyes open wide as she tries to gasp for air, but she can't. Her chest feels caved in like it was crushed like a soda can. She feels vulnerable and fragile. All she can see is a blur. She hears people screaming and yelling. Now, she feels nothing. Her pain is numb. Her thoughts are numb.

She feels her long black silky hair cover her entire face as Dakota yells something she can't understand. The voices inside the car and outside the car are faded out as she only hears a loud piercing ringing in her ears.

She closes her eyes for what seems like a decade. She slowly opens her eyes. She knows she's not breathing. She feels a burning sensation in her lungs. She can't feel her breath anymore. She sees strangers in dark navy blue uniforms approach her. She sees their lips opening and closing in slow motion. They make eye contact with her and they are talking to her, but she can't hear their words. Their words are blared out by a continuous truck horn.

She closes her eyes. She hears nothing, feels nothing, and sees nothing, but a turning, whirling, spinning, black abyss. Her lungs no longer sting. She's floating. She slowly opens her eyes. She sees a blur of people in a circle surrounding her. They are moving their lips. She doesn't know what they are saying. She closes her eyes and hears a very familiar voice. She feels his large, callused hands on top of hers. His palm was large against the top of her hand. She feels him smiling. His warmth is all around her.

With his hands on top of hers, she hears her grandfather's voice. It was soothing. She feels the love within his voice.

"Ah, My Lady," he says, "My sweet, beautiful Lady, you're home."

And she closes her eyes.

Chapter 2. The Challenger Deep

"No matter what happens or where you go, this is always home, my Lady."

-Frank Nez

It's 1993. She's eight years old. It's the beginning of the year. It's still dandruff in the mountains season near Dibé bi to', New Mexico. Dibé bi to', New Mexico is three miles North of Tohatchi, New Mexico. Dibé bi to' is a place, an actual generational landmark. It's not on any maps as it doesn't exist in the White people world. So, with that I will take you to the place, three miles South of Dibé bi to', that does exist on the maps, a small communuty—Tohatchi, New Mexico. Tohatchi is on the Navajo reservation. It's near the four corners—where Utah, Colorado, Arizona, and New Mexico meet in a perfect perpendicular manner. It's the only place in the United States four states meet in a perfect ninety-degree corner-of-a-box angle. It just so happens she lives near this perfect grid wonder. She knows the Navajo reservation as "the Rez". To White people, the Rez is better known as the middle of nowhere, the real "ghetto". It's her home. The Rez is rich of Navajo customs and traditions.

The Rez is the complete opposite of any place in the Universe.

Obviously, a city is well-equipped with a large population—large buildings, easy access to schools, universities, access to a bus line, food, and work. A city is a deep sea-dwelling fish with its' colorful rainbow scales screaming in color. Its' brightness strains the eyes at night. It never stops swimming. This colorful fish is alive, well, and sought out for fish tanks of the white people.

A town is much smaller than a city—doesn't have as many resources as a city has and very few to no tall buildings. Most businesses are closed down at night. There is not much of a nightlife. That means this deep sea-dwelling fish is not only scaled of its' rainbow colors, but its' skin and head is ripped off. This fish is not much to look at now. Its' headless body still spasms time-to-time, but it's still beautiful. It only feeds hunger to the eyes because of its' meat.

And then, there's the Rez. The Rez is like removing the meat off of the fish. Much like the Navajo, Diné language compared to the English language, only the bones and tail remain. A rare few would still see the beauty left in the bones and tail that was once a beautiful, colorful, living fish. It exists like a faint ache echoing in the bones of what once was healthy tissue. No one wants a headless, dry-boned, fish skeleton in their fish tank.

That's the Rez. It's all land. It's like scraping off the colorful scales of that rainbow-scaled fish with a sharp knife, chopping off the head, scraping off every morsel of meat leaving a thin, fragile, exposed skeleton that nobody wants. The Rez is just like that skeleton—clean of loud noises, dry, and bare.

Days on the Rez are complimented with a scorching wind that stings the surface of the skin. A rebound of sunshine rays burst through the atmosphere burning straight through to the soul if one is not used to it. The dust bowl of the early 1930s doesn't have anything to prove on the Rez. Just like the super bowl, the Rez has its own dust bowl every year, if not, more often. The only difference is the Rez's dust bowl is never in the news. The Rez is never on the news because it is off the grid from the rest of the universe.

The Rez is like the ocean's Challenger Deep, untouched, rarely gone to, and holds a different population than any other part of the ocean. No one knows the Rez exists unless they are from the Rez—that's isolation at its' finest.

The Rez has no tall buildings, including two-story buildings. There are more tumbleweeds than stoplights. There are a few stop signs that blow in the dust here and there—that's where the post office may be. The only paved roads are the main highway, places where the very few fast food franchises struggle to breath, where the tribal government buildings sit on, and maybe the post office. Majority of the roads, up and down on, is on mother earth's bare skin. When it rains, it pours. Ninety percent of the roads get washed out, but it's not ever too muddy to drive through. Everyone on the Rez is born to drive not only in the rain and snow, but also in the mucky, thick, mud. Most houses are a few miles off the paved main road. Navajos don't have time to walk the plank of shame getting their truck stuck in the mud. Navajos have things to do just like everyone else. They don't schedule their day around the weather. They have been doing what they have been doing for centuries. They have adapted to this lifestyle and they are proud of it. It's a culture. It's a way of life.

The only scenery in Tohatchi is the Chuska Mountains that lie as a beautiful backdrop. When she is there, the mountains remind her of a lonely iceberg out in the stretch of the wide-open ocean.

To Navajo people, traditions, and old customs coexist with the land. The Navajo culture respects the aspects of fours—four seasons, four cardinal directions, four states of life, four sacred colors, and the four sacred mountains.

Every house visible from the main highway showcases the sacred fours as every home faces east. The east represents the awakening of life and beauty. Therefore, every home greets each morning with the blessing of the sunrise and new life.

There are a few small towns that surround Tohatchi. The nearest town is Gallup—a half an hour drive south.

Tohatchi is not a town, but more of a very, very small community. There are no grocery stores, no restaurants, and no hospitals in Tohatchi.

There is only one gas station. The post office, smaller than an upper-class white man's walk-in closet, sits in the back of the community surrounded by dirt. An old abandoned trading post sits next to the post office about fifty feet. Next to the abandoned Trading Post sits an abandoned laundromat. Both have accumulated sand and the timeless vintage look of the old Native American hood screaming assimilation. In front of the post office are a few clusters of several houses that make up a few small "neighborhoods". Along with no neighborhood watch, there is no landscaping, grass, landlords, street signs, and ice cream trucks neglect to roam. Some houses' yards are sprinkled with sheep and horse. On the border of the small housing community, lies one elementary school, middle school, and high school. Three churches somewhat suffocate the community's north side. The small grouped community is a mile in radius.

The Rez is where snail mail soars like the mighty eagle. It is impossible to get packages and tree-killing paper delivered to the front door. Just like the White House and Santa Claus, houses on the Rez do not have a deliverable address. And just like the White House and Santa Claus' north pole, houses only pose as a landmark-ish rather than a slot for deliverable snail mail. So everyone on the Rez owns a post office box in order to be a part of the snail mail communication network, bleh. The Rez doesn't experience the euphoria of their significant other yelling, "the package is here!" while still being at home, like white devils in the city. Yes, the Rez is a different kind of ghetto. At least one can still get mail in the city version of the ghetto.

The Rez is never thought of being the real ghetto, but it should be.

Ghetto is the modern translation of "poor living" or "poor means". Living in the ghetto is known as living a hard life. Most people think they know what the ghetto is. According to most dictionaries, the ghetto is defined as, "a restriction of an isolated or segregated area or group". Famous rappers, movies, media, and the universe agree the ghetto is living in an area that is labeled as being the poorest area. In reality, all of these people living in the ghetto can easily flip a switch to turn on the heat during the winter and flip a switch to turn on the air conditioning in the summer. They can simply turn a facet to get fresh water. If they need to cook something they don't have to worry about manually hooking up the propane or building a fire to heat their meal like the world of the Rez does. "The ghetto's" resource for food is just down the street a couple blocks away. Is that what one calls hard living?

Navajos, and Native Tribes alike, have been living off the land since they were forced to exile off of their home and have been living off the land ever since. Navajos have it so hard that most live with no electricity, water, plumbing, and resources for food, gas, and jobs are slim to none.

Cold in the winter? One better have hauled truckloads of wood and have it chopped long before the bone-cracking cold, winter settles in. Out of the purest form of hydrating liquid? One must drive up the mountain in their war pony to get their water from the well. Need food, but have no car to get it? The wide elephant, known as the bus, is non-existent on the Rez. Most people on the Rez repeat what their ancestors did hundreds of years ago—they walk. They walk for miles and miles on the side of the road to get that loaf of bread and diapers for their little one.

Need a paycheck to live off of? The nearest town is a minimum of a thirty-minute drive, but for most it can be hours. The 9-1-1 emergency calls that happen in the city is replaced by relying on the oldest in the family and driving, if one has the car to do so, and get help in the nearest small town. To the Rez, the ghetto's modern definition is majorly overrated and merely a walk in the park. Living life the indigenous way is the real ghetto.

Everyone's ghetto on the Rez resides at his or her grandma's house. Melissa is no exception. She loves Grandma's house. Grandma's house is a three-mile drive north on the main highway from the gas station in Tohatchi. Grandma's house is another fourth of a mile drive on bare mother earth going west of the main highway. Grandma's nearest neighbor is her sister less than a hundred feet from the main highway on the same dirt road.

A huge hill layered with mother earth like tiramisu is visible from the main highway a half a mile away. The tiramisu hill is the perfect backdrop for Grandma's house. This legendary hill is known as Dibé bí tó or Sheep Springs. The hill is a fourth of a mile high and half a mile wide. Looking at the hill upside down it looks like a cursed white man's butt chin.

Grandma tells Melissa a long time ago Navajos made caves in the big hill to hide from U.S. soldiers. She tells her she's not allowed to go up into the caves because many people died there.

Then there's Grandma's house. Just like Grandma, the house is inviting. It's more than just a home—It's her security blanket.

Grandma's house holds memories and plenty of tea time stories. Grandma tells one of Melissa's favorite teatime stories, of course. It's about the time Grandma's daughter and son made bread dough. Grandma found her one-year old son playing in bread dough on the kitchen floor. It was Grandma's daughter's responsibility to make bread dough. The little girl finished making the bread dough and gave it to her little brother to play with. Grandma's attempt to get after her eight-year old daughter for letting her little brother play in the dough had failed.

Grandma said in Navajo, "You wasted good dough."

Her daughter responded in Navajo, "What?.. Floor is clean. Baby's clean".

Melissa always smiles when Grandma tells her that story. She knows thirty years later Grandma will still be telling that same story.

If cleaning were a sport, Grandma would always come home with the gold. Grandma's floors are always clean—cleaner than the whitest person with the most compelling OCD cleaning disorder.

Grandma's house is sky blue. Inside has the flare of the 80s, 90s, and a slight touch of the 50s. The atmosphere is very calming. It would put the most stressful CPA during the last days of tax season at ease. There is one window on each side of the front door. Each window is a three-panel window measuring four-feet tall and five-feet wide.

The floors are tiled with white laminate foot-long square tiles. The walls and ceiling is painted white. The white paint has a soft texture lifting off the walls and ceiling. The floors, walls, and ceilings alike are always immaculately clean—a clean that would put a museum's cleaning staff to shame.

The front yard stretches out twenty feet from the front door. A four-foot by five-foot gray cement porch sits just below the front door. The cement-poured porch is six inches thick. The walkway is gray with a dusty brown color. The walkway is made of cement and flagstone and connects the porch to the front gate.

During the summer there are patches of Rez grass on Grandma's front yard. Not bright green city grass, but a darker species of green grass that has to be watered often because of the dry clay soil that soars indigenous to the Rez.

Here is where the Rez is. Here is where things happen that most people don't ever experience. Here is where her childhood ends and where she begins her womanhood, Grandma's house.

Welcome to the ghetto. Welcome to the Rez. Welcome to the Challenger Deep.

Chapter 3. Preparation

"Grandma doesn't think we're ready, but we're ready. I've been ready
even before you were born and you'll do a perfect job."
-Frank Nez

She wakes up to the sound of Grandma's slippers sliding against the
white tiled, double Pine-soled, and triple Cloroxed floor, "shooooook shooooook
shooooook shooooook". It's coming from the other side of the house. It must be 5am.
The dragging sounds of the slippers come to a halt. She hears the sharp, long,
creak of the black, cast iron, wood stove door coming from the other side of the
house. She lies in bed staring at the white ceiling listening to the sounds of
Grandma's house. It's alive and well.

Looking from the sky downwards on Grandma's house, the roof has light
gray tiles and the house is shaped like the letter "L". The front door of the house is
on the bottom line of the "L" in the middle. A black iron cast woodstove greets
everyone whom enters the house. Coming inside the house, the woodstove
separates the living room. The living room sits to the left and the dining room sits
to the right. Her grandparents' bedroom is behind the living room.

Past the kitchen there are two stairs leading up to a small narrow hallway.
The bathroom is to the left at the end of the tiny narrow hallway. There never
seems to be a problem with four grandkids, two grandparents, two parents, and all
who comes through the front door, and one bathroom.

The bathroom is located at the bottom left part of the "L" shaped house.
Just past the bathroom is Melissa's parent's bedroom complimented with a dark
cocoa colored bedroom door. Walking past their bedroom to the middle part of the
"L" shaped house is a top loading washing machine on the left. Next to the washer
is a second fridge.

Finally, moving to the top left of the "L" is her bedroom. She shares her
bedroom with three older brothers. Entering the bedroom there is a black, iron
cast, stove to the left. A chestnut colored wooden desk with a beat up rolling chair

with one squeaky wheel sits a few feet from the cast iron woodstove. Off and on her brothers would bring in the wooden desk with two drawers to do homework on and then move it back into the storage. The storage resembles a plain, no candied, tiny gingerbread house about twenty yards North of the house.

Next to the desk with the beat up chair with a squeaky wheel sits a wooden bunk bed with twin mattresses. A full sized bed with a wooden frame and mattress sits to the right upon entering the room. There is a small closet against the wall behind the full sized bed.

A large wooden entertainment center that has hues of blood red mixed into the wood's stain holds a RCA brand VCR, video cassettes, a boom box, and a nineteen inch, old school, gray television sits in the middle of the entertainment center. The entertainment center sits against the wall separating the beds. The top of the entertainment center showcases what her brothers spent their time in. There are several golden-colored figurines of men frozen in action either running or throwing a basketball. It represents her brother's basketball, track and field, and cross-country achievements. Each trophy has three medals stacked on it. Among the dozens of trophies, two are gold women figurines frozen in time, which represents Melissa's achievements.

There is no door to separate the bedroom she shares. The bedroom is completely open to the rest of the house. She usually sleeps on the top bunk of the bunk bed made of two by four lumber.

She quickly sits up, hops off the top bunk, and puts on her faded, yet favorite, navy blue Nike running shoes and faded navy blue Puma hoodie. Her sleeves of the hoodie were becoming frayed, fragile, and thin from wearing it so much. Her clothes smell like smoke and ash because she kept the fire going all night. Her brothers snore loudly hibernating harder than the two large frozen trees outside in front of the house. The abrupt chilly air in the bedroom doesn't make them shiver much less flinch. She pulls the black hair tie off her wrist and ties her long black smooth hair into a messy ponytail.

The wood she brought in last night is all gone. She got up every few hours to keep the fire in the black iron cast stove going all night in her room and in the living room of the other side of the house where her grandparents sleep. Not wanting her Grandma to go out into the unsympathetic winter, she rushes outside to get more wood.

She walks through the house from her bedroom past her parents' room, past the bathroom, down the two steps and past the kitchen to the front door. She opens the first front door. The first door is brown with three long diamond-shaped windows on the top half of the door. The second front door is a white screen door. The top half of the door has two screens; one screen has hundreds of tiny four-millimeter squares and the other screen has hundreds of five-millimeter squares.

During the sweltering summer, the brown front door is left open and the screen door remains closed. The two screens on the screen door prevent all small and unwanted visitors from entering such as flies and mosquitoes. There is a familiar distinct sound as the front door is closed almost as if the slam of the front door is the voice of the house.

Not only does everyone know the distinct sound of the front door, but everyone knows the familiar sound of Grandma's barking dogs, as well. The barking dogs are Grandma's household trademark, like a white woman with her minivan, pink scarf, and plants in the kitchen window, it was a given. Three dogs run out of their doghouses as soon as they hear the front doors close. They are always happy to see Melissa coming outside. They pant and bark in an eager tone. Each dog's breath turns to a brisk fog as they bark in the early morning's cold winter air.

The cold greets Melissa's exposed skin with what feels like an avalanche of frozen ice. It burns uncontrollably tingling her exposed skin. The cold chills go up and down her body as she walks and breathes in fresh oxygen. She feels her body getting colder as she inhales and exhales each breath. It's still dark outside.

The bitter cold wind whistles through her ears. Her clothes become quickly frozen with stiffness. She feels goose bumps popping up on her skin. Every minute feels like ten. She grabs her gloves from her back pocket, puts it on, and grabs the wheelbarrow with both hands. She walks east until she reaches the woodpile in two hundred feet. The dogs follow her with smiles and happy tail wags.

An early sunrise later, she stacks pieces of wood in the 3x4 foot wood box that's 3 feet deep against the wall in front of the dining room. She puts more wood in the other wood box outside next to the cement porch. She stacks the wheelbarrow with an overload of wood and leaves it next to the cement porch.

She comes back inside the house. She uses the small, metal, black shovel to scoop up the ashes in the woodstove. The scrape of the small cast iron shovel makes a loud scraping sound against the cast iron woodstove. Her ears are annoyed by it, but she continues to scrape up the ashes and dump it into a metal 10-gallon bucket.

When it comes to building a fire, Grandma doesn't like using lighter fluid or kerosene to start a fire. She wants to make sure the fuel will last. So to start a fire, she piles small wood chips and lights a match. Then she, blows on it until it is a full-fletched fire. Once the fire is burning and roaring, coal is added to make sure heat will percolate later from the hot coals. Once the flames of the fire are out, wood is added to the cherry-red lava-colored coals off and on.

This is the routine before bed, midnight, and 3am and again at 5am. It doesn't matter if it was snowing, raining, or hailing, a fire is needs to be built, as it is the sole source of heat for the entire house.

The light is on in the kitchen. Grandma is pouring coffee grounds into the blue coffee pot as Melissa walks by. Melissa walks by Grandma, walks past the bathroom, past her parent's bedroom, and goes to her bedroom with the metal bucket. She empties out the ashes from the woodstove into the metal bucket. She walks back through the house and out the front door with the metal bucket filled with ashes. She walks east through the snow just past the woodpile to a large metal barrel. She dumps the ashes in the large metal barrel.

She comes back into the house. She gets down on one knee and starts a fire in the living room. She then starts a fire in her bedroom. As the fire crackles in her bedroom, she looks at the clock on the wall behind her and realizes it's 5:37am. The cast iron door makes a high and long 'screeeeeech' as she closes it.

The energy of the flames roars fiercely as she closes the woodstove door. Through the crack of the stove's door just under the hinge, the fire's flames cast bright orange shadows on the white tiled floor. She goes back to the other side of the house where Grandma is. She sees steam rise from the hot water as Grandma pours it into a large metal bowl.

That large metal bowl is Grandma's trade secret; her famous biscuits made from scratch. Grandma's biscuits are always perfect. It's so good it saves lost souls. It heals all wounds. It makes a "no carbs, no bread" diet repent two biscuits later. There is no other food in the universe that you'd feel guilty and enjoy simultaneously, than Grandma's bread. Her bread is a screaming temptation to have an affair on your fruity strawberry and kale smoothie. There isn't anything more pleasing in the entire universe than the first bite of Grandma's hot bread. Her bread could save the whales if only they could have a piece.

Grandma is always doing one of three things, cooking, cleaning, or getting after someone that even includes the crazy cats that she claims she never lets in the house, but feeds them next to the gas stove ironically.

Grandma's little old lady chic closely resembles the pancake syrup bottle brand of Aunt Jemima, but a Native version. Grandma is genuinely old school. Her style consists of a one-piece house dress that stops just above her ankles, comfortable white lace-up tennis shoes, white or beige calf-high socks pulled up covering her grandma calves, and her signature blood-red polyester apron. The blood-red apron wraps twice around her waist. She ties a bow against her belly button. Her apron has two front pockets. She always has safety pins on the bottom of her apron, for just in case. Grandma's blood-red apron only comes off when she goes to town with Melissa's grandfather. Grandma's hair is always tied up in a neat bun. She only takes a shower at night. Her hair is only down at night when she takes a shower. Once it's dried with a towel, she makes a single braid. Sometimes Melissa braids her hair. Come sunrise, it's placed into a neat tight bun with a hurricane of black, wavy, bobby pins. Grandma has streaks of white lightning in her hair.

It seems as though Grandma always has a remedy for everything and is always prepared. She once took a bobby pin out of her hair and gave it to grandfather to help fix the truck when it broke down in town one day. The bobby pin held until they came home. Grandfather fixed the problem the truck had that same afternoon and gave Grandma her bobby pin back. Grandma grabbed the bobby pin, washed it, and put it back into her hair.

Grandma's hands told the story of just hard she cleans and cooks. Her hands are small, always clean, and feel like there is a hard shell on top of her skin. Her fingers are short and square at the tip. When Melissa looks at Grandma she thinks Grandma looks old, small, and sweet. Grandma's less than five feet stature doesn't stop her feistiness. Her muscles are visible in her arms when she makes dough. Just like disinfectants, Grandma's definition of clean is cleaner than a can of disinfectant, and 99.9 percent of the time, she is a nice little old lady just the same.

Grandma uses the bottom of her blood-red apron to wipe her hands.

Grandma flicks her pointer finger in the direction of the hallway, and says, "Go wake up your brothers, we need to get ready".

Melissa walks up the two steps, walks past the bathroom, her parent's bedroom, and goes to the bedroom she shares. She tells her brothers to get up. Her brothers hear her. They sit up and stretch. She hears her parent's bedroom door open and close.

Her dad walks into her bedroom. He's wearing blue sweatpants with a banded bottom and a comfy cotton t-shirt that reads, "10th Annual Gallup Run". It has an image of a purple man running towards a sunrise up a large mountain.

Her dad smiles, walks up to Melissa, and grabs her shoulder, "Good morning, my daughter, are you ready? It's going to be a long week, but we are here and we are ready. Go help your mom get the hogan ready. The medicine man will be here soon."

Her dad looks similar to the movie actor Jackie Chan. He is maybe a little bit taller than Jackie. Her dad stands six feet tall. Her dad has dark-black shiny hair and has the same facial expression as Jackie when he smiles. Her dad works for the state. He makes a forty-minute drive west just a hairline past the Arizona state line. He is a supervisor for one of the state departments.

Once he is off the clock he preoccupies his time with filling the needs of the family or his need to fix something. He is always working on a project. One week he's making repairs to the roof, other weeks he's hauling wood, fixing vehicles, fixing the sheep corral, or helping someone with their problems when their aura, spirit, health, work affairs, or financial means are out of balance.

Her dad is a medicine man. He holds a healing power. Being Navajo, she is taught there is a particular balance she must maintain within her body, mind, spirit, and in the universe. When one's balance becomes compromised by sickness, financial problems, or something else, her dad finds out how to put everything back into balance. He restores the balance by intense spiritual prayer and sending the evil and bad vibes back wherever it came from.

Her mom is as close to Melissa as a grumpy old cat is to a dolphin. Well, one could say it's not to the standards of the happy white people she sees in movies. Her mom is very skinny just like she is. Her mom has long hair like she does. Melissa dresses like she does either in sweatpants or jeans and a simple cotton blue or black t-shirt. They don't go shopping, get their nails and hair done, or even go to the movies. Instead, her mom teaches her how to survive in the life they live. Instead of baking, cooking, or going out for pizza, her mom taught her how to filter water from the well in the mountain, how to cook meat on a fire for lunch when they haul wood, and how to obey Grandma's indirect rules on being the proper little Navajo Lady.

There is a hidden family hierarchy, but everyone covertly knows the ranks. Oddly, they don't talk about it. It's just there like the sand that lies naturally on the ground. Grandma holds the highest rank and the family tribe obeys. That's right. A woman, a tiny little old lady holds the highest rank, not a man, and not even the strongest man holds the highest rank.

Grandma's rank is followed by her husband, Melissa's grandfather. Except, no one calls him "grandfather", "grandpa", or "papa". Grandma doesn't call him, "my husband". Grandma doesn't even call him, "darling", "sweetie", or "honey", like Melissa sees in almost every movie that has couples. Instead, everyone calls Grandma's husband, "Cheíí". "Cheíí" is the Navajo word for "grandfather".

"Cheíí" is the combination of the words "cherry" and "hey". To pronounce it take the beginning of "cherry" taking only the "ch" sound and take the ending of the word "hey", taking the "ey" sound. That's how to pronounce his name, "Cheíí".

Following Cheíí's rank are her parents. Of course, her mom comes first in rank over her dad. She never sees or hears her parents argue about anything. She knows there would be some trouble when there is a sigh, but it is always followed with the hopeful smile and the phrase, "We will figure it out".

Within this Navajo family hierarchy, women hold the most say when it comes to decisions. Melissa is well accustomed to the family's Navajo traditions, but she doesn't live in Tohatchi. She doesn't know exactly why she doesn't. She figures there is no room for her. So, she visits.

Just last week Melissa came to visit her Grandma for spring break.

Melissa lives in Flagstaff, Arizona. The woman Melissa stays with in Flagstaff doesn't seem to like it when Melissa wants to come to Tohatchi to visit. She becomes annoyed by it for some reason.

It was just the second day at Grandma's when Melissa's stomach started aching complimented with a stabbing pain. Her lower stomach underneath her belly button felt like a washrag being rung out. Her pain worsened, but she didn't think to tell anyone. She just thought it might be her hunger or something bad she ate. Just as abruptly as the pain started, the pain stopped.

It was just like every other week. Her grandparents take the half-hour drive to town to pay bills, visit the town's famous restaurant Earl's, the town flea market, or get groceries when they need it. About ninety-nine percent of the time there is always a human home at Grandma's. When she got back, Melissa does as she always does when Grandma is not around. She digs around in Grandma's closet.

Digging in Grandma's closet fills her eccentric void of her youthful curiosity because she never knows what she is going to find. Grandma's closet reflects the preparation of a possible and very near apocalypse. Grandma's closet reminded her of a sheep stomach. There were pockets and infinite folds of goodies. Grandma's shelves held canned goods and boxed preservatives, such as: canned fruit cocktail and peaches, canned corned beef hash and Vienna sausages, an array of vanilla crème and windmill cookies, boxes of jell-o, chocolate pudding cups, boxes of chamomile tea, coffee tin cans, and Melissa's favorite, an array of candy that range from exotic chocolates and hard candies to licorice. For some odd reason, Grandma had three pairs of everyone's clothes folded and stacked together in her closet. Among the food and clothes, she had piles of new blankets, house slippers still in its' original packaging, bottles of unopened body wash, shampoo, and a collection of soapboxes. The curiosity monster fed itself as Melissa opened box after box that's filled with sugar highs, new socks, small toys from McDonald's, and other small trinkets. Among the boxes there was a pile of thin canvas two-strap bags, leather purses, and piles of blankets and new towels with the tags still attached.

Nothing matched in Grandma's closet. Each time Melissa opened the closet door, her excitement held its' breath in anticipation and her heart raced. The last few times she found a new box of 64 count crayons, the good brand, and a new box of colored pencils, but the excavation is not as easy as it seemed as Grandma had professional packing tactics that could fool anyone. Once, Melissa found a round, purple, and shiny tin that had a variety of yummy shortbread cookies pictured on the cover of the tin. She instantly became ecstatic. Her mouth watered imagining the soft bite of the sweet powdered cookie. She imagined opening the tin. Her taste buds would fall in love with the different types of shortbread sweetness, but when she opened it, she was welcomed with an array of sewing supplies. Strangely, another time there was an opened 12-pack of Red Crème soda, but all the cans inside the box were different brands of soda. This storage tactic intrigued Melissa. The closet doesn't have any open spaces other than the middle of the closet to take a single step inside. Everything inside the closet is packed and stacked tight and neat. Grandma's Tetris score would be groundbreaking and undefeatable.

Melissa felt like everything she could ever need and want in the universe was in Grandma's closet, but her Grandma wanted her treasures to be kept a secret. Melissa knew this because she had never seen Grandma in her own closet. She had never seen Grandma put anything in her closet much less take anything out. With all the goodies and undiscovered bliss that was waiting to be found in her closet, Melissa found it just a little but strange also knew Grandma didn't want anyone to know about her deep treasured abyss. The times Grandma caught Melissa digging around she yelled at Melissa. Melissa wanted to have easy access to the hidden wonders and treasures, so she kept her small, purple, duffel bag in the closet when she visited.

On this particular day, Melissa went to her purple bag to break off a corner piece of an almond chocolate bar. All of a sudden, she felt wet. She looked down at her blue jeans. She saw a red spot bleeding through her jeans in between her legs. Confused, Melissa changed out of her stained pink-colored panties and stained blue jeans. Standing in the closet she changed into a clean white pair of panties that had rainbows and unicorns on it.

She wiped herself clean with the toilet paper Grandma had stocked in her closet. She figured she'd wash her stained panties and jeans later. She rolled up her blood-stained panties. She folded her jeans in half so the legs of the jeans met. She put her stained panties in her stained jeans and rolled it up. She placed the wrapped jeans on top of her purple duffel bag and closed the closet door.

She went to the kitchen and washed her hands. In the middle of the kitchen was a light green and white marble 1950s kitchen table. She opened the yellow Dutch oven lid that was always on the middle of the table and grabbed a tortilla. Grandma's Dutch oven was always full of her handheld miracle of cooked perfection, Grandma's bread. Melissa put her purple puffy coat on. She sat on the cement porch in front of the house. She ate her tortilla and played with the dogs.

The dogs barked as the sun reached the middle of the blue Rez sky. Grandma and Cheíí drove up in their 1980 Ford F100 truck. It was their war pony. The truck a.k.a. war pony was dark blue with light blue trim. The family named all of their war ponies. The two-tone blue truck, Tubby, was no exception. Tubby was Cheíí's war pony. Melissa ran to Tubby and helped bring in the groceries. Grandma got out of Tubby on the passenger's side. She grabbed a brown paper grocery bag that held her own personal goodies. Cheíí stayed sitting in Tubby. The Navajo Times newspaper crinkled as he turned the long wide pages and chewed his Juicy Fruit gum. Grandma walked inside the house and went straight to her closet. She restocked her hidden cave of treasures. Melissa wanted to see Grandma restock her treasures so she hurried as fast as she could to get the groceries out of the bed of the truck and onto the kitchen table. She knew if she put the groceries away quickly, there could be a chance that she could see exactly where Grandma puts her goodies of gold.

While Melissa was speeding to put the groceries away, when it happened. The noise Grandma made when she was in her room stopped. Grandma stumbled upon Melissa's stained jeans and stained pink panties.

27,000 square miles of the Navajo reservation heard Grandma's holler, "Heeeyyyyyyyyyih haaahhhhhhhh!!!!!!"

She yelled as if she stubbed her pinky toe on the bottom of the bed frame. It never meant anything good when Grandma yelled. It meant she was a volcano about to erupt and just like a volcano, the eruption was always an epic catastrophe.

Melissa froze as she opened the fridge door. She bent over and slowly put the eggs in the fridge. She heard Grandma's feet shuffling against the floor. The footsteps became frantic. Then Grandma yelled some more. Melissa looked toward Grandma's room with a puzzled face. Grandma walked out of the bedroom. With a fast pace, she went outside. The front screen door slammed behind her. Cheíí was still sitting in his war pony shuffling the newspaper. As Grandma approached the truck, he leaned forward and rolled down his window. He shuffled the crisp newspaper as Grandma spoke frantically. He never looked up at Grandma as she yelled waving her arms.

Melissa ran towards the front door and looked out the screen door. Grandma continued yelling at Cheíí. She waved Melissa's panties around in the air as she talked with her hands. Melissa didn't really understand anything Grandma was yelling other than they have to go visit someone now and start getting ready. Melissa saw that Grandma stopped talking. Cheíí put down his newspaper, looked at Grandma, and nodded his head. Melissa hysterically stumbled back to the kitchen and quickly took groceries out of the brown paper bags making sure Grandma didn't know she was standing at the front door watching the drama unfold.

Grandma walked with a fast pace back inside the house, put on her blood-red apron, put Melissa's pink stained panties in a plastic bag, put the bag in her apron pocket, and picked up the house phone. When the other line picked up, Grandma spoke in Navajo. Cheíí came inside the house and walked up to Melissa.

Cheíí pat her on the head, smiled, and said, "Ahhh, the little Lady is not a little Lady no more. That's good. That's really good. Grandma is acting crazy because she thinks we aren't ready, but we are. I have been ready for a long time, more than eight years I've been ready. Awwww, The Lady! You will do well. You always do well. Awwww, My Dear Sweet Lady."

Cheíí gave Melissa another huge grin and hugged her tight.

"Cheíí is so tall and so skinny", Melissa thought.

Melissa felt his boney chest against the left side of her head. As he squeezed her, her ears listened to his heart beating. His heartbeat was calm and relaxed. She smiled and closed her eyes as she listened to his heartbeat. Cheíí kissed the top of her head and combed his large, rough, hand through her hair smiling down at her. He went back outside and stood on the front porch. He stood tall and skinny. Cheíí took out his rolling paper, loose mountain tobacco out of his left front shirt pocket, and rolled a smoke.

Cheíí always wore the same type of clothing day in and day out regardless if the weather was scorching hot or bone cracking cold. Whether he was healthy as a fox or sick as a dog, he always wore the same type of clothes. His wardrobe was consistent like Charlie Brown.

Cheíí's signature wardrobe consisted of a dark navy long sleeve button-up collared shirt that always had a front left pocket. He always folded his long sleeve shirt three-quarters up his arms.

Part of his body armor included Japanese style tattoos. He had a tattoo on top of both of his forearms. His right side was of a woman's face against the moon and stars. On his left forearm was a naked 1950s woman. The woman was bled into skin like a pinup doll style tattoo. She wrapped in a U.S. flag. Melissa always looked at his tattoos. She admired his body war paint. She knew he got his tattoos when he served in the military. During his military era he went to Japan. Melissa raised her left eyebrow when she looked at the naked Japanese woman wrapped in a United States flag. The woman's shoulders, arms, the top of her thighs, and legs were the only skin that she bared. This woman was to be forever painted on his arm and this made little tall Melissa chuckle to herself.

His third war paint decor splashed on the top right hand just below his thumb. It was a tattoo of a cross. He fought in the Korean War. Melissa thought having a tattoo of a cross meant that a life was taken and maybe the tattoo meant the death would never be forgotten. The permanent body war paint that once bled through his skin was always visible. Nobody ever asked him questions about his war paint. He always tucked his shirt into his dark wash contrast yellow stitch wrangler jeans. That was Cheíí, blue button-up shirts, long dark blue jeans, permanent skin war paint, and his humbling face, that was Cheíí.

Cheíí had a Navajo name, but in his time it was not appropriate. So, the U.S. government gave Cheíí a government name and birthday. There was no official record of where he was born and when he was born.

When asked about his birthday, he would smile and said, "G, I don't know. When I was little, I once asked my mother when I was born. My mother held up her hand about three feet off the ground and told me I was born when the corn in the field was this high. That's all I know about my birthday."

Early on, the family gave him the birthday of St. Patrick's Day.

When he was younger, he was forced to attend boarding school far away from home. As a young adult, he trained to be an auto mechanic at Stewart Indian School in Carson City, Nevada. He then retired from El Paso Natural Gas Company in 1986. Upon retirement, he built a home from the ground up, which turned out to be "Grandma's house" and better known to Melissa as "home".

Cheíí's Saturday mornings were like clock work. Cheíí and Melissa rarely stood up the Gallup flea market on Saturday morning. After a quick slurp of hot coffee, he would start the truck. That was Melissa's signal. Melissa's long legs ran her as fast it could to the truck. The Gallup flea market was on the north side of Gallup on a huge dirt plot. The flea market was surrounded by small dirt hills covered in sagebrush and small cedar trees. The train track lied east of the flea market, but a single caboose never choo choo'd by. Cheíí liked leaving early so that he can not only get V.I.P. parking, but to get hottest, freshest lamb stew, fresh frybread, and hot steaming blue corn mush before the food stands ran out of food.

The Gallup flea market held the best food of the universe next to Grandma's. There were homemade gifts for every occasion. The Gallup flea market stands displayed Navajo arts and crafts from jewelry to pottery and everything in between, such as: healing herbs, livestock, and antiques that people in the area franchised. After getting the perfect breakfast, sometimes she walked next to him and looked at once beloved treasures. Other times, she separated from him and looked at different things by herself.

Cheíí was always drawn to the antiques people sold. Of course, antiques must intrigue to everyone at a certain extend, but Cheíí was always interested in the antiques that served no purpose. Once, Grandma sat at the kitchen table drinking her tea as Cheíí happily put his new finding of a 1940s typewriter on the table. He was proud of his new finding. Grandma on the other hand was not fond of his hobby. She saw it only as junk that took up space, since he wouldn't ever be using anything he brought back.

Cheíí smiled looking at his glorious treasure. Grandma sneered and sternly said,

"What is that? You don't type. The keys are broken. I don't even want to know how much you paid for that!"

No matter how much Grandma rejected Cheíí's treasure, Cheíí spirit remained bright.

Other times Cheíí brought home things that were of use, but he ended up paying a toll for it later. One time he brought home a used three-wheeler ATV to assist in herding sheep. He looked at it as an opportunity of adventure. He made his own petite roads in the desert of the Rez. Melissa only rode the ATV a few times, but the times she rode it, she felt invincible as her hair flew behind her. However, the outcome was different for Cheíí when he rode it one last time.

On this particular day, someone let the sheep out of the corral. Later on in the day, there was no sign of the wooly group. A storm was moving into the grey Rez skies quickly. Cheíí, being the only one home, used the ATV to retrieve the sheep. He drove towards the "clanging" sound of the sheep bells hanging around their neck. Cheíí knew he was close to them. The sheep were just around the steep hill. He didn't want to lose them. So, he decided he could go up and over instead of around. He was going too fast and in an instant, the ATV flipped over. The three-legged machine revved as it fell on Cheíí breaking his leg. Instead of screaming and panicking like the average outside world, Cheíí got as comfortable as possible on the steep hill. He took out his playing cards he kept in his shirt pocket, and started playing cards until a rescue team arrived.

Soon, evening arrived. It started to rain. The family set out to look for the long lost old man. Some walked and others drove pick-up trucks making their own roads on the Rez terrain. In the distance, they spotted the upside down ATV's red shell. The wheels were upside down. The long silly old man was not too far away. As they walked up the side of the hill, Cheíí simply lied there on his side playing his cards. It was just Cheíí on the Rez terrain, just Cheíí, an upside down red ATV, playing cards on the damp dirt, and his broken leg. Cheíí was just like the little Navajo kids that ran off and got into mischief and Grandma yelled at him for doing just that. This happened at the mercy of the flea market. Except, Cheíí paid no mind for the Gallup flea market as it called Cheíí's name like a wild tiger on the hunt. It came hand-in-hand for he loved the Gallup flea market.

There were times when Cheíí was a very peculiar man. The mornings Melissa woke up early enough, which was often, she would see the finale of Cheíí getting ready as would everyone else sitting at the table eating breakfast. Melissa chewed her freshly made tortilla at the table. Cheíí quickly turned around facing his back towards the kitchen table. He pulled down his pants exposing his rear end of his tidy whities. He pulled up his pants and moved his hands around his slim to none waist tucking in his shirt. He tucked in his shirt. He fastened up his brown leather belt. Cheíí's dark wash jeans were worn high above his waist probably clear up to his belly button. He wore a brown formal leather belt and comfortable white tennis shoes.

He was done getting ready and the entire kitchen table bared witness to this strange morning ritual. Melissa raised her left eyebrow, slowly chewed her tortilla, and tried not to chuckle, but ended up giving a chuckle nearly spitting the tortilla out of her mouth.

Grandma always told him sternly, "Go do that in the bathroom!"

Regardless, Cheíí turned around smiled, ignored Grandma's comment, opened his arms, and said.

"Well, good morning to you beautiful ladies!"

Grandma's response is always the same. She rolled her eyes. After breakfast, she smiled as her husband walked out the front door.

For the next two days, Grandma's bossing around rank went from a drill sergeant to a colonel. She bossed everyone around making sure everything was ready. She checked everything fifteen times. She even bossed around the dogs and told them to keep an eye out on who comes and leaves. She yelled at the cats and told them they can't come into the house because she needed the space for people when they come.

Each time she fed the cats, the cats stopped eating and looked at her as she yelled at them in Navajo.

"I mean it! I better not find you in the house, you're terrible!"

Melissa and her brothers filled Grandma's orders. They went up and down the lower Chuska Mountains to haul wood with her dad's 1980s brown Chevy quarter-ton truck. Three tanks of gas later they were done hauling wood. The long, thin, tree stalks were chopped and stacked. Then, Melissa helped Grandma clean the already spotless house from the ceiling to the floor. She swept seven times. She swept corner to corner, and then mopped another five times getting every single grain of dirt and speck of a speck of human cells into the trashcan and water bucket and out of the house.

Grandma's house now had the aroma of a swimming pool and pine tree sap with a touch of lemon.

The house was so clean the overpowering aroma burned every sin to the ground and much less every nostril that inhaled within fifty yards. Melissa crinkled her face and thought the inside of her nose stung a little bit when she took a breath. Bodies exited the house with the essence of Clorox that lingered on their body and as well as a clear, clean conscience. Every dish, pot, and pan was washed twice, soaked in boiling hot water, dipped in Clorox diluted water, and rinsed twice before it was dried and put to its' resting place in the cupboards. Next on the list was the hogan.

The hogan faced east and stood in front of Grandma's house to the left about fifty feet. The sides of the hogan had eight sides like an octagon. Melissa's dad, oldest brother, and oldest cousin on her dad's side made the hogan a decade ago. The walls were made of alternating layers of cement and horizontal whole logs. The hogan's front door was white and faced east. The hogan's floor was mother earth's bare crust. There were four medium-sized windows in every other one of the sides. The roof tiered to a cone-like shape. The roof made a slightly high point in the middle and was tiled with light gray shingles. Cheíí and Melissa's dad were medicine men. They used the hogan to help people. Many people were very familiar with the inside of the hogan.

Over time, the hogan became storage for the family as belongings were placed in boxes and stacked against the wall. When a ceremony took place, the hogan was immediately cleared out and cleaned.

Now Melissa has to clean and clean since Grandma found the gleaming pair of panties in the closet. Melissa cleared out the large brown boxes that surrounded the walls of the hogan and placed the boxes in the square hogan.

The square hogan was next to Grandma's house behind the hogan about a hundred feet. The square hogan resembled a tiny house with four sides. It was thirty feet long and twenty feet wide. It was gray with a brown door and two windows on the sides. Surprisingly, the trend of the doors facing east didn't phase the square hogan. I mean, that is, after all, what most people care about, tangible things. So, why not have belongings and memories blessed, right?

A long time ago there was an ancient hoop ceremony performed for Grandma's relative in the square hogan. Melissa wasn't sure what the ceremony was exactly for. All she remembered was that her Grandma's relative was very sick and the white people medical doctors told her there wasn't anything they could do. She was on her journey to leave this world. Unwilling to accepted that fate, the family got together and decided to cure her illness through Navajo traditional means instead.

Melissa remembered several medicine men and Cheíí spending the early morning hours making a huge five-foot-by five-foot sandpainting on the square hogan's dirt floor. The sandpainting was a picture made completely of fine sand dust. She remembered Cheíí's voice. She sat at the edge of the painting while Cheíí told her a very old story. She watched three men crouch on the ground. Slowly the beautiful, yet sacred art work came together. The men wore white, sheer handkerchiefs on their head. The handkerchief was worn horizontal much like a sweat headband. The knot of the handkerchief was exposed on the side of their head. They wore short moccasins. Two of the men had long hair wrapped up into a Navajo bun and tied with buckskin. The other men had short hair. They all wore the "Cheíí wardrobe" like it was protocol. Their sleeves were unbuttoned and rolled a third up their arms. They all wore sterling silver rings, turquoise bead necklaces, and a large sterling silver and turquoise bracelet.

Near their feet were several medium-sized, steel silver-colored bowls. Each bowl was half-filled with a different color. The colors of the sand were sky blue, mustard yellow, rusty red, midnight black, dark forest green, white, light brown, dark purple, and dark grey.

They grabbed a handful of sand. They made their hands into a fist. They straightened their thumb and placed it against their folded pointer finger. The sand seeped through under their thumb unto the ground. Their fisted right hands hovered over the ground about an inch and a half. The tiny sand particles fell onto the ground just as pixie dust would. The sand looked soft like beach sand. Each color contrasted against mother earth's crust.

They didn't take a break until the sandpainting was done. As soon as the sandpainting was done, they called the patient over, and the ceremony began. Melissa remembered the medicine man singing a long sacred Navajo song and cited long prayers. People came in and out of the square hogan to help. Each time she went into the square hogan, she always remembered the sandpaintings that splashed across the dirt floor. Although she was small, she remembered the ceremony that was in the square hogan. Nowadays, the square hogan was back-up storage.

After Melissa emptied the hogan out, Melissa and her mom beat the dust out of two couches and two upholstered chairs with a broom. Next, they dusted off an antique dresser with a mirror. Not too much dirt accumulated since Grandma's last cleaning a few weekends ago. Melissa and her mom took the good blankets out of the storage. The blankets were Pendleton and were only used during ceremonies. The blankets were folded and stacked against the hogan wall.

The hogan's dirt floor was sprinkled with cool water from a glass pitcher. Then, the floor was gently swept with a broom. The aroma of wet dirt filled the air. The aroma went through Melissa's soul and soothed her mind. She sighed happily and smiled as she finished lightly sweeping the dampened dirt floor. The hogan was now ready. Melissa went back to the house to see what else she needed to do.

Grandma was finally off the phone. She was done telling the entire Navajo Nation that Melissa had her period. The ceremony was about begin. She told Melissa to run out to Cheíí, whom was sitting in the truck, and tell him that they have to go back into town. Melissa ran out to the truck.

Cheíí smiled and told Melissa, "Okay Little Lady, let's go to California. Tell your Grandma she better pack her bags".

Grandma quickly changed into her town clothes. Melissa went back to the house, helped Grandma walk to Tubby, and got in. Melissa sat in between Cheíí and Grandma.

Grandma only wore her best turquoise and silver jewelry when she was going to town. Melissa never saw Grandma put jewelry on in the house. She always saw her put it on as Cheíí drove to town. As Cheíí drove pass the sign that read "Tohatchi", Grandma placed her purse on her lap, unzipped it, and took out a clear sandwich bag that 'clinked' as she took out her jewelry.

Melissa always loved looking at what Grandma chose to wear to town. Grandma had four sandwich bags of jewelry filled with various items of jewelry. The first piece of jewelry she put on was her wedding ring. Her ring was yellow gold with an array of huge, white, shiny diamonds.

As she put on her diamond wedding ring, Cheíí said, "That ring right there is worth about twenty horses, ten sheep, and a few bails of hay."

Grandma quickly glanced at Cheíí and smiled. She continued to pick out the rest of her jewelry. She usually picked out three or four turquoise rings, a turquoise necklace, and a silver bracelet. She then got her cold cream lotion and rubbed it onto her hands, wrists, arms, and elbows. The cold cream smelled of baby powder and fresh roses.

After her jewelry and lotion ritual, Grandma smiled and said.

"Theeeerrre now! I'm ready!"

Melissa smiled back as they continued the drive to Gallup.

They drove the twenty minutes and reached the small town of Gallup, New Mexico. They drove near the middle of town and were going to the town's supermarket, called, "California Supermarket". It wasn't what Melissa imagined as being anything close to California, but it sure brought her the same excitement as if she were going to California for real. Even with no roller coasters by the oceanfront, smelly seagulls, surfboards, or modern edge of the hip life, Melissa absolutely loved going to California Supermarket. Going to California with Grandma and Cheíí was Melissa's Disneyland.

Just as she saw in commercials, California brought her happiness, smiles, and bliss. She loved being part of the comic book magic. It gave her happiness when she saw the new comics that came out. Although she didn't see the comics until check out, she was patient. She loved seeing the new toys and different types of candy on the shelves. That moment was her Christmas morning, as she didn't know what kind of new toys and candy there was in California.

Most of all, she loved watching this little old lady walk up and down the aisles shopping. She enjoyed grabbing things high up off the shelf and grabbing the heavy food items that Grandma couldn't carry. She didn't know what to expect this shopping trip though, and that, to her, was exciting.

California Supermarket was the size of six gas stations combined. Pass the motion-censored glass sliding doors, customers were greeted by tall brown bins of fresh vegetables and bright colorful fruit. Behind the bins were aisles of canned food, boxed food, and everything anyone could need to cook, or in that case, anything anyone could need food-wise for a Kinaałda, the womanhood ceremony.

Cheíí usually sat in Tubby reading the most recent Navajo Times newspaper with his loose tobacco in his front shirt pocket ready to roll. Melissa knew Grandma's grocery list down to the single bag of white onions.

Grandma always went to the fresh produce section first. Melissa walked behind Grandma as she walked up and down the fruit and vegetable bins. Melissa helped Grandma grab several bags of potatoes, oranges, and apples. While Grandma decided what to get and how much, Melissa stood on the other side of the bins touching and smelling the fruits and vegetables.

One of her favorite bins was the tall, clear, bin filled with loose pinto beans. She stood next to the pinto beans, smiled, and stuck her hands into the loose beans. The light brown spotted beans felt light, smooth, and cool against her hands. The 'clicking' and 'clacking' sound of the beans as they moved was addicting. No more than a minute later, Grandma's eyes in the back of her head "bust" her.

Grandma told Melissa in a stern voice.

"Don't do that!"

Melissa smiled at Grandma and slowly pulled her hand out of the beans to hear the 'clacking' sound of the beans one last time. Grandma walked pass Melissa and walked into the Moses' split aisles of canned goods.

Five aisles and forty pounds of food later, Grandma's silver wire cart was filled with white onions, lettuce, potatoes, canned tomatoes in every style: stewed, peeled, and chopped. There was fresh whole kernel corn, canned green beans, fresh bags of carrots, a variety of Campbell soups: chicken noodle, tomato, broccoli and cheese, Chicken and Stars, Cream of Chicken, and Cream of Celery. There was canned corned beef, canned corned beef hash, a small white and pink box of Sweet n' Low sugar sweetener, powdered coffee creamer, a large green can of Folder's Decaf Coffee, Rice Chex cereal, Cream of Wheat, a few bags of Bluebird flour, ten pounds of ground beef, five big packs of chuck roast, seven packs of t-bone steak, and her ever so famous get-up-in-the-morning-and-make-toast-to-go-with Grandma's-awesome-bowl-of-Malt-o-Meal cereal. Of course, Grandma never forgot the food that still holds a legacy today, the almighty can of Spam.

In the checkout line, Melissa eyeballed the comic books. It was right before the conveyor belt. When she reached it, she twirled and twirled the comic book stand. She looked at the Looney Tunes and Pink Panther comic books. She bit her bottom lip. She hesitated. She grabbed three comic books. She stood next to the cart holding the comic books and waited for Grandma to look at her. Grandma took a quick glance at her. In that sudden glance, Melissa held up the comic books. Grandma smiled and responded to Melissa's silent plea with a soft laugh.

Grandma pointed to the conveyor belt and said,

"Yes, little Lady, go ahead."

Melissa happily stared at her two Looney Tunes comic books and Pink

Panther comic book. Grandma agreed to Melissa's one final plea, a bag of orange Cheetos. Melissa was very happy to end her grocery shopping in California.

They walked out with a cart full of ammo ready for the week long haul. Grandma could feed more than the Army, Navy, and Marines, with the food she bought. Melissa looked at the cart full of food. She thought it was a lot of food for the ceremony. It was more food than she thought they needed. When they have the usual ceremony, Grandma bought about a fourth of groceries purchased that shopping trip. That made Melissa nervous. She now knew a lot people were going to show up for her ceremony.

A few minutes later, Melissa put everything in the bed of Tubby. Melissa hugged Grandma and told her thank you for the food. Grandma smiled, pat her on the back, and pointed at Cheíí. Melissa got into Tubby and hugged Cheíí.

Cheíí smiled, patted her back, and said, "Ohhh Okay, okay, Lady. You're welcome."

Night time came. Melissa fell asleep wondering how it would all come together. She closed her eyes and smiled as she fell asleep with the Looney Tunes comic on her chest.

*   *   *

Today is the day. She is excited and nervous. Melissa gets out of her bed, builds a fire, and goes to the restroom. She comes out of the restroom. She hears Grandma putting a batch of biscuits in the oven. Melissa smiles and walks to the kitchen. Grandma's special brew of liquid gold fills the kitchen with the essence of coffee beans. Grandma tells her to go get ready. Melissa takes a quick shower and walks back into the kitchen in less than twenty minutes. She is ready head to toe.

Cheíí takes the last gulp of his coffee, and says. "Ahhh! The little Lady is ready."

He puts his empty cup on the table. He motions his arm, "let's go." He walks out the front door. Melissa quickly grabs three biscuits and puts it in her kangaroo hoodie pocket.

Before Melissa closes the door, Grandma yells in Navajo with a stern voice. "Make sure it's the freshest!"

Melissa makes a puzzled facial expression and closes the door.

The truck starts as Melissa gets in and puts on her seat belt. Cheíí revs Tubby's engine and they drive down the dirt road and get onto the main highway. Melissa hears nothing, but the sound of the truck's engine, the wind going against the truck windows, and Cheíí chomping on his gum every now and then. Cheíí is usually not much for words when it comes to trips.

Melissa is used to reading his cues and being comfortable in his presence of silence. There are times when they ate at the table and Cheíí pointed at the salt making the hand notion to pick it up and pass it to him. Without a word from

Cheíí, Melissa grabbed the shiny gray saltshaker and gave it to him. Cheíí would smile in exchange for the giving of the salt.

Then Cheíí always said, "That's me, salt, that's where I come from."

He would say his clan, Salt People, in Navajo. There was almost a hidden routine with Cheíí that Melissa caught on to.

Not wanting any more silence, Melissa leans over and turns the dials to turn on the radio. It's programmed for the A.M. Navajo radio station, KGAK. This is Grandma and Cheíí's only radio station they listen to. The radio station plays old country music, Navajo song and dance music, and some other Native ceremonial music from other tribes. The radio announcer speaks fluent Navajo, except for the times when he says the ironic radio's motto, "KGAK, all Navajo all the time" in English. Melissa doesn't mind the station. Even though she only understands about half of what the radio announcer is talking about, it brings her comfort in listening to it.

It's still really dark outside. Melissa realizes she didn't check the time before she left. With how dark it is outside and no trace of the sun coming up, she guess-timated that it's around 4am. She has no idea where they are heading. She only knows that they are heading towards the opposite direction of Gallup. Heading north and with Grandma's clue before she closed the door, she guesses that they are going to either see the medicine man and get herbs from him, get hay, or get sagebrush from the mountains.

Cheíí always has this gleam in his eye when he is going to Farmington. She notices the gleam is there in his eyes, but it is a much happier gleam than usual this time. This tells her that since they are heading in that direction, they must be going to Farmington. With country music playing on the radio, she looks out the window at the brush along the highway. The brush is rushing by fast.

As the sunrise slowly turns into the tone of light orange, she looks at the other trucks that pass by going the opposite direction. Just as she is falling asleep, the route he usually makes to Farmington becomes unfamiliar. They drive through Farmington, but she's never been on this small road before. The small road is paved and surrounded by tall trees. The houses are very close to the road. The speed Cheíí is driving is much slower.

Just as she is about to say she is hungry, Cheíí turns into what looks like a small, white, adobe, house right off the road. There is only one yellow old truck parked in front of the small white house with people in it. Cheíí parks in front of the white, adobe, house next to the yellow truck. She sees a black sign hanging on the white screen door of the small white house that reads, "Closed" in red text.

Cheíí turns off the truck and gets out. He pulls out the rolled mountain tobacco smoke out of his front left pocket and lights it. Melissa sits in the truck in silence. There is only the sound of trucks driving up and down the paved road behind her every now and then. She remembers she has one of her comics she left in the glove box. She gets out her Looney Tunes comic and a small flashlight from the glove box. She holds the small, red, flashlight up to her comic. She grabs a biscuit from her pocket. She takes bites of her biscuit and reads her comic.

As the sun is coming up, more and more vehicles park beside her. Soon the entire dirt parking lot is full. People park on the side of the road. Cheíí gets back in and starts the truck. He turns on the heater and turns the truck off when the cabin of the truck is warm. Moments later, the screen door opens. A Navajo man in his forties with a white t-shirt, and white apron turns the sign around and signals for them to come inside.

Melissa and Cheíí get out of the truck with everyone following behind them. Melissa steps into the house. The small house is a butcher shop. The floors are old wooden planks and creaks with every footstep. Cheíí looks at the glass counter, which is just as tall as Melissa is. Inside the glass counters are rows and piles of fresh mutton. There are different parts of mutton. The man that opened the door and two other Navajo men stand behind the counter. Behind the counter to her left, a back door is wide open. She looks and sees two men cooking on a propane grill outside. The aroma of roast mutton, green chile, seasoned potatoes, and frybread fill the air.

The butcher smiles at Cheíí and says in Navajo, "Good Morning, Cheíí. How are you? Long drive?"

Cheíí smiles and says to him in Navajo, "Not as long of a drive to get back to my lady from Japan."

The butcher laughs, nods his head, and looks down at Melissa.

The butcher points at her and asks Cheíí, "Who's this little lady? I've never seen you bring anyone before. You hungry?"

Melissa feels the shyness consume her words. The shyness consumes her body with stiffness. She can't move. She hesitates, but manages to nod her head.

Cheíí laughs, puts his arm around Melissa, and says, "This is my Lady, my sweet little Lady I was talking about, but she's not a little Lady anymore, she's a nice Lady, proper Lady, now. We are going to have her ceremony this coming week. I am very proud of the Lady."

The butcher smiles at Melissa and says in English. "Ahhhh! I see! Well, that's good. Make sure you're strong to the very end. When you want to give up, find your strength, tell yourself to be stronger than your weaknesses, okay little Lady?"

Melissa understands the butcher's Navajo, smiles, and says, "Okay, I will", in English.

Cheíí continues to talk Navajo to the butcher. He points at the meat and tells the butcher he wants three mutton legs and some freshly cooked mutton sandwiches with green chile wrapped in a fresh tortilla. The butcher smiles and nods his head. Moments later, he tells Cheíí to pick up his fresh food at the other end of counter.

A few minutes later, the butcher calls out. "Cheíí, here is your order!"

The butcher reaches over the counter and gives Cheíí five big mutton legs and ribs wrapped in thick white butcher paper.

Cheíí grabs the wrapped mutton. He looks at the mutton. Cheíí tells him that he gave him extra mutton and ribs by mistake. He tries to hand it back to the butcher.

The butcher smiles and says, "Oh, that's for the little Lady. It's my gift."

Cheíí smiles and tells him thank you in Navajo. Cheíí gives it to Melissa and tells her to put it in the ice chest in the truck and that he would be out with breakfast. Melissa grabs the wrapped meat from him and goes out to the truck.

The sun is bright yellow and up now. She puts the meat in the ice chest and gets into the truck. She takes out her comic book and starts reading where she left off. Cheíí opens the driver side door. She puts her comic on the dashboard. Cheíí reaches over and hands her an ice-cold grape Shasta cola, salt, napkins, and a hot tortilla sandwich wrapped in wax paper and butcher paper. He gets in the truck and takes a deep happy sigh. Melissa puts her sandwich on her lap and salts the meat of her sandwich.

"The sandwich smells sooo good", she thinks.

While Cheíí is smiling prepping his mutton sandwich, Melissa is smiling on the inside. She makes a faint smile and looks at Cheíí.

Cheíí raises his sandwich to Melissa and says, "Cheers to the best food in the Universe!"

Melissa's first bite and every bite thereafter is complete and utter bliss. Her taste buds are going crazy begging for more. The mutton is cooked to perfection. It has just the right amount of char to the meat. As she chews, the juicy meat falls apart in her mouth. The green chile gives the sandwich a fierce and bold personality. She thinks anything she could ever crave, anything in the universe, that that taste of the green chile, hot tortilla, and muttony mutton, satisfies that every crave she could ever have.

As they eat, a man comes out of the back of the white house with a live sheep. The sheep is fat, clean, and yelping in fear. Cheíí chews his food and points to the back of the truck with his thumb. The man loads the sheep onto the back of the bed of the truck. The man ties the sheep's legs together, closes the tailgate, and walks back behind the house. He waves to Cheíí before he disappears around the corner. Cheíí waves back with his greasy mutton hand. They are only half way finished with their heaven-sent mutton sandwiches when Cheíí starts the truck and they head back home. Melissa takes her time finishing her sandwich savoring every juicy bite.

An hour later, they arrive home. Cheíí and Melissa put the newly bought sheep with the rest of the sheep in the corral. They pull up to the house. Melissa takes the wrapped meat out of the ice chest and puts it on the kitchen table.

Grandma smiles, claps her hands together, and says.

"Goooood, NOW we are ready!"

Melissa faintly smiles and asks herself mentally, "Am I?"

Chapter 4. The Ceremony

"Ah ha! My Lady. It's official. You're a Lady now and a beautiful one from your spirit to your soul to the tip of your toes!"
-Frank Nez

Melissa opens her eyes. She lies there in her sleeping bag staring at the wood logs and two by six lumber that make a cone shaped ceiling. She thinks to herself the lumber and logs look like a giant spider web. She didn't get much sleep as she kept the fire going all night. The fire is now out and she had maybe a couple hours of sleep when her body warmed up. She slept in the hogan alone. She can hardly feel the weight of being tired. She feels wide-awake. Her energy is rising. It's the second day of the ceremony and so far she thinks it's not too bad.

She continues to stare at the ceiling wondering if she should get up and go run now. She listens for voices outside or someone's truck engine starting, but all she hears are the distant 'clangs' of the bells that are tied around the sheeps' neck at the corral. The bell 'clangs' are accompanied with sheep cries. The sheep must be curious as to what is going on.

After a few minutes, she sees orange lights flickering from the right front window of the hogan. She knows the sun will rise very soon. She sits up and gets out of the sleeping bag. She turns around and looks at the gold antique clock with roman numbers hanging on the wall behind her. The second hand and long hand is stuck on "XII", midnight. All evening into the night and even right now, the clock reads midnight. She keeps forgetting the golden clock is broken. The second hand on the clock is vigorously stuck and ticks in the same place between the first and second second.

She folds up the cream white Pendleton blanket. Next, she rolls up her sleeping bag that's under it. Lastly, she folds up the thin foam mattress. One by one, she stacks the blankets and thin mattress on top of a clean small red rug against the wall in front of her. She takes the few steps to the vintage dresser. Standing in front of the dresser mirror, she dusts off her long, purple, cotton, three-tiered skirt going down to her ankles. She's wearing a collared, pink, velvet, long-sleeve blouse. She looks at herself in her reflection with a stoic face. She gives herself a slight smile.

She opens the top dresser drawer and changes her white, long socks into clean ones. Her shiny black bushy hair is tied into a ponytail. The ponytail is tied with a long piece of beautiful buckskin. Her hair runs down her back and is slightly bushy from sleeping on it.

Around her tiny eight year-old waist, she wears a dark red sash belt with white and green-colored trim made of high-quality yarn. If the yarn were a type of car it would be a fancy, shiny, and smooth running Mercedes Benz and not an everyday-teacher-driving-dusty-window-cracked-heater-not-working-Volvo. The ends of the sash belt have twelve inches of fringed loose dark red yarn.

She wears the sash belt so that not only her body stays thin, but to prevent bad posture. Grandma gave no mercy when she wrapped the sash belt around her waist. She could tell the last thing Grandma wanted her to do was breath. The sash was more than snug around her waist, as it has become a natural indentation of her body in less than a day.

On the vintage dresser in front of her is a light brown Navajo basket. The basket is old. The designs on it are faded. It has been through many ceremonies. One of which, she saw the basket being used in her brother's blessing way ceremony last year. The aroma of sage, buckskin, and fresh, soft, damp dirt fills her soul with a calmness she only gets in the hogan. The earthy aroma doesn't exist anywhere else in the universe. It made her soul smile.

Inside the basket is a pile of turquoise and sterling silver jewelry. She sits on the ground and puts on her moccasins. Her moccasins are thick, off-white colored with buckskin soles. The top piece surrounding her foot is one solid piece of dark red brick-colored buckskin that is softer than suede and goes up covering her ankles. There is a vintage, sterling silver, inch-long in diameter, round button on the side of each ankle. On the silver button is an etching of a kachina face. Under the silver buttons is a thin buckskin tie. She wraps it around the back of her ankle and around the top of her ankle. She then ties it making sure it meets behind the silver button. She ties each moccasin snug, tucks in the ties, and stands back up.

She stands in front of the dresser mirror. She grabs the jewelry in the basket piece-by-piece and slowly puts it on. She puts on her vintage, sterling silver, squash blossom necklace, two large sterling silver bracelets with an abundance of turquoise, two long turquoise earrings, a large turquoise pin for her blouse on her chest, and four large turquoise rings. She wears the rings on her middle fingers, ring fingers, and pinky fingers. She remembers not to wear it on her thumb and pointer fingers. Cheíí told her not to wear rings on those fingers as they are only worn by the dead.

She looks at herself in the mirror with all of her jewelry on. She smiles. She thinks she's a splitting image of Grandma. She thinks she looks exactly like Grandma, but younger, taller, and skinner. She wonders for a few seconds if Grandma looked like her when she had her ceremony many decades ago.

As she looks at herself in the mirror, she hears Cheíí's voice in her head. She remembers how cold it was sitting on the hogan's dirt floor just the night before. She could feel the coldness of the dirt through her long, cotton, skirt. She sat on the damp ground. Her back was straight and her legs were straight out in front of her. Her hands were palm up on each leg ready to receive the offerings from wise Cheíí and honor it.

She wore her Navajo dress, moccasins, and jewelry while Cheíí stood next to her, talking to her. She didn't look up at him. Instead, she stared straight ahead. She stared at the hogan door while Cheíí talked to her in Navajo. He knelt down on one knee and grabbed her hand.

Cheíí looked at her and said, "My dear, my Lady. I don't want you cutting your hair. You can trim it, but don't cut it. Your hair is your thoughts, your mind. The only time you cut your hair is when you are grieving. When someone dies or you go through something and you can't let it go on your own. That's when you cut your hair. You leave that grief behind and you cut your hair."

She caught herself spacing out in front of the mirror thinking about what Cheíí told her.

She's been to other ceremonies like hers and the young girl's own Cheíí always got after his granddaughter. The Cheíí would tell his granddaughter how disappointed he was in her and why. Once, she even saw a Cheíí whip the granddaughter with his belt and tell her she has a long way to go to grow up. Melissa inhales a deep breath and exhales slowly. She snaps out of thinking about the other girls whom were disciplined in front of everyone because they weren't doing what they were supposed to. She looks at herself in the mirror and remembers what happened the evening the before.

Melissa remembers sitting on the hogan's cold dirt floor. She was nervous and mentally prepared herself for the offering Cheíí was about to give her. As she sat on the floor, Cheíí stood up beside her. Nervously, she took a quick glance at Cheíí's brown leather belt and wondered if she would be embarrassed to be whipped in front of Grandma.

After Cheíí told her about her hair, he opened the hogan door. She looked outside. She felt the fresh, cool, breeze come inside. She looked into the dark night. She could see the stars twinkling against the deep, dark, black sky. The world outside was quiet. The space outside looked peaceful and beautiful she thought. As she stands in front of the mirror in the hogan remembering, she grabs her necklaces hanging around her neck, and closes her eyes. She hears Cheíí's voice talk about the first woman to exist in the Universe.

Cheíí's voice in Navajo says, "See that out there? This universe is bigger than you can imagine. Just like your way of thinking. Your brain is strong. Keep it sharp. Through the years you will learn and teach your brain how to think. I want you to always think of yourself of being a Lady. Changing Woman is the personification of mother earth and how the universe should be in balance. She worked hard and fought many battles for you to be here. She was very intelligent and she was very beautiful. After she was born, she grew up to be a lady in four days. Her life cycle represents the seasons and your life cycle. Birth represents the spring, maturing of age represents the summer, and growing old and dying represents the fall and winter. Changing Woman had the first puberty coming-of-age ceremony. She ran towards the sun three times a day: sunrise, noon, and sunset. You must do the same as she did. She didn't walk. She ran gracefully Her heart beats and flows through your body now. The runs you make represent life's journey. Her father, the sky, told her she must run with grace. The energy of the sun will bless your life with longevity and balance. During the ceremony, Changing Woman wore precious jewels and was blessed with corn pollen. Sacred songs were sung to protect her throughout her life. So, that's what's going to happen now. You're not a little Lady anymore. You're a Lady, '*The* Lady'. You have a long life to live. Live it well and live it so you can prosper. One day, you will see why our ancestors suffered. One day, it will make sense. Be proud of who you are and where you come from. You're a warrior. It's in your blood and always will be. So, take it with you wherever you go."

Melissa closes her eyes, takes a deep breath, and listens to herself take her breath in. She exhales, opens her eyes, and looks at herself in the dresser mirror. She walks clockwise to the front door. She washes her hands. She goes outside. She stands tall in front of the door. She stretches her arms to the sky. Her breath is warm and turns into steam in the cold morning darkness. She faces the east to greet the sunrise.

About twenty feet to the right in front of the hogan, she sees her brothers standing around a large fire. The fire is roaring and crackling on the crust of mother earth. They look at her and smile. They cup their hands on both sides of their mouth and start hollering. Their holler is the holler she would hear in those old western movies that featured Indians on horses wearing fringes; their faces splashed with paint ready for war, and have feathers for days.

The dogs come running to her with their wagging tails and start barking and jumping up and down at her side. Soon, all four dogs surround her and they start stretching. She can see their steamy doggy breath against the dark, cold, morning air. As the dogs bark sharply and her brothers continue to holler, Grandma's porch light flickers.

There are dozens of muddy cars and trucks parked between Grandma's house and the hogan. Melissa's dad comes out of the house wearing blue pants, a puffy navy blue vest over a navy blue hoodie, and running shoes. She sees him raise his arms waving to her standing on the porch. He joins her brothers hollering. People that had slept in their cars and trucks last night hear her dad and brother's hollering. They get out of their vehicles, start stretching, and join the hollering.

Her brothers throw more long pieces of wood into the fire. The fire crackles. It grows just as tall as they are, six feet tall. The east hills that sit on the horizon reveal the break of the bright yellow and mango-orange sunrise. She takes a deep breath and starts running. Her dad follows behind her running along with family and people that came to see her.

All of the men running behind her are hollering. An older teen tries to pass her and her dad tells him not to pass her. Her heart is pounding through her chest. She feels her throat and chest suck in the piercing cold, brisk, morning air. Her long skirt flares out in front as she runs. She holds down her large and heavy squash blossom with one hand to prevent it from bouncing up and down.

She runs east on the declining dirt road for half a mile. She reaches the main highway. The main highway and dirt road are separated by a cattle guard. A wire fence runs parallel along the highway. The highway lies north to south. She carefully runs across the cattle guard. She decides to run north along side the highway turning left and runs against highway traffic.

Every few minutes a car or truck drives pass her. There are dozens of people trailing behind her. She hears vehicles slow down in the distance behind her. Moments later, she sees a white Chevy truck in the distance driving on the highway towards her. It slows down on the highway, pulls off to the side of the road. It turns on its' hazard lights. The truck is fifteen feet in front of her. Now ten... five. She is face to face with the truck. She doesn't stop. She can't. She runs around the truck staying on the side of the highway.

She hears three doors of the truck open and shut behind her. She hears hollering coming from the white truck. She sees vehicle after vehicle pull over on the side of the road. Everyone that stops hollers. They all turn on their hazard lights. The passengers of the vehicles get out and start running behind her. Four green highway mile markers and a bright sunrise later, she turns around clockwise and runs back towards the hogan. As she turns around, she sees ten times the amount of people running behind her when she left the hogan. She only recognizes family and friends.

The bottom of her feet pound on the loose asphalt on the side of the highway. Her father is behind her. He tells her to run as fast as she can all the way up the dirt road. She nods her head. She makes a right turn onto the dirt road that leads up to the hogan. Now it's time. Her chest is piercing in pain. Her thighs are burning. She tells her body to dig deep for more energy. She finds it. She widens her stride. She runs the fastest she has ever ran in her entire life. Her legs feel like its' dragging weights as the hill gets slightly steeper and steeper.

She runs faster to pick up her pace. Her father yells to her in Navajo, "Beautiful! Faster! You're stronger than you know, go, go, go!"

As she gets closer to the hogan, the hollering behind her gets louder and louder. She abruptly stops in front of the hogan. She goes inside. She's breathing heavily. Once inside the hogan, she walks clockwise in a large circle around the fireplace that is in the middle of the hogan. She comes out of the hogan. Family, friends, and the strangers from the highway follow her footsteps inside the hogan and come back out. As she tries to catch her breath, she sees dozens of vehicles coming up the dirt road. They park along side the dirt road. The vehicles are parallel parked bumper to bumper.

From the house, Grandma sees the Lady and goes outside to greet her. Grandma smiles, claps her hands, and tells her to come and get the food to feed the medicine man. The Lady is sweaty. She gathers all of the food. There is freshly grilled steak, scalloped potatoes, sweet roasted corn, steaming hot yeast bread, roasted green chile, lamb stew with carrots, onions, potatoes, and celery, and of course, the gold nugget of the meal, the fresh, hot, traditional, fluffy and bubbly frybread. The medicine man only comes to the hogan in the morning after her morning run for the first, second, and third day. On the last day of her ceremony, the medicine man comes in the evening.

It's now the third day, the Lady is a private and the family is her drill sergeant. She does everything she is told to do from chopping wood to cooking to cleaning to herding sheep to hauling water from the well in the mountain to help cleaning the sheep that is butchered. She is not allowed to slouch, laugh, get angry, talk back, yawn, sigh, disobey, or move her long bangs that dangle in her face.

The ceremony is a very organized and respected process. In the mornings after her run, the medicine man sings sacred songs while her aunts, female cousins, and other females hold up blankets so she can wash. Before she is washed in a sponge bath-like fashion, the water is blessed with corn pollen. The soap that is used to cleanse her body is the root of yucca. The yucca root was dug up by Cheíí days before the ceremony began. The blessed water and yucca soap is placed in a beautiful Navajo basket. She is washed with yucca so that her hair grows long, healthy, and she won't get any allergies as she ages.

She runs a little farther every sunrise and sunset. She races the sun. The people that follow her represent her future children that she will teach to be strong in character. They will follow her teachings that she brings them throughout their life.

Each morning she gets up a little earlier than she did the morning before.

No matter what she endures, she is not allowed to stay up late nor sleep in. Except, for the last night. On the last night she has to stay up all night. She cannot go to sleep until the next sunset. Aside from behaving properly, and taking orders from the colonel, one of the most important things during the ceremony is the creation and labor of making the traditional Navajo cake.

On the first day of the ceremony, the men in her life, Cheíí, dad, and her brothers dug a large, round, six-foot in diameter hole in the ground. The hole is round in shape and about three feet deep. A fire is built in the hole. It is going to be cooked in the ground on the third day, which is today. Just as white people preheat the oven for their cake, Navajos did just the same. The fire burned in the hole all day and night until the last day. Today, the cake batter is going to be poured into hole. This cake just isn't any cake. This cake holds more importance than a birthday cake and wedding cake. This cake holds the future story of the woman's, the Lady's, life journey, her legacy. It's The Lady's turn to make the cake from scratch. Sweat will pour. Muscles will be sore.

Just as high-class white people respect the quality of food, it is the same for the Navajo cake, but it means more. The corn was harvested. It was torn of its' ears and was hung out to dry. The kernels were taken off the corn and stored in large Bluebird flour sags. The corn is used throughout the year for stews and for occasions like this one.

The corn is grinded with two stones. The two stones resemble very large, very smooth, river rocks. Both of the stones are very large, flat, and rectangular in shape. The stones are very heavy weighing about hundred pounds together. The larger stone of the two is three inches thick, thirteen inches long, and nine inches wide, The large stone is placed on the ground. The smaller stone is the same in thickness, but a fourth size of the larger stone. The kernels are crushed with a back and fourth motion by the small stone.

The Lady is almost done grinding corn. She's been kneeling down on her knees for the past three hours. She places the last handful of dried, whole, white corn colonels in the middle of the largest stone. She grabs the small stone and places it on top of the corn. The corn makes a loud 'crunch' as it breaks between the stones. The Lady holds the smaller rock with both hands applying her body weight and strength as she grinds the corn back and forth crushing it. It has taken her sixteen hours total to grind two ten-gallon buckets of corn kernels.

It's the third day. Today is nearing the close of the ceremony. The early afternoon has settled comfortably. She's finally done. Her hands, arms, and shoulders are sore. For the past three days, her legs and feet fell asleep from grinding the corn on the ground, but she didn't stop. She couldn't.

Her hair sticks to her face as sweat slowly drips down. She can feel the tightness of her abs. She felt a little tired yesterday from grinding and butchering a sheep, but she tells herself she is almost done. She gets up slowly. When she gets up she wants to grunt in pain, but she knows she can't. She holds in her pain by closing her eyes. She carefully pours the last of the grinded white corn into the top of the filled ten-gallon bucket. She smiles inside. She is done. At that very moment, she has never felt so accomplished in her entire life.

Just in the nick of time, Grandma comes in the hogan and tells The Lady that she now has to make the covers for the cake. Grandma has a large tub full of dried cornhusk. The cornhusk no longer carries its' fresh bright green color. The cornhusk has taken on a light tan color now that it has dried.

The Lady has to make two large covers for the cake, one for the bottom, and one for the top. She overlaps two ears in a circular motion sewing in a clockwise pattern. She makes sure the ears are facing the direction of how the corn comes out of the ground. She knows the ears of the corn need to be sewn close together to keep the cake batter from seeping through. She takes her time and soon enough she's made a cinnamon bun-like swirly pattern with the thread.

She remembers Cheíí telling her she must think of what she wants in life as she threads. So, she does just that. She starts thinking about trusting her confidence. She thinks about having the passion of living life. She thinks about what her happiness is. She thinks about how much she wants to be a good person. She loves writing. She wants to fall more in love with writing. She thinks later on down the line when she is much older that maybe a family of her own is in her path. She wanted a family that is close to her. She thinks about going to college. She thinks about having a nice house and being able to become better at everything she does. She mentally asks the Creator to be able to get through all obstacles that she might have in the future.

As she carefully sews the corn husk together, she quietly whispers, "Oh Creator from up above, I am praying to you to tell you that I appreciate the universe you have created. I see the stars every night and think about how beautiful life is. You created the different worlds and I appreciate the beauty of it. I am still learning and don't really understand what I need to do in life, but I am hoping the best from the universe and the good things it will give me. I was taught that this universe is infinite. Please bless all of the creatures and beings in this world and in the next. Bless my home and my family. Protect me. Help me to see my great-grandchildren. I want to have children someday. Help me find what I want to do in life. Right now, I am still seeing life through the eyes of a little girl. Most of the time, I cannot see what I need to see in order to prepare for the future. Many people have told me that I am still little, but now it is time to grow up. I am still at a lost as to what they are talking about. Please guide me. Help me to know what to do when I come across an obstacle. I want to be happy, but I don't know what that means. Happiness to me is being able not to worry about things that I shouldn't be worrying about. Protect my future. Help me to be strong when I need to be strong. I thank you for bringing me this far in life and taking care of me. Thank you, My Creator. I say this to be blessed by you with all the beauty in the universe. I ask to be blessed by the sunlight and the moon, O' Creator, O' Creator, O' Creator, O' Creator."

Three hours later, the covers for the cake are completed. Soon after, the cake lady that Grandma hired to help with the cake batter comes into the hogan. The cake lady is in the-reinforcing-grandma category. Her purpose serves to not only follow a recipe of the cake, but to make sure the cake is cooked correctly down to the very science of its' texture and temperature. The cake must turn out immaculate. The cake lady is old in her sixties, maybe even seventies. The Lady can tell the cake lady has seen enough life to be trusted to make sure the cake is stunning in every way.

There are taboo stories about the cake. If the cake comes out too dry, the young girl will grow to be extremely stubborn not able to strive due to her stubbornness. If the cake comes out undercooked, the young lady will not only fall short of her expectations that she sets for herself, but she will have a hard time in life and she will not get out of it. If the cake is overcooked and burned, the young lady will be lazy and forgetful causing her future to not be a successful one. If the cake doesn't cook at all, then she will never come home once she leaves and she won't be proud of where she comes from. She will be forever "lost". The cake must turn out clean cut. It must be like a fresh mud pie, moist, and fresh in color. If so, the young girl will strive in her life and raise good children.

Even with the perfect recipe, it is very difficult for the cake to come out just right on all aspects. Not only does the cake need to be cooked just right, but the taste, flavor, and texture of the cake must be on point, too. The cake must have the right amount softness, yet firm texture to it. It shouldn't be hard to chew or be bland. Some recipes call for raisins, others don't agree with the cake having raisins. Melissa feels the trust from the cake grandma that is hired to help her make the perfect cake.

The cake grandma reminds her much of her own Grandma. She's miniature, bossy and knows exactly what she wants. She's easy on the eyes. Strangely, contentment is alive and well in the presence of her royal bossiness. The cake grandma tells the Lady how to stir the cake and just how many raisins to put in each batch. The Lady makes six large batches. The cake mix is mixed in large ten-gallon plastic buckets and brand new, very large, metal tins that are usually used to feed horses or cattle. The Lady guess-timates the large metal water tins are about fifty-gallons of her future. She begins mixing the cake with clean, thin, sticks, known as stirring sticks. She adds each ingredient little by little as instructed by cake grandma.

The cake batter reminds her of thick pancake batter but with a thicker and meatier texture. It smells sweet like carrot cake. It also smells like wet, damp, and clean dirt. It reminds her of a perfect rainy day. She thinks nothing beats the aroma of the clean rain hitting mother earth's soil.

An aching back, sore arms and a set of sore abs later, the Lady is finally done. The news spreads of the cake finally being done. It's ready to be put in the ground. The men relocate the fire and ash that is in the pit. When they finish, they await for the instructions from cake grandma.

The Lady walks in the hogan and grabs the bottom cover of the cake. She counted two hundred ears of corn she sewed to make the bottom cover. The bottom cover is six-foot in diameter. The Lady, cake grandma, her mom, dad, and other people she doesn't recognize, carefully lay the cover down into the steamy dirt pit. The pit is steaming radiating with heat.

The cover is a perfect fit. So far, so good. Next, comes the grueling task of hauling the hundreds of pounds of cake batter to the hot pit. The Lady comes to the pit with the first ten-gallon bucket of cake batter. Before she pours it, cake grandma tells her to take corn pollen out of her small buckskin bag hanging on her sash belt. The Lady pours a small handful of corn pollen onto her right hand. She closes her hand making a fist. She kneels down onto her knees. She feels heat on her face. She feels the heat seep through her clothes. Her clothes start to feel hotter than if it was fresh from the dryer.

The pit radiates heat five times hotter than when the stove is at 400 degrees when she's taking out meatloaf. Sweat quickly percolates down her face. She slowly leans over. She stretches her right arm out over the middle of the hot pit. She sprinkles corn pollen onto the middle of the pit. The corn pollen feels like fluffy yet starchy, clean, corn meal in her palm. Then, she sprinkles in the direction of the east and then again from the middle to the south. She repeats the same technique sprinkling slow and in a precise line for the west and finally the north. She is now drenched in sweat. For some reason, the heat doesn't make her nervous or hesitate. It's almost as if the heat is feeding her strength and making her body sturdy from the ground up.

She is on her knees. The cake grandma tells her to slowly pour the cake batter onto the middle of pit. The Lady has a hard time picking up the ten-gallon bucket of cake batter, but manages to lift it off the ground. For half a second, she is a little terrified thinking she could fall into the pit, but she quickly pushes past the thought and tells herself she can do it. She knows her strength has to come from her arms and core in her stomach since she has to lean as far as she can to pour the batter.

One hand tilts the bottom of the bucket. The other hand is on the wire handle. She discreetly shakes as she slowly tilts the white bucket. She does her very best to balance her weight. She aims the batter on the middle of the pit. She slowly pours half of the batter. As the weight of in the bucket slowly decreases, it gets easier to pour. The cake grandma tells her to stop. Now everyone can help pour. The cake grandma tells the Lady in Navajo to make sure she handles every batch of cake batter. After ten-back-breaking-and-arms-shaking-in-lifting-and-pouring-minutes, all of the Lady's homemade cake batter is now in the pit.

The pit is completely full. The Lady sprinkles the raw cake batter with corn pollen in the same manner as she did earlier. She goes inside the hogan. She grabs the top cover and places it on top of the raw batter. Everyone in the front line helps to ensure the ears do not rip. The cake batter is now covered. There is an inch gap between the top of the cake and the ground. Cheíí, the Lady's dad, brothers, and other men begin to shovel fresh, clean, dirt on top of the cake. Once the cake is fully covered with dirt, the fire is moved back onto the top of cake.

The Lady is ecstatic the cake is finally done. Grandma hugs the Lady and tells her to come to the house to help prep for dinner. The Lady cuts carrots and other veggies that are going to be put into a lamb stew later. While she is cutting the veggies, Grandma tells her how special this last night is going to be. She tells the Lady in Navajo that she must listen very closely to the medicine man.

The Lady isn't nervous for tonight. It's the last night of the ceremony. She just wonders if she'll last staying up all night. She's stayed up all night before. In fact, she's done it several times, but this time it's different. The times she stayed up all night were to watch a VHS movie and to go to a squaw dance with Grandma and Cheíí. Other times were when she helped Cheíí with an all-night ceremony for people that came for help. She was in charge of the fire all night, but this time she knows it's different.

She remembers going to other coming-of-age ceremonies. Just a few girls were young just like her, but most were older in their late teens. She remembers one ceremony in particular. The girl was older than her, 16, maybe 17 years old. The young girl kept crying on the last night because she complained of her legs and back hurting. She wanted to go to sleep. While the medicine man sang, the girl whined endlessly to her mom and grandma. As the medicine man continued to sing, her mom and grandma allowed her to fall asleep. The Lady sat up against the hogan wall. She saw the young girl fall asleep. She saw some people shake their head in shame and disbelief as the girl was allowed to fall asleep. Other times the older girls having the ceremony were disciplined when they gave attitude to her elders. She saw girls get whipped by their grandparents. Even after the whipping, neither their attitude nor their demeanor changed. The Lady scrunched her face as she saw the young girls in each ceremony get whipped and even slapped. The first time the Lady saw this she was horrified. It scared her since she knew it would be her turn to have a ceremony. The Lady quickly caught herself spacing out thinking about the young girls she saw before. She walked into Grandma's house.

The Lady helps Grandma cook the glorious food that will be served to the entire Navajo Nation since it will be the last day of the ceremony. Grandma's house filled with the aroma of freshly grilled lamb meat, scalloped potatoes and onions, fresh frybread, and posole stew. There was always food cooking, but this was nearing the last day, the most important day of the ceremony, and the amount of food cooking is quadrupled. People are grilling food outside the house while others are helping Grandma with chaos in the kitchen. Food is everywhere. The Lady falls in love with a large watermelon. It stuck out like a white man at a kinaálda. It's amongst the different breads, meats, and sweets. The Lady wonders how someone has the means to get watermelon in the winter time. She is grateful for it. She'll eat it after she serves the medicine man food, which is very soon.

Grandma has stacks of large, thick, plastic trays to serve food on. After having several ceremonies in the hogan times before, the Lady knows to bring coffee and cookies first. She places a small kettle of freshly, brewed coffee, coffee cups, sugar, powdered creamer, spoons, and a variety of freshly baked cookies onto a bright yellow plastic tray. The tray was heavy and uneven in weight, but the Lady has no time to fret. She must take it to the hogan as fast as her little eight year-old legs can walk.

Halfway to the hogan, she feels her arms get stiff. Her arm muscles burn in tiresome and soreness. She fights it. She tells herself she can do it. She can serve the food. The Lady makes sure to walk clockwise once she's inside the hogan. She stops a few feet in front of the medicine man. The ceramic coffee cups 'clink-clink' as she slowly sets the heavy tray down on the mother earth. She gets on her knees and serves the medicine man his coffee and cookies. The Lady grabs the empty tray and asks the medicine man if he wants a tortilla or frybread. The medicine man slurps his coffee and tells her he wants both. She nods her head once, walks out the hogan's front door, and back to grandma's house.

Once in Grandma's kitchen, she says out loud to the kitchen staff that the medicine man wants both a tortilla and frybread. A foreign grandma she doesn't recognize pops out in front of her and yells at her in Navajo. The foreign grandma yells at the Lady in Navajo that she should know not to ask the medicine man anything and to not let it happen again. The Lady doesn't feel anything. She doesn't feel ashamed nor does she feel like she made a mistake. She just takes a mental note and remembers it for next time.

After she is done being grilled by the foreign grandma, the Lady asks one of her cousins on her dad's side if they saw her Grandma. They point to the back bedroom behind the living room. The Lady slowly walks over to the bedroom. The door is closed. She hears people yelling and arguing in Navajo. She can't make out what they are saying. She quickly recognizes her Grandma's voice. She stands still leaning towards the crack of the door to make out the argument.

She hears footsteps coming towards the door. She quickly bolts back into the kitchen grabbing another tray and piling on more food. The Lady piles a bowl of lamb stew, a bowl of posole, a piece of freshly grilled lamb meat, charred green chile, two pieces of frybread, two pieces of tortillas, and a large, juicy, watermelon slice. The Lady tries to take her time, but knows she can't. She's eager to see whom Grandma is arguing with. She wants to know if there is any way to find out what is going on.

Grandma usually yells out in the open. That's normal. Yelling in a bedroom with the door closed isn't normal for Grandma. Just as the Lady picks up the heavy tray, the bedroom door opens. The Lady gets easily distracted wanting to eagerly see who comes out of the bedroom and nearly drops the food off the tray. She can't believe who she sees coming out of the bedroom with Grandma. She makes a puzzled facial expression before being ambushed by the foreign grandma. The foreign grandma shoves the Lady in the back. The stews come even with the bowl's rim nearly spilling.

The foreign grandma yells at the Lady in Navajo, "Get out of the way! Why are you so slow getting the food out the door?! Move!"

While she's multitasking trying not to spill the hot stews over the bowl's rim and being yelled at, she thinks to herself, "Why in the world would they all be in that room? What possibly would they be arguing about? What is she doing here? Did I do something wrong? Maybe, Grandma will tell me later. Nah, I don't think she'll tell me, but she has to, doesn't she? I just don't get why…"

The foreign grandma shoves the Lady again, yelling in Navajo, "What are you doing? Can you be any slower? Get a move on you good for nothing! Get outta here!"

The Lady retains the pushing blow from the foreign grandma. She quickly forgets about whom she saw and gets to the hogan.

As the Lady kneels down on her knees taking everything off the tray and placing it on the dirt floor in front of the medicine man, the medicine looks at the Lady as he slurps his coffee.

The medicine man is a Navajo man possibly in his late fifties, maybe early sixties. He is wearing old, very worn, jeans that have gone passed its' expiration date. His moccasins are rusty red in color. He looks like he knows how to be Navajo. From the first time she was introduced to him when she was younger to the first day of the ceremony, the Lady thought his facial expression always expressed how serious life is and how serious she should take this world. She thought of just how many secrets of life and distant life in another world he knew of. The Lady thought that maybe he has seen enough life for five life times. Every question anyone has for him, he always had an answer.

When Grandma asked him in Navajo how he needs to be paid in order for him to conduct his protection and coming-of-age ceremony, he replied, "You pay me what you think is fair."

Grandma nodded her head.

The Lady thought, "Well that *is* only fair. That also seems like a trick question, I mean, it kind of says, 'let me see how much my granddaughter is worth', but on the other hand, it also makes it seem like the more the family gives in gifts, the more they want for her future. Wow. If humans were antiques, he'd be behind that glass collecting dust, that's for sure."

The medicine man ate first. The Lady ate second. Everyone else ate third. The silence while eating doesn't make the Lady feel uncomfortable. She's used to silence. The Lady keeps her head down as she eats. The sounds of ripping crispy frybread, spoons 'clink'ing against the metal bowls, chewing, and slurping, take over the hogan. It almost creates a faint echo among the hogan's whole log walls.

The Lady remembers being a part of this moment in other coming-of-age ceremonies. The silence is usually too much for the young girl having the ceremony and she almost always ends up complaining about something to her mother or grandma, but not the Lady. The Lady takes refuge in the silence. She's finishes her meal. She closes her eyes. She takes a deep breath. She hears the crackles of the huge, roaring, fire outside. She hears her brothers and dad talking and laughing around the crackling fire outside the hogan. She wants to smile hearing their laughter, but she knows she will get whipped. Instead, she lightly bites her bottom lip and takes another deep breath to shake off the urge to smile. The silence breaks. The Lady opens her eyes as she hears a spoon slide against the metal bowl as the medicine man puts the metal bowl on the ground. He tells the Lady in Navajo the food was really good and was the best-cooked mutton and lamb meat he's had in several years.

The Lady quickly gets up, gathers all of the empty plates, bowls, trash, and puts it all on the tray. She takes the tray and dirty dishes back to Grandma's kitchen. Grandma is sweating still making frybread. Grandma wipes the sweat off her forehead with a paper towel and yells for one of the Lady's cousins to help bring the rest of the dirty dishes back from the hogan. Within what seems like microseconds, the hogan is cleaned up.

The Lady goes to the bathroom. She washes her hands and quickly goes back to the hogan. She enters the hogan and walks in from the east entryway. She walks clockwise, in front of the medicine man, and sits down next to him. With her back straight, legs straight out in front of her, she looks forward at the door.

She hears the medicine man tear off a paper towel.

As he wipes the salt and cooled fat from the mutton meat off his mouth and hands with the white paper towel, he continues to talk in Navajo, "The mutton, did you butcher the sheep yourself or did someone do it for you like everyone else?"

The Lady looks down at the dirt floor, looks at the end of her long three-tiered skirt, then glances up at the medicine man and calmly says in English, "Yes, I butchered it."

The medicine man claps his hands, smiles, and says in Navajo, "That's good! That's really, really, good! That's one of the main reasons of having this ceremony, for you to really start doing things yourself. No one is going to do it for you. If you want things done right, you do it yourself. When you do something, you do it with care, with love, and do your best. I want you to set the bar high for yourself. This ceremony is a huge part of growing up. I know a lot of people have probably already tried talking to you. They might say this and that, but it's up to you on what you want. It's all there for you, your future. The songs I sing are about the first-coming of this universe and this earth. The songs are very old. My great-grandparents told me from their great-grandparents that the earth is very old, and just like an elder, the earth needs to be taken care of. So, you do that, too. This world is bigger than you think. The stars that you see in the sky are a sign that the universe is old and that us, humans, will never really solve everything. We are just here to live, live life, but I want you to live life in a good way. One thing that you must know is that you have to trust yourself. You have to find the strength when you think it's not there. You have to fight for what you want in life. In this life, there are many things that we don't understand. I want you to remember these past four days. Remember the things you did. Remember that no matter what you will endure in your future, you are protected. When the times are tough and you think and feel like giving up, that's when you make that choice to fight for what your heart wants. Your mind is what you need to make strong. Once your mind is strong, your heart will follow. Don't be worrying about what people may say to you, even your own family. You keep going. A long time ago, your great-great-great-great grandparents were forced to leave their home. During the winter, the white people came, the soldiers. They made all the Native families walk, different tribes. For hundreds of miles they walked. The soldiers rode on horses. For months, our people, your people, Navajos saw their children and grandchildren raped, killed, and left behind, but they finally made it to a camp. We were prisoners of the United States. The United States tried to kill us, but we made it through. My great-grandparents told me their great-great-grandparents were given spoiled food. The flour and corn the soldiers gave them had bugs in it and was stale. So, your great-grandparents decided to fry the bread dough that was given to them to prevent them from getting sick. That is where you come from. That is who you are. Don't ever forget who you are and where you come from. This is your home. Just like any home, where you live, even if you're only there for a little while, you must take care of it. That's what you do to mother earth, too. You take care of her. Don't get caught up in the white people world. White people will mess with your way of thinking and might say church this and church that, but religion is the white people way to control you. They don't want you to be who you are and they want you to forget where you come from. When I was young, many religious people tried to tell me that who I am and where I come from is wrong and evil. Being young you don't understand that until you get a little older. Those white people that tried to tell me I was wrong to be Navajo, they forced me to try to think like they did. They punished me for speaking my own Native language. I saw them beat small children until they could barely walk. There were times when they beat the children so much that sometimes I never saw those children again. That didn't scare me. I thought of what my great-grandparents told me, about how to survive, and that I have to fight to live. Many young people have to leave home now, just like we did a long time ago. Times are changing, but don't ever lose your voice, that's yours. Be proud of who you are and where you come from. I can feel the strength and pride you have in yourself. I can tell you are always thinking. You are very smart. Your Cheíí tells me that you got a poem published in a journal? That's good. I read it. I couldn't' believe what I read. The poem was very powerful. It spoke to me. It told me you are proud to be Navajo. It touched my heart and soul. Your Cheíí also told me that you love to write. He says when you're not working and helping, you're writing. That's good. Don't lose that. Don't let anyone tell you, 'you can't do what you love doing'. Don't allow anyone to tell you any different. When you succeed in what you want to do, people, even family will not like it. When that happens, leave it alone. Don't act on it. Just leave it be and let them drown themselves in their own poison. There are a lot of people that want bad things for others even though they are family. It's sad to see. There are very few that have good intentions, but they make the most difference. I know that is going to be you. I have done many, many, many ceremonies and it's been a very long time since I have been to a ceremony like yours. Every time I drive up the road I smile and I think to myself, 'this little girl, this young lady is special. She is marked by something good by the Gods, the Holy People' I see it. Every day that I have come here, even before your ceremony, you are always doing something. I sit in my truck before I get out. I see you chopping wood. I see you helping your dad. I see you talking to Cheíí. I see you helping Grandma. I see you cooking. I see you playing basketball. I see you running hard and running as fast as your body can take you. From here on out, you work harder on the things that are important to you. From here on out, you do things on your own. From here on out, you trust yourself, okay? Don't be sleeping in. Sleeping in makes you grow old faster. Make sure you make your bed. Otherwise, you will carry the bad with you the next day and can't move forward, okay? The songs I am going to sing tonight will protect you. They will protect you and your future, okay? I know you don't really truly understand Navajo, so if you don't understand something, you let me know right away, okay? I am going to go home, feed my dogs, feed my cattle, feed my sheep, go get some more propane, take a short nap, and shower. After that, I will return. This evening when the sun sets, the last time that you run, run and think about your strength. Ask the Gods, the Holy People from up above for your protection and strength. When I come back, we will have a small dinner, then I will sing all night. I don't want you to doze off. You sit right here next to me and sit up straight. There are four long sacred songs that I will sing. If you listen closely, you can learn it, but you have to listen to the song. Then after the songs we will pray together. Then, you will pray by yourself. When you pray by yourself, you pray about the things that are bigger than you first, the Holy People, the Universe, the planets, the stars, mother earth, all the creatures on this earth, and other humans. Then, you pray about your family. Then, the very last thing you pray about is you. You pray about what you are grateful for, the problems you might have, then you pray for what you want. I, too, will pray in this order. The Navajo I will use when we pray together is very old. A lot of Navajos don't really understand the old language. Try to listen to what I am saying. I will pray for your protection, okay? When you are about to go through life and it gets hard, remember that it will never ever be as hard as it was for your great-great-great-great-Grandma and Cheíís. They really fought to live, so that you could sit here next to me. Now, you are here, alive, and grown. Navajos are very different from white people. You will have to learn their ways in order to survive in this world. Promise me when you get old, too old to drive, too old to worry about money, that you will come home, okay? I want to let you know that I really enjoyed watching you work, help your family, and be a little girl. Now, I want you to know that all the hard times will only be for little while. Don't allow the hard times to get the best of you, okay? Thank you, Miss Lady, The Lady. You are a good Lady. Grandma and Cheíí are really proud of you. You good? You understand what I have told you?"

The Lady again, wants to smile, and oddly enough she understood every word he said to her. She bites her bottom lip and wants to hug him, but knows she can't.

The Lady looks at him with a grateful twinkle in her eyes. She nods her head and says in English, "Yes, I listened to everything you said. I understand."

The medicine man claps his hands once. He gets up off the dirt floor with a grunt.

He says waving his hands in the air with excitement in English, "Yes! Good then! See you all later!"

The Lady watches the medicine man walk out of the hogan. She hears him start his truck, honk his horn, and start to slowly drive down the dirt road. The dogs bark as a few more vehicles drive up the dirt road. She gets up and goes to Grandma's house to see if Grandma is okay. She has never seen Grandma sit down in the last week.

The Lady goes to the kitchen and tells Grandma she will finish making the frybread and tortillas so that she can sit down and eat. Grandma agrees. She wipes sweat off of her forehead, washes her hands, wipes her hands on her blood-red polyester apron, and sits down. The Lady places raw dough into the crackling grease and serves Grandma fresh stew and a frybread.

A stand-byer, a mom in her early forties, asks Grandma, "What next?"

Grandma slurps her coffee and says, "We prepare for tonight."

The Lady goes through all the raw dough. She puts the red ice chest filled with hot, fresh, frybread on the empty chair next to Grandma. She washes the dishes thinking of what she needs to do next. Grandma tells her that she must stay up all night no matter how tired she feels. The Lady nods her head giving the notion that she is listening to her. As Grandma is talking to her about the morning that follows, the Lady can't help to think about why Grandma would be so upset coming out of her bedroom earlier. The Lady's thought is interrupted as Grandma tells her to go find Cheíí so he can get more propane. She goes outside and finds Cheíí. Just as she is about to tell Cheíí Grandma is out of propane, he tells her that he knows he needs to get more propane. He tells her to start the truck and load up the propane. She starts up the truck, drives to the back of the house, and loads up the propane. She parks the truck back in front of the house. She goes back inside the house and gives the keys to Cheíí.

The chores and orders are fulfilled. The day passes quickly. The evening is finally here. The Lady makes frybread. The medicine man has returned. She serves the medicine man food. She eats. She cleans up. The last night of the ceremony begins. The hogan is packed with people most of whom she has never seen before. Everyone is sitting on the ground against the hogan wall. She is sitting on the west side of the hogan. She sits facing east. She stares at the hogan's white door eager to start. To her right, a few feet away sits the medicine man. On the right of the medicine man sits Cheíí. Cheíí smiles at the Lady off and on as the medicine man speaks to her. To her left a few feet away sits Grandma, her mom, and several other Navajo faces.

The hogan becomes deaf to sound. There is nothing, but silence.

Everyone is quiet and listens to the medicine man as he speaks.

The medicine man asks her in English, "Do you remember everything I told you earlier?"

Melissa nods her head and says in English, "Yes."

The medicine man smiles and says in English, "Okay then, good. We start now."

The medicine man closes his eyes and clears his throat. He starts to sing. The song sounds very old. It sounds older than the earth. It sounds older than before traditions became tradition. The Lady sits on top of her turquoise Pendleton blanket on the ground. Her legs are out straight in front of her. She places her hands palm up on her thighs as the medicine man begins to chant in Navajo. The words sound very ancient. The chant is soothing and calming. The Lady wonders exactly what the chant is saying. The words in the chant are so harmonious. It sounds like one long run-on sentence. The medicine man takes a second break in singing to catch up in his breath.

The songs are long. She notices there is a pattern with the repeating phrases of the songs always being in fours. The medicine man sings twelve sacred songs. The Lady forgets about keeping track of time and feels like she's in a time loop. The night is no longer young and vibrant for it is the earliest of the awakening dawn now. As the medicine man sings into the last song, the Lady realizes that she was multitasking. She prayed the entire time the medicine man sang, but she also was able to listen to what he was singing. She ends her prayer and opens her eyes. She feels lightheaded when she opens her eyes. She feels as if her spirit and mind left the hogan when she was praying.

As the Lady opens her eyes, the medicine man grabs white corn pollen and sprinkles it on her. He grabs large stones and puts it on her body starting from the bottom of her feet going up her legs, stomach, chest, up her back, and finally, touching the stone on top of her head. He grabs a tiny, rusty-red, ball. The tiny ball is clay-like. He crushes it with his hand. He wipes the clay-like substance on her forehead and cheeks. Sheep fat aroma enters the Lady's nostrils. The clay-like ball feels greasy and sandy as he wipes it on her face. He cues her asking her with his eyes if she's ready. She nods. The singing comes to a halt. He sits back down on the ground and starts to pray. Every two phrases he takes a brief pause making sure she keeps up. The last hour of praying seems like an eternity, but she finishes. She's happy.

The prayer is done and the sun is now up. Strangely, the woman she stays with in Arizona takes her ponytail down. For a second, she wonders why her mother isn't fixing her hair. The woman brushes the Lady's hair with a straw brush and puts it in a Navajo bun. The Lady stands up and goes outside to greet the sunrise. She comes back inside the hogan.

The medicine man smiles and says in Navajo. "Now, you *are* a Lady! *The* Lady!"

The medicine man makes one last speech and tells her that from here on out she is not a little girl anymore and must carry herself with respect and dignity. The medicine man hugs the Lady and tells her congratulations.

The medicine man packs up his things and leaves. As soon as he leaves, Grandma and her soldiers start running around like it's midnight on black Friday. Kids run around outside playing and laughing. Days before, everyone helped make hundreds of brown paper bags full of goodies. All of the goodies are placed behind the Lady so that she can give it out. Before the goodies are handed out to everyone, the Lady lies face down on her belly on top of a Pendleton blanket. Her arms are stretched out parallel to her shoulders. The woman from Arizona starts to massage her. She starts from the Lady's feet. She goes up the Lady's legs and up her back, then her head.

Grandma tells the Lady in Navajo with a comforting tone, "I want my Lady to be smart, beautiful. Nice and tall. You will be so beautiful my sweet baby, my precious, my sweet baby girl."

Earlier when the medicine man sang the last song for the Lady, the men took out the cake. The Lady overheard some of the foreign grandmas say that the cake is perfect. She smiled.

The Lady gets done being stretched and stands up.

There are hundreds of brown bags filled with fruit, candy, soda, water, and finally, the Lady's triumph, her cake. With all of the bags and boxes of goodies behind her, the Lady stands holding a Navajo basket in front of her. Her mom grabs the premade brown bags and places it in the Navajo basket. The first in line is Cheíí. He sings her a song. After he sings the song he tells her that he sang the same song when he first held her when she was a newborn. The song is old and talks about how precious, beautiful, and wonderful this new baby is. The baby is protected with the mountains, powerful storms, and his prayers. The Lady smiles. This time, she can't contain it. She feels fresh air from outside fill her lungs.

The Lady says in English, "Thank you, Cheíí. I love you."

Cheíí greets her with a smile and says happily, "Awwww! My Lady! Look at you! Smart! Beautiful! My Lady! Good job! My strong and smart Lady!"

He reaches in his front right pocket and takes out his wallet. He sifts through his crisp bills.

Cheíí places a clean, crisp, 50 dollar bill in her basket and says, "Here you go My Lady! It's not about what you earn or how much money you make, it's about you having passion and loving what you do. This is for you! I know there will be plenty more where that came from and it will all be for you."

He grabs his goodies in the basket with a smile and kisses her forehead. The Lady always feels the love and warmth from Cheíí. Soon there is a line of people going outside of the hogan. Some people leave money, some leave gifts cards and others leave words of wisdom. Some tell her they saw how hard she worked and it touched their heart.

As she finishes giving out all of the goodies, the ceremony is officially over. The day is long and she starts to become overly exhausted as the sun takes what seems like forever to reach the sunset. After the hogan, house, and the last dish is cleaned, the Lady is finally able to sit on the couch in the living room. She sits next to Cheíí. Cheíí hugs her and tells her she did well. She can go to sleep now if she'd like. The Lady holds onto Cheíí not wondering when to go to sleep, but wondering why she can't stay. She doesn't want to leave back to Arizona. She closes her eyes. She squeezes Cheíí tight until she finally falls asleep.

The next morning is here. She is able to change into normal clothes and it's time to leave. The woman waits in the car as the Lady goes around to the kitchen hugging Grandma and Cheíí. Grandma starts to faintly cry as she hugs her.

The Lady hears Grandma's sadness in her voice when she says in Navajo, "Take care of yourself, my baby. My Sweet Little Baby. I will miss you, my sweet, sweet, precious baby. My Lady."

The Lady can't find her mom and dad. She wants to wait, but the woman is impatient honking the car horn, so she gets in the passenger seat. Driving down the dirt road she looks in the right side mirror. She bites her bottom lip in sadness as she sees the big hill that sits as Grandma's backdrop. She turns around and takes a last look at Grandma's blue house as it gets smaller and smaller and then finally disappears as the car gets onto the highway and drives further away.

Three hours later, they reach a small apartment on the university campus. The Lady brings in her bags and puts it on her bed in her bedroom. She goes to the living room and sits on the futon.

The woman tells her, "Give me all the money you have. I gotta go. I have some stuff to do. I'll see you later."

The Lady reaches into her pocket and gives the woman $149. The woman grabs her backpack, a few books, the car keys and leaves. The Lady turns on the black twenty-inch tv as she sits on the futon and watches Tiny Toon Adventures.

Chapter 5. For the Money

"You're gonna work like a dog even when you're sick as a dog, but that's what you do. You keep going."
-Frank Nez

It's Monday morning. The sunrise's orange juice bursts through the horizon—it's 5am. The Lady goes back to the normal city life she lives. The small apartment is a casket in disguise, except with less life in it. This must be what the mummy's tomb in Egypt feels like. She brings life to the crypt keeper's cell and turns the tv on—channel 13. The tv screen's flashes can be seen from the hallway. She keeps the bathroom light on and door open. She watches the classic 1940s cartoon Pink Panther off and on. She brushes her hair and ties it into a simple ponytail. She's ready. Her keychain jingles as she locks the front door behind her. She walks down the street to the bus stop. Behind the bus stop is a twelve-story college dorm. The dorm is white with large, square windows. She turns and looks behind her. For a second, she wonders what it looks like inside.

She waits at the bus stop. University buildings swallow her little-girl-in-a-backpack presence up like the legendary kraken swallows pirate ships for a light snack. Sounds of the bus take over her morning. The bus stops with a 'pssshh'. The door opens and closes as she steps in. She gets off at her stop. She walks across the street to South Beaver Elementary. School for her is much like a dog getting its' head stuck in a fence—helpless, sad, and kind of funny simultaneously.

After school, she sometimes walks through the university campus instead of riding the bus. She likes walking through campus because the student union building gives out free samples of food.

Time presses on like a pregnant white woman wanting her baby out of the womb. It's been a month since she left the Rez. She starts to panic. She notices there is little to no food behind the small, dark brown, squeaky-hinged kitchen cabinets. Her small hands grasp onto a half a bag of pinto beans and less than half a bag of white rice. That's her city norm—her stomach starts to ache in the evening more often now.

At school, kids give her their unwanted food at lunch. She stops taking the bus after school. She goes to the student union building. She gets free samples of the daily special, ice cream, and a few french fries. There is a large, heated, canister of soup near the tables against a pillar. The staff can't see the soup canister when they work. The canister holds the soup of the day. She watches them work and notices they are busy often.

One day she's at the student union building. Her starvation is scratching the inside of her gut much like an angry wolf looking for his next meal. She decides she can't stand the stings of hollowness any longer. Her heart beats just as much as her stomach aches for nourishment. She takes a deep breath and she goes for it. When the cashier's back is turned, she walks as fast as she can over to the silver, hot, soup canister. She frantically grabs a paper bowl. Her little hands tremble, making the ladle rattle against the canister's rim. Her taste buds scream as she scoops the soup into her equally empty bowl. She takes her steaming soup and quickly sits down at a table. She feels a wave of relief as her lips caress the silver spoon.

She slowly slurps and whispers, "Oh, my Waterloo, I finally got you."

She takes her time eating. She does her homework. Waves of college students with backpacks pass by her like a school of fish. Some rush by. It reminds her of a little white rabbit she once read in a book. The little white rabbit was carrying around a watch with a chain. Others walk slow reading their book not really watching where they are going. Others run into people they know and have a brief happy college conversation before they hug and part ways.

Evening hits. There is a shift change with the food staff. She grabs more free samples and soup. She is tired of being there. She finishes her soup. She grabs a handful of crackers on the condiment stand and stuffs it in her backpack. She heads back to the apartment. She arrives at the apartment. She sees dirty dishes in the sink. The woman must have been there for a while and left. She washes the dishes. She cleans the small apartment, gets ready for bed, and falls asleep looking at her red '93 Lamborghini panoramic poster hanging on the wall in front of her.

A few months later, the food manager, a young white man, nearly a baby himself, maybe in his early twenties, catches onto her array of free samples. His skinny pencil of a body walks over to her table and tells her that they will no longer be giving out free samples. He stands in front of her table with his arms crossed against his skinny, brown tie telling her she now has to buy something. She doesn't find a word to muster. She packs her notebooks, pencils, homework, and leaves with an empty stomach. She walks across campus back to the apartment. Just as she's crossing the main street back to the apartment, she sees college students holding stacks of pizzas headed to the dorm.

She is so hungry today. The chicken salad at school did nothing for her hunger. She looks down at her stomach as it growls in bitterness. She looks up. She walks in a fast pace, but trying to act normal following the pizza. She stops in front of the doors just as it closes. She spots the pizza going into the elevator. Her heart is racing. Her palms are sweaty. She squeezes her eyes for two seconds and walks with a fast pace straight into the elevator. The doors take what seems like forever to close, but she makes it and quickly regrets it.

The elevator 'dings' past each floor. She closes her eyes and inhales the potent stench of garlic butter, yeast bread, and mozzarella cheese heaven. The elevator doors 'ding' open to a huge living room-like set up. It looks like two living rooms, side-by-side. There are tables and chairs against the walls. There are huge, yellow and blue beanbags on the floor. Everywhere she looks, there are college students. It was aberrant to her. Like mosquitoes in the summer over the lake, they are ubiquitous. Her heart is beating through her chest rapidly. The palms of her hands are clammy. Her face is getting flush. She takes shallow breaths. She realizes she doesn't fit in. A young, white woman sitting on the couch turns, and looks at her for a few seconds, then turns back around.

As she looks around she sees college students. Some are watching tv on low, some are reading on the couch, and others are sitting at the tables highlighting their textbooks. The tenth floor is hosting a study hour. There are tables of pizza, burgers, fresh veggies, and iced tea. She's ecstatic. She sees the food and then quickly realizes she has to leave. She starts to walk towards the elevator when someone notices her leaving.

A white woman stops her. She looks young, in her twenties, maybe mid-twenties. She is very skinny, has no hips that couldn't possibly bare children, and she has no muscles which means she's probably never worked a day in her life. Her hair is thin which means she probably doesn't drink much water. Her hair is blonde and in a lazy ponytail. She is wearing a cherry red t-shirt that is clearly three sizes too small. Her t-shirt reads, "Coca-Cola" in cursive. She is wearing black sweatpants and sandals. Melissa quickly notices that she reeks of chicken soup. The aroma is rancid. She tries not to react to the musty, chicken soup perfume.

The white woman asks her, "Where are you going?"

Melissa turns around, opens her mouth, but nothing comes out. She can't muster a word much less a sound.

The woman laughs, "That's okay. You can start in that hallway. Come on, let me show you where all the cleaning supplies are."

Melissa doesn't know what to do other than follow her down the hallway.

The woman says, "Okay, so here is everything you need. I need you three times a week around the same time, if that's okay, and I will pay you cash every Friday. Is that okay? Oh, and you are always welcome to the food here. We usually have food. Something is always going on."

Melissa is shocked. She quickly realizes that she could easily work here, get paid, *and* eat. She mentally tells herself that her shoes are starting to hurt her feet and her clothes are getting thin and worn. She thinks maybe she could do the job right after school.

Melissa hesitantly responds, "Yeah, okay…yeah."

The woman smiles and tells her, "Good. I'll let you get to work."

Melissa vacuums the carpeted hallways. She cleans the bathrooms and showers. She goes to work right after school three times a week. Sometimes the college students request her to clean their rooms for five dollars. She starts to think how else she could get money.

On one of her days of cleaning, she comes up with the idea of babysitting when she overhears some of the women talking about working as a babysitter and how it interferes with being at study group. She hears the women talk about how they wish they could get paid more for the babysitting jobs. One of the other women asks if babysitting is easy and what they do when they babysit.

Melissa slowly wipes down tables and chairs listening to the conversation. The women explain how to care for babies, such as, how often to check diapers, and babysitting babies were the easiest since they often sleep. They posted flyers on the bulletin boards on campus with their phone number and that's how they got the jobs.

The next day at school, Melissa sneaks colored paper from the art room during a bathroom break. She works on her flyers during recess. She uses a black magic marker and writes on each flyer in big letters.

BABYSITTER!!! DO YOU HAVE KIDS BUT CANT STUDY?
WEEKENDS ANYTIME
TUES & THURS 4-12. CALL 928-863-1757

After school, she posts flyers in the student union bulletin boards and other bulletin boards outside of the university buildings. She waits tentatively for the phone to ring back at the apartment. After only a few days, she gets her first call. She doesn't know what to say, but listens to what they need. It's a college student and she lives on the other side of the apartment complex. She tells the college student she can do it. The college student asks her what she charges. She tells them she charges whatever they think is fair.

So far, she only has one babysitting job and it's tonight. She's excited about it. It's now evening. She goes to the apartment. She nervously knocks on the door. A white woman answers. She is an older white woman. Melissa could tell she is stressed as she has thick wrinkles on her forehead and heavy bags under her eyes. Her dark, blonde hair has streaks of white lightning in it and is tied in a messy bun. The woman is wearing light brown khakis, a white t-shirt, and hiking boots. The woman tells her the baby is playing in his playpen and she will be back in a few hours after class. The woman tells her she is welcome to any of the food there is.

Melissa sees her leave and goes to the baby's room. The baby is quiet playing in his playpen. He turns around and looks at her. She remembers what the women at the dorm said about how to take care of a baby and how to check if the diaper is wet. She bends down and squeezes the baby's diaper. It's squishy. She picks up the baby slowly.

She tells the baby, "Geez, you're heavy baby. Almost as heavy as a sack of blue bird flour, oaff, twenty pounder."

She takes the twenty-pounder, bald, and round-headed baby out of the playpen. She finds a baby blanket, places it on the carpet, and slowly lies the baby down. She remembers babies cannot support their own head so she places her hand behind the baby's head as she lies him down. She changes his diaper.

She is not sure how old the baby is, but gets the just that he is not walking yet. She sits on the ground holding the baby as the baby stands against the couch. She gets up and turns on the tv. She puts on cartoons. She is shy and doesn't know what to say to the baby. She feels a little weird talking to the baby.

She calmly tells the baby, "You're a cute little guy. Are you hungry? Do you want something to eat?"

The bald-headed, cute, baby smiles and babbles baby talk to her. For the next few hours, Melissa becomes more comfortable with this little, bald, human being. The baby smells of clean, cotton sheets, lavender fabric softener, and some sort of rose-scented lotion. She plays, tickles, and holds the baby, before changing his diaper, again. She feeds him, burbs him, and puts him down in his crib for his night of slumber. The baby immediately falls asleep.

She leaves the bedroom door open a few inches and turns the tv down in the living room. Just as she dozes off on the couch, there is a bang at the door. The bang startles her. Her chest tightens. She doesn't know what to do. There are two more bangs. She looks out the peephole in the middle of the front door. She's on her tippy toes. It's a white man. He looks old, tired, and angry.

He bangs on the door again.

He yells. "Open the door! Hey, look. I'm sorry. Open the door!"

The white man bangs on the door four more times. She continues to watch him through the peephole. He finally walks off. She tries to see which direction he goes. She quietly checks on the baby. The baby is in a deep slumber. Melissa is wide-awake and hungry. She goes to the small kitchen and opens the fridge. She makes herself a plain Jane turkey sandwich—just two slices of turkey and two slices of bread. When she is done eating, she cleans up her mess, and decides to make herself an extra sandwich for later. She makes the sandwich, puts it in a sandwich bag, and stuffs it in her pants pocket. She goes back to the living room and finds something to watch on tv. Every so often she goes into the baby's room to check on him.

Moments later, the woman comes back. She pays Melissa ten dollars. Melissa is very happy about the ten dollars. Tired, but happy. The woman thanks her and Melissa leaves. She tiredly walks to the new department store near by. She buys half a gallon of milk and a small box of cereal. Drained, she goes back to the small apartment and goes to bed.

Days go by since her first babysitting venture. She is cleaning at the dorm today. However, today she is particularly excited. Today is Friday. She finishes cleaning the wings of the dorm of the tenth floor. She doesn't know what to do after she is done cleaning. A few students invite her to movie night. They tell her Stacy, the dorm resident advisor, is in class and will be back soon to pay her. Melissa sits on the big comfy couch. She mentally tells herself that the couch is more comfy than her flimsy, spring, twin mattress in her room. She accidentally dozes off on the couch watching the movie when Stacy wakes her up and gives her money.

She sits up and puts the money in her pocket. Just as she is about to say good-bye the fire alarm goes off, but it doesn't sound like a fire alarm. It's a loud 'buzz'ing sound. The alarm stops. The elevator 'dings' and a dozen police officers flood out of the elevator.

Cops with noisy jackets point guns at everyone and yell. "Freeze! Campus Police! Freeze! Don't move!"

Women scream. Some are still sitting. Some run. Melissa gets scared and looks around for a place to run to before they see her. She doesn't know why she runs, but she feels like something isn't right. She runs towards the stairs at the end of the far hallway. As she gets to the stairs, two white women give her a big, clear, bag with something green in it. She thinks it looks like tea. She doesn't know what it is.

The older white woman in a concert t-shirt and jeans, tells Melissa in a frantic voice. "Here. Keep this for me. Come back in a few weeks. Don't worry about the pay. I'll make it up to you. Just keep this for me and just go, go, go!"

Melissa grabs the bag of tea, puts it under her shirt, and runs down the stairs. She goes out through the back of the dorm. She runs towards the apartment. She runs as fast as she can. Her heart is beating faster than any drum she's heard in any ceremony. Once in the apartment, she locks the door, runs to her room, and flops on her back onto her bed. She manages to calm down. She pulls out the tea from under her shirt. She looks at the tea the white women gave her. She sniffs it. She makes a puzzled facial expression. She thinks to herself what it might be. She has never seen tea that reeks of skunk before.

She puts the tea in her bag and puts the bag on the top shelf in her closet. She quickly remembers the money Stacy gave her. Her excitement punches through the ceiling and counts it—fifty-five dollars. She decides to buy herself a new pair of shoes. She walks ten minutes to a sporting goods store and buys herself a pair of basketball shoes. The cashier asks her if she wants to throw away her old shoes. Melissa smiles and agrees. She leaves the store wearing her new shoes. Her feet feel like their walking on firm marshmallow clouds. She smiles and is proud of her shoes. She stops at a small farmers market on the way back to the apartment and buys ten dollars worth of groceries.

A few weeks go by and she returns to the dorm with the tea. She is nervous and doesn't know what to expect. She comes out of the elevator and is immediately greeted by all the college dorm students. The two women that gave her the tea tell her Stacy was caught with weed and she got kicked out. Melissa takes the tea out of her bag.

She dangles the tea and says, "You mean because of this?"

The older woman laughs. "Oh yeah, I forgot about that! Girl, you can keep it!"

Melissa doesn't really want to keep the tea, but puts it back in her bag. She starts cleaning the floor of the bathroom, when the older woman approaches her.

"Hey little lady," she says. "How would you like to move some weight?"

She stops cleaning and looks up at the woman puzzled, "What are you talking about?"

Over the next hour, the two white women tell her they want her to be their delivery person. They would pay her triple what she's getting paid cleaning. She asks how it works. The two white women laugh and tell her the tea is weed. They tell her the weed would take her places she's never gone before and it helps with stress. She tells them she's never seen weed before. They explain that weed comes from the earth and not harmful.

The women explain to the tall, thin, pony-tailed, third grader that plenty of college students are all about stress-free leaves. Hesitantly convinced, she agrees. The women hand her a small, midnight-black, electronic box with a olive-green colored display screen. The device is smaller than her hand.

They explain to her she'll only deliver to four places. They explain how the small, black, electronic box works. The small, black, box 'beeps'. When it 'beeps', a phone number and a series of numbers will display. When she gets the code "143", she'll pick up a delivery. The women tell her they trust her and will tell her where to go.

It's been a month. They give her six hundred dollars. Melissa was beyond herself and didn't know how to react. She asks if they are sure about giving her that much money. The women laugh and tell her she worries too much and she needs to chill. Melissa wants to hang out with them, but she knows she can't. She has errands to take care of. So, she tells them she will stop by later. She leaves. She goes to the nearest plaza that has a grocery store, sports store, and clothing store. She buys herself a new backpack, a bike, roller blades, some new clothes, and groceries. She saves the rest of the money for future milk and cookie runs.

Melissa ends up working for them off and on for three years.

Time flies and Melissa is now in sixth grade.

One day, police officers come and visit the classroom. They are wearing black t-shirts with blood-red text that reads "D.A.R.E." over their bulletproof vests. Three police officers talk about gangs, drugs, and alcohol. Much like watching paint dry, they tell the class the dangers of alcohol, marijuana, and other drugs. After a torturing session of listening to cops that got degraded to talk to a room full of virgins and kool-aid palm lickers talk of peer pressure and the damage of alcohol to the liver, they hand out a survey.

She lightly sighs and thinks, "Seriously? They should be fined for this waste of time."

The snitches say the survey is anonymous.

She wonders why they talk slow.

The tallest one says slowly, "You won't.. get into trouble for telling the truth on the survey. The results are for research purposes only."

The survey cards are a dark magenta pinkish color. That reminds Melissa of the construction site she's been riding her bike by everyday. She saw that color on a tall canister. The yellow canister had that exact color, but on a skull and crossbones. The color automatically lights flares in her brain—a signal for danger or caution. She starts to read the survey. She checks the "yes" box to the questions:

"Have you ever smoked weed?"

"Have you ever seen anyone drunk or pass out because of alcohol?"

"Do know someone who sells weed?"

She writes in a short answer to the question, "Do you think weed is dangerous? Why or Why not?"

She writes, "It helps migraines, body aches for the elderly, and cancer patients. Weed is from mother earth. Weed is not tarnished like pills."

The high-on-adrenaline cops start talking about an event that is going to be held on campus. As the cops talk, Melissa looks at her classmates' pink index cards and realizes that she is the only one that marked any of the "yes" boxes. She quickly erases her pencil marks in all of the "yes" boxes and erases her handwriting in the last question. She marks the "no" box on everything and leaves the question blank. The bell rings ending the school day. The class turns in their index cards.

Melissa tries to push pass the other kids, but she can't. She ends up being the last one to turn in her card. She faces her pink index card upside down and walks in a fast pace out of the room. Before she reaches the door she feels the blue meanie take the top card and read it and quickly look up at her. She dashes outside to her bike. Her heart beats faster as she unlocks her bike on the side of the school building. She gets on her bike and leaves faster than a rabbit running from a fox. She feels like the blue meanie will call after her and want to ask questions.

She gets on her bike and as soon as she rides her bike across the street, she hears her teacher yell her name. She doesn't want to turn around. Her teacher yells for her name two more times. She pedals her feet as fast as her long legs can take her down the street and out of sight. It turns out that she had merely won the door prize, a D.A.R.E. t-shirt.

In the last two years, the two white women and Melissa have grown very close. It was more than just an underground stress-free leaves business. They were her friends. They tease her about liking boys telling her she needs to wear dresses and not be so damn serious all the time. She laughs and tells them she's not thinking about boys right now and just wants to make money. She sometimes wonders if the women really know how old she is. The two white women teach her how to roller blade and fix her hair. When she first met them she always wore a simple, third grade ponytail. Now, she's a chic, sixth grader with TLC-curled side bangs, and an opened portal of endless beautiful hair.

Because she is making so much money, she only babysits if it is an emergency. She likes knowing she can help others that really need it. Off and on she sees the woman she stays with at the apartment, but more often than not, Melissa is not at the apartment. When she isn't delivering, she's out roller blading with her friends from school or riding her bike. During winter when the snow is deep, a snowball fight with the two white women from the dorm, and a fifteen-foot snowman were her play dates.

She seldom buys herself new clothes including the number 32 jersey, Shaquille O' Neal, her favorite basketball player. She saved just over six thousand dollars. She keeps it in three red metal coffee tins in her closet.

One night after counting her bundles of money, she excitedly, but quietly says to herself, "This is crazy."

She quietly screams and falls back onto her bed holding her money on her chest. She looks at her red Lamborghini poster on the wall. Then, she looks up at the loft-high ceiling and skylight. The stars out beyond the skylight are a blur, but bright against the dark night sky. She feels at peace. She thinks about Grandma and Cheíí. She wonders what they're doing. Grandma is probably drinking her cup of tea at the table winding down her day. Cheíí is probably sitting on his brown, fluffy, recliner falling asleep.

Her excitement and peace is temporarily taken away when she hears the jingles of keys and the front door handle twist. The front door opens and slams shut. She hears stumbles of footsteps. It's the woman. She's back.

The woman yells in a slur. "Aaaay! Ew back?"

Melissa gets up and shoves her money under her pillow. She runs to her bedroom doorway. The woman walks into the other bedroom and slams the door. Melissa hears the woman talk gibberish behind the closed bedroom door. Melissa goes to the living room and checks the front door. The hallway stinks of old fruit. The aroma of spoiled grapes is overwhelming. She wants to throw up.

As she is about to close the front door, a man says. "Wait, wait, wait."

He pushes the door past her.

Melissa figures he knows the woman. He smells like spoiled fruit and spoiled yeast bread, too. He stumbles to the woman's bedroom door and bangs on the door.

In a slurring voice he yells. "Aaayy! 'pen da door!"

The woman opens the bedroom door, giggles, lets him in, and slams the door. Melissa hears the bedroom door lock. She hears them talking and laughing. She doesn't feel like listening through the paper-thin walls. So, she puts her shoes on, grabs her money, puts it in her bag, and walks to the playground. The playground is behind the complex. The playground is abandoned. She thinks of all the kids in her class. She knows they're at home with their mom and dad having dinner and getting ready for bed. She sits on the swing. She starts to slowly swing. Her legs droop. Her feet drag lightly scraping the top of the soft, beach-like, sand under her feet. The squeaking of metal rubbing against the chain echoes as she swings slowly back and forth in the dark. She looks out beyond the dark-orange streetlights. She looks up at the college dorm. She decides to go visit the two white women at the dorm.

She gets to the tenth floor and there they are. They giggle as Melissa steps out of the elevator. They ask Melissa if she wants to go get some food. She happily agrees. They make the five-minute walk. They share heavy doses of dopamine laughs and a pepperoni pizza. They laugh about an elderly couple that buys weed from them.

The old couple is Melissa's favorite client. They live in an old farmhouse just outside the campus walls. They always invite her inside. The old lady reminds her of Grandma, but a white version. She's in her seventies. She seldom eats due to a medical condition. She wears an apron just like Grandma. She loves baking. She always makes Melissa something—sometimes it's banana bread, other times it's an apple pie, and other times it's pumpkin cookies. Melissa savors every soft bite. During lunch at school, she shares her baked gifts.

The two white women laugh and say that they hope they don't die soon because they will lose their best customer. Melissa faintly smiles wondering how that's funny. They take the leftovers of the pizza back to the dorm. For the rest of the night, they watch a movie on the couch. Melissa accidentally falls asleep on the couch. She wakes up to the 'ding' of the elevator. The sun shines bright through the glass windows.

She slowly sits up says. "Shit."

She can't wait for the elevator. She's going to be late for school so, she runs down the flight of stairs and makes it just in time. She gets on the bus and sits down. She shakes off her tiredness and gets to school just as the bell rings.

"Crap." She says as she sits down at her desk.

She forgot her backpack along with her homework in it. During morning recess and in-between class nonsense she spends her time re-writing her essay. She manages to turn it in at the end of the school day.

She goes back to the apartment after school. She goes inside the apartment and finds all of her clothes, belongings, and bags scattered all over the room. She sees the red coffee tin cans on its' side on the ground in the closet. All of the lids are gone. She rushes and picks it up. The red cans are empty. She goes to the woman's bedroom. The woman looks at her angrily and asks her where she got the money.

She says, "It's not mine. One of my friends asked me to hang onto it for her."

The woman is drunker than a sailor back from war.

The woman slurs. "Ew lil' piece of shit! It's a damn lie! What have I 'ver done t'you? I didn't ask you to live with me. Don't you want to be here? I told you, you live with me, you… bitch."

The woman pushes Melissa out of her bedroom and slams the door in her face. Melissa goes to her bedroom. She starts cleaning the mess the woman made. She closes her bedroom door and locks it.

She leans up against her door, and says. "Fuck."

Seconds later, she hears the woman's bedroom door open followed by the front door slamming shut.

She lifts up her long, white and royal blue, basketball jersey exposing her belly button. She holds up her jersey with her chin. She takes out a thick wad of money folded in half, and wrapped with a thick, light brown, rubber band. She's glad she took all of the money with her last night when she left the apartment. The woman merely took three hundred dollars from her red coffee tin. She knows she can make that money back in less than month. She's not worried about it. She now knows that she has to keep her money with her and wherever she goes.

She cleans her room and then goes to visit the two women. They are studying. They tell her their classes were canceled because a college student committed suicide. Melissa is shocked and confused. She can't grasp onto why someone would take their own life. She feels sad for a moment or two. The two women sigh and tell her sometimes people don't want to face their fears and get through life. There is a slight pause. They tell Melissa to sit by them and do her homework. For a few hours all three little ladies write and study. Just as Melissa finishes writing her history paper, the two women are done writing their paper, too. They put their pens, paper, and books away and decide to go to the new department store that is just a few blocks away off campus.

They go inside and start to horseplay around the store. The women go to the accessories section and try on an array of sunglasses, hats, scarves, and 'clanky' costume jewelry. Melissa laughs as they make fashion statements in what is her world right now. Next, they go to the toy section. They find an enormous, red, bouncy ball. They each grab a ball, sit, grab the handle, and start racing down the main aisle. One of the women gets off the ball. She picks up the ball and hits the other woman with it. The woman being hit screams, laughs, and falls onto the floor. Melissa laughs hysterically still bouncing on the ball going down the aisle.

Like a mortuary, there is no one around except the employees. Before they exit the store, the women buy baby lotion, shampoo, and some snacks for later. On the way back, the women tell her one of their friends works at the campus movie theatre and the concession stand is hiring. They tell her she can get all the free movies she wants. She tells them she's willing to do it. For a few months, she works at the movie theatre on campus. The two women visit her at work. They throw popcorn at Melissa when she gets them their popcorn and drinks.

Like everything in life, things must change. The past three years were some of the happiest moments she's had, but now it's time to say good-bye to the two women. Over the years, they have watched out for her. They made a cake for her on her birthday, went to the movies with her, took her skiing, and they even smoked weed a couple of times with her.

The farewell is final and embedded by the two women's college graduation. After the graduation ceremony, they go to a house party at the old white grandma's farmhouse. Her house is on the edge of campus less than a block away. The house is a two-story, with a large porch, a deck on the second floor, and beautiful grass on the lawn in front. Melissa blows up balloons and hangs blue and yellow decorations. She hangs up white Christmas lights in the backyard and helps start the grill. She has fun watching the house get occupied by other college graduates and their family and friends.

She drinks the non-spiked lemonade and eats. She's never had shrimp before. She loves it. She's never seen that type of food anywhere. As the music blasts, the women sadly tell her that they are moving back to California. They tell her they are leaving in two days. Melissa is bummed out. She hugs them and says her final farewell. She tries to give them back their beeper. They tell her she can keep it. They tell her they will send her the code "143" which is the code for, "I miss you". The numbers represent the amount of letters in each word. She lightly rubs the beeper's screen and slowly puts it back in her pocket.

Even though her friends are gone, she still finds bliss in her childhood. For a few months she doesn't work. She does her homework at the student union and now buys her food. The young white manager is no longer there and he is replaced with a woman that looks like she is always stressed.

On the day the two women from the dorm left, they gave Melissa a pound of weed to part their friendship. They told her she could smoke it or sell it, if she wanted. She makes some joints out of it. She doesn't smoke it. She just makes it and thinks about what she wants to do with it. She keeps two joints with her, for just in case. There is no particular reason why she keeps two joints with her. She just does.

One day while doing her homework in the student union, she notices the manager crying a few tables down from her. The manager is doing shift paperwork and stops doing the paperwork because she's crying. Melissa decides to offer the woman a joint. The woman calms down and asks her what she owes her. Melissa tells her not to worry about it. Melissa thinks maybe she just needs something nice on a bad day. Melissa packs up, leaves the building, and feels good about her small gift.

For the next several months, Melissa notices her money is slowly deteriorating and needs to figure something out and fast. She still visits the farmhouse grandma, sells her weed, and sometimes smokes with her. The farmhouse grandma tells her she is going to leave this world very soon. She now wears a yellow silk scarf on her head to cover her baldness. Her cancer is progressing quickly. She's going back home to Wyoming. That is where she wants to be buried. Melissa gives her all the weed she has left—half a pound. The grandma tells her she can't accept it. The grandma walks out of her 1950s style kitchen and comes back into the kitchen minutes later with a parting gift. She gives Melissa another pound of weed. The grandma tells her she's an intelligent little lady and not to take life for granted. Melissa asks her when she's leaving. The grandma tells her she's leaving the day after tomorrow. The grandma asks Melissa why she looks so worried.

Melissa tells her she knows she will need to get a job again and this time it can't be weed. Melissa takes her last baked gift of banana bread, hugs the old grandma's frail body, and parts ways. She takes a bike ride to the student union. She goes to the bulletin boards and sees a flyer that quickly gains her interest. She rides her bike the two miles across town. She locks her bike outside the building and goes inside. She sees rows of desks, computer desktops, and white people running around frantically like they lost their car keys and they're late to go somewhere. She walks up to a woman that looks like she's the meanest in the room. The woman stops yelling at her employee and looks down at her.

Melissa tells her firmly with confidence, "Hi. I'm interested in delivering newspapers. I can start tomorrow."

The woman stops and looks down at her and says sternly, "The job is open, yes. You have to finish your newspaper route by 5am. That means you get here no later than 4am. Have the papers delivered before 5. Can you do that? How old are you? Never mind that, go pick an area on the map over there on the wall, memorize it, draw it on a piece of paper, do whatever you have to do to remember your route. See you tomorrow morning, kid."

The woman continues to yell at her employee. "I told you to change the headline. Or is finding less than six words too much of a job for you?!"

Melissa walks over to the wall and picks a neighborhood a few blocks down from the university campus. She walks out of the building and rides her bike back to the apartment. She figures it will take her thirty minutes to get back. She should be able to have the newspaper route done before school starts. She gets back to the apartment, quickly makes spaghetti, cleans up, gets ready for bed, and crashes for the night at 7pm.

The next morning, she gets ready for the newspaper route. She dresses warmer than usual. She takes the 30-minute bike ride and finishes her route at 530am. She hopes she won't get into trouble for being thirty minutes over the deadline. The student union is open and near school. She doesn't want to make the drive back to the apartment on the other side of campus. She goes inside the student union and sets her watch alarm to go off at 730am so she can head to school. She finds a couch in a dark corner and falls asleep. Her alarm beeps at 730am. Her eyes feel heavy. Her energy drags like a cat not wanting to get off the couch. She buys a breakfast burrito and heads to school.

It's nearing the end of her sixth grade year. Her hustle is a well-known highway—babysitting, newspaper route, cleaning the dorm, and once in a blue moon, selling weed. Twice a semester, the woman in the apartment drops her off at McDonald's in Holbrook. Holbrook is halfway between Flagstaff and Tohatchi. She's ecstatic because she gets to see Grandma and Cheíí. When she returns from Tohatchi, she goes back to her daily grind. Soon, she's thickening in dead presidents. She's worn-out. Sometimes she falls asleep on the swing or under the slide during recess. Other times she tells the teacher she's not feeling well and lies down in the nurses' office.

Her teacher is calm and surprisingly, also Navajo. Her teacher is around her mom's age. She's just as feisty as Grandma. She often talks Navajo to Melissa.

Melissa understands her, but ignores her sometimes because she feels like she picks on her. She asks Melissa if she knows how to butcher a sheep, make bread, and haul wood. Melissa just nods her head to whatever the teacher asks. Melissa thinks she doesn't have time to be chit chatting. She just wants to finish whatever project or lesson they are doing so she can move on to the next one.

The Lady is tall for a sixth grader—standing on the brink of five feet and three inches. She's still slender, has her long, black, shiny hair, and wears prescribed contact lenses. She mostly keeps to herself. She observes the other sixth graders. She notices kids are having boyfriends and girlfriends. Kids are getting in trouble for holding hands during recess. She wonders why someone would want a boyfriend. She hasn't really thought about having a crush on any boys.

She laughs to herself about the fun times with the two white women from the dorm. She remembers what they said about liking boys—make sure the boy she likes is nice and treats her with respect. She sees the drama in relationships on tv and movies it makes her not want a boyfriend.

Suddenly, a thought pops in her head. When she was five years old, she remembers Cheíí telling her something she hasn't forgotten. She was playing outside Grandma's house with her yellow, Tonka, dump truck in the dirt. Cheíí came up to her. She stopped playing and looked up at him.

Cheíí bent down and patted the top of her head, "Hey, my little Lady, what are you doing?"

Melissa answered, "Paying in the sand whiff my sruck."

Cheíí quickly changed his facial expression and tone of voice to a serious one.

He said in Navajo, "My Lady, My sweet little precious Lady, I'm not sure how to tell you, but the Holy People are greedy with you. They came to me. Told me you are not meant to be with anyone, but only with the Moon. You're smart. Beautiful. They made you this way. Made it this way. I can't explain why, but I want you to know. You will have your time, I promise. Where the Moon's stars were and where the stars were when you were born were aligned alike. I have seen him. Your love is not among the stars, but with the Moon. When you can't see, don't know which way to go, the stars can't be there for you, but the Moon will. The Moon will light the way for you, take care of you. The Moon will fall in love with you. So, don't be upset when I tell you this, My Lady. I am just telling you what the Gods have showed me."

Then Cheíí patted her little head and walked back inside the house. She stopped for a few seconds, pondered, then continued playing with her toy truck.

She still remembers. She hasn't figured out what it means, but knows it's important. As she gets older, she still thinks about it.

Over the years, she's made some new friends. All of her friends are unique. She only makes friends from the same class she's in. Sometimes after school she goes to NiMarco's pizza a few blocks away. They sell pizza by the slice. It's the best pizza she's ever had. She admires her sixth grade class because the class is diverse. There is an Italian, a few Hispanics, an African American, Asians, and even other Native Americans from different tribes. Minority make up half of the class and the other half is white. A few of her friends also live on campus. She becomes close to some of them over the next few years, but never close enough to tell them the tough times she's had much less her interest in stress-free leaves.

Seventh grade is a slap in the face. She's hit her peak growth spurt. She's grown out of her shyness, but still keeps much to herself. She's grown out of her little girl appearance. Her seventh grade chic is similar to the popular trio TLC—side bangs, high ponytails, and baggy overalls. She joins seventh grade volleyball, band, and basketball. She ends up dropping out of sports because she doesn't feel like making the six-mile bike ride home after a late night game.

She's now on "bad terms" with the woman at the apartment.

The woman at the apartment is always pissed off. The woman is clearly stressed about classes. For some unexplainable reason, the woman starts to question Melissa what she does after school. Melissa wonders why the woman is being clingy and nosy all of a sudden. It doesn't bother Melissa, she just wishes the woman isn't home when she gets back.

There are more times she's working and alone after school than there are times she's playing with friends.

She soon finds something she can do on the weekends. She finds a job with the university volleyball games. She's a volleyball retriever. During the games, she sits on the corners of the volleyball court. She retrieves the ball when it bounces off the court. She's paid five dollars per game. She doesn't do it for the money. She likes the hot incentives—fresh, steaming hotdogs, grilled hamburgers, cheesy nachos, hot pickles, and fizzy soda from the concession stand. Since she's working hard by white people standards, they give her as much hot incentives as she can eat and drink. Unfortunately, there's a down side. Sometimes the games end late making her ride her bike late at night back to the apartment on the other side of campus. She's not scared, just exhausted. She always makes sure she takes the butterfly knife Cheíí bought her years ago.

One late night, Melissa finishes her job at the volleyball game. The university wins the title. It's an exciting night. The MVP gives Melissa the volleyball to keep. Melissa's ecstatic. She gets back to an empty apartment. It's just after midnight. She lies on her bed. Laying on her back with the winning volleyball on her chest, she looks up at the stars shining through the skylight. The skylight is crystal clear, clean, Grandma clean. She thinks the apartment complex must have cleaned it. It's the cleanest it's ever been since she's stayed there. She lies on her bed thinking about Grandma and Cheíí. She misses them. She hasn't seen them in over six months. Every time she asks the woman if she can take her home, the woman gives her a loud annoying sigh and tells her she can't because she's busy.

Melissa stares at the peaceful moon. She gently rolls the volleyball on her chest. She thinks when she'll be home again.

Chapter 6. One Way Ticket

"No matter what you go through, remember you handle it like a Lady.
Like 'The Lady' should."

-Frank Nez

In the wake of seventh grade, things are out of whack like a caterpillar strolling the chicken cage—being eaten is in inevitable. The woman at the apartment starts to notice Melissa "gone" more often and doesn't like it. Regardless of the woman's drunken rants when she's at the apartment, Melissa leaves for work. Taking the woman's drunken stress as a grain of salt, she finds her own peace. She remembers the Rez back home is quiet. She hears its' heart beat. Melissa carries the Rez with her—it's the only way to find her peace.

She enjoys getting lost in the hurricane of bookcases at Newman's used bookstore. Inside, dozens of slender, carrot-orange bookshelves form a wide maze. She tilts her head as she walks amongst the maze of books. She's mesmerized by the titles of books—Fear Street Saga, Oranges, Scary Stories to Tell at Bedtime, and Chariots of the Gods. Like a puppy at the pound, she picks one. She sits on the firm, velvet, tufted, ruby red, winged-back, chair against the bookshelf, and starts to read. The aroma of coffee grounds and books swallow her baby lotion charisma. For now, she's home. She doesn't have to answer to stressed out undergrads. She doesn't have to drown barf in Clorox off college toilets, or deal with the grape-foul smelling, sloshed, roommate. All she has to do is browse amongst the other outcasts—aliens, ghosts, conspiracy theories, corrupt governments, Egyptian Pharaohs, loch ness monster, bigfoot, and the yeti, pick a book, pick a spot, get comfy, take a breath, and flip pages one-by-one. She likes visiting another reality. It didn't matter if was real or not or even just a mere theory. She doesn't have to go anywhere or do anything. All she has to do is flip a page. When she is anywhere else, she has to deal with the unrelenting hustle or the sour aftertaste accumulating from the woman in the apartment.

Today is the third day of the month. The woman takes Melissa to the post office across town. She makes Melissa check the mail. Melissa catches onto the fact that there is always one piece of mail waiting at the beginning of the month. She wonders why the woman doesn't want to check it herself, but checking the mail doesn't bother Melissa. This one piece of snail mail in particular always seems to strike happiness in the woman, well, at least for the moment.

The woman waits in the car. Melissa walks through the clear, glass, post office doors. She takes a left after entering and then passes six pods of shiny, golden-colored, mailboxes. She finds the mailbox—#6003. Melissa's small hands grab the long, white, thin envelope. As Melissa comes out of the post office and hands the woman the single piece of mail, she wonders what she could possibly get in the mail that makes her so happy. This is one of the very many rare occasions the woman is happy and not intoxicated simultaneously. Other than those days on the third of the month, the woman is stressed, wasted, and just not a person anyone would want to be around.

There are a lot of times Melissa gets annoyed being at the small closet of an apartment. The woman brings back a different being of the opposite sex every now and then. For some reason "every now and then" seems to happen more often. They go straight to the bedroom, blast music, and laugh. Annoyed, Melissa leaves and heads somewhere else. She wonders if it will ever stop. Things don't change since she's been living with the woman. There is no promising moment of peace. Drunken rants are like the sun rising. It's clock work. Melissa knows drama happens between the woman and the man she brings back because she never sees the same man twice in a row.

The one time Melissa felt sorry for the woman, she asked her what was wrong. Melissa is unbeknownst that the woman was merely someone's emotional welcome mat and is stomped on quite often.

One night, the woman was sitting on the toilet in the bathroom crying. She was crying like someone she knew died. Melissa thought maybe she did lose someone, or if it wasn't that, maybe the bills may have been too much. She wanted to help her.

Melissa heard her crying when she was doing her homework on the small kitchen table.

She slowly walked to the bathroom, "Are you okay? What's wrong? Do you need help?"

The woman sat on the toilet. She looked up at her. The white in her eyes were red, under her eyelids were puffy, and her black mascara ran down her cheeks. Her hands held her head up as she cried.

The women looked up and screamed. "GET OUTTA HERE!"

The yelling startled Melissa, but she still stood there. Melissa had $40 in her pocket. She took it out of her pocket.

Melissa calmly asked, "Do you need help with the bills? I have money.

Here."

The woman looked at the money in her hand. Like a monkey at the zoo, she snatched the money from Melissa's hand scratching her wrist. She pushed Melissa out the bathroom and slammed the bathroom door.

Behind the door, the woman yelled. "GET OUT! MIND YOUR OWN FUCKING BUSINESS!"

Since then, Melissa leaves her alone and doesn't feel like being at the small apartment all day much less at night. Sometimes Melissa sleeps on the couch in the dorm across the street. Even though the two white women have gone she still has friends at the dorm, but they weren't as close as friends to her as the two White women were.

Melissa decides to plays the flute in the school band.

Just after the drunken monster in the bathroom incident, something odd happens. The drunken monster lets Melissa borrow her flute. Melissa plays everyday. The high-pitch tooting hits the walls of the small apartment and the walls of her soul. After a few months, she gives up babysitting, working the newspaper route, and housesitting so she can practice.

She practices the different keys. She practices with passion and imagines a crowd is cheering for her, screaming her name, and roses are thrown at her feet as her playing comes to an end. She gets up and bows to her imaginary crowd. She practices for the all-state band competition. It's going to be held in Phoenix, Arizona. It will be the first time she will be going to Phoenix. She's never been there before.

During seventh period band class, she notices a conversation among other students. They happily talk about their parents and families being at the competition to cheer them on. They tell each other of their distant relatives coming out of town and are planning to celebrate with a nice dinner after the performance. She lightly bites her bottom lip as she listens to the conversation and feels a hollowness in the pit of her soul. She wants that. She wants to eat a greasy, bacon cheeseburger with someone after the performance.

She is so good at playing the flute she has been appointed for an important solo. The solo is the longest solo in the entire performance. She wishes someone could be there to be proud of her much less her solo performance. She works hard on it day in and day out. She thinks maybe the woman could take the time to come and see her. So, everyday for three weeks she leaves yellow, sticky notes on the bathroom mirror. In the morning before school, she puts sticky notes on the woman's driver's side window and side mirrors.

The sticky notes she leaves behind reads.

I have a flute solo in PHX
I hope you can come!!

Info on fridge, read it
I really want you to come

She is so excited about the competition she packs a week before. The flute becomes a part of her veins. Today is a few days before the competition. She decides to leave early from school and help out a family she's been babysitting for off and on for the past two years. She feels bad for them. They are going through a divorce. The wife needs to fill an extra shift at the restaurant she works at. At 2pm, Melissa gets to the door. She rings the doorbell. The ring of the doorbell echoes inside the house. The wife answers the door. She is dressed ready for work. She gives an exhausting smile and tells her to come in. The bushy-haired wife walks through the hallway leading to the living room where the twins are. Melissa smiles takes a deep breath and greets the twins.

Melissa claps her hands together and says happily. "Hey my babies! How are my sweeties? Oh my, you both are growing. Look at you!"

The twins turn their head as they sit bored on the floor. Their faces light up. They smile and scream happily. The wife walks back and forth from the bedroom to the kitchen scrambling for something she lost and can't obviously find. She finally finds it and comes into the living room. She kisses the twins good-bye and sets off.

As the front door opens Melissa hears the wife quickly yell. "There's food in the fridge if you're hungry! Be back right after my shift!"

She hears the front door close. She spends the rest of the afternoon playing with the twins in the living room. It's dark outside now. The toddler twins' dad comes home with boxes of Pizza Hut. As their eating, Melissa tells their dad she can't help them anymore. He doesn't say anything. He puts pizza on the kitchen table. He hands her two slices in a large clear sandwich bag.

He thanks her for all the late nights, emergency situations, and date nights that she helped them through. As he sits at the kitchen table, he starts to cry and tell her that he doesn't know how to fix his marriage. Melissa feels the slight awkwardness in the air and walks off to check on the toddlers looking at their books on the floor in the living room. Melissa walks back to the kitchen table where the husband is helplessly sobbing.

She tells him, "I don't know what to say. I'm sorry, but I have to leave now."

She grabs her backpack and says, "You'll figure out what's important. That's all that matters, but right now your babies need you."

She slowly walks to the twins, wraps them in her arms, kisses them on the forehead, and heads for the front door. As she closes the front door, the husband sobs sitting on the floor with his toddlers in his arms.

The door creaks and her last image she sees are the twins telling their dad, "Don't pie, daddy."

She puts the pizza in her bag and gets on her bike. She decides to take a stroll by the plaza. She hasn't been there in while. She noticed the other day that there are new stores and restaurants in the plaza. She slowly rides her bike down the pathway in front of the plaza. She thinks to herself that she is getting tired of this hustle. She begins to wonder if this is how her life is going to be. She stops and gets off her bike for a second as she sees a happy family going into the plaza restaurant. She looks through the window and sees kids smiling. She sees teenagers laughing with their parents. She realizes she misses Grandma and Cheíí. It never really bothered her before because she still goes home once in a great while just for the weekend. She guesses that Cheíí is probably bringing in the sheep right now and Grandma is sitting at the table drinking tea with her stash of vanilla crème cookies. She smiles, sighs, and takes her time riding her bike back to the small apartment.

 ***

Today is the day! Her white, leather, Puma bag is finally ready to serve its' purpose. She kisses the photo of her grandparents on her dresser.

She says quietly, "I promise I'll make you proud."

The small apartment is tidier than the White House. She makes sure the sink knobs are tightened. She makes sure the oven knobs are turned off. She skims the floor to make sure there are no crumbs. She's been at war with sugar ants the past month. All dishes take their rightful place in the cupboards. The fridge is a hotel for a dozen eggs, a half-gallon of milk, an untouched carton of bacon, small bag of potatoes, blue box of veggie noodles, and a small bag of pinto beans.

She smiles knowing she has groceries when she returns. She doesn't have to rush to find a job since she has groceries for a few weeks. She is done judging herself harshly on her cleaning ethics. The sting of satisfaction pimp slaps her. She knows it's time to leave. She opens the front door, stops, looks back at the apartment, smiles, and closes the door. She holds in her excitement. She arrives at school and gets on the bus. She decides she doesn't want to sit by anyone on the way to Phoenix. She gets comfy with her pillow and presses 'play' on her Walkman cassette tape player. Two flips of Tupac Shakur later, the bus arrives at the hotel.

She gets to her assigned hotel room. She decides to call Grandma and Cheíí to tell them the good news. The last dozen times she's called, her mom tells her they are busy, has to go, and hangs up the phone before she can even tell her mom the good news. She is hopeful this time. As she dials the 10-digit number, she gets a knock at her hotel door. She listens to the phone ringing and someone answers. It sounds like Grandma.

Melissa excitingly says. "Grandma! It's The Lady. Hello, Grandma?"

The banging on the door gets louder.

A woman outside her hotel room door yells. "Open this door right this instant!!"

Melissa hangs up the phone and says. "Fuck!"

She opens the door. It's her band teacher.

The band teacher asks, "Were you on the phone?"

"Yes, I was."

"You can't be using the phone. Every call costs fifty cents."

Melissa reaches in her pocket, hands the teacher twenty dollars, and replies, "Don't worry about it."

The teacher is shocked and quickly changes her tone to a nice one.

"Breakfast is early. Did you have a chance to look on the schedule?"

"Yeah, I already looked at it."

"Okay. Are you going to the movies with the rest of the group?"

Melissa doesn't want to go anywhere. She just wants to relax and watch some tv and maybe get some snacks across the street.

Melissa replies, "Nah, I'm not going."

Melissa closes the door. Melissa hears knocking on the next hotel door.

She falls onto the hotel bed on her tummy and turns the tv on.

She's too excited to watch tv. She leaves the tv on and rolls to lay on her back. She looks up at the ceiling. She imagines the woman finding the sticky notes and is planning to come to Phoenix. She imagines the curtain going up and the woman is sitting in the front row. The woman happily waves to her and she waves back. The woman gives her a thumbs up. She imagines her solo leads to a standing ovation. The audience and judges are screaming, "Bravo!"

Her daydream fades. Her reality hits her hard. She feels alone. She falls asleep hugging a puffy, feather-down, pillow with the tv on. Hours later, she wakes up, takes a shower, and goes to bed.

The next sunrise, she gets up early and gets ready. She curls her hair with a curling iron. Each curl is long, black, and shimmers. An hour after breakfast, the group walks a couple blocks to the Orpheum with all of their instrument cases in hand. They arrive and head straight to the back of the stage. Music notes float and echo through the halls as several school bands perform. Hours and a grumpy stomach later, her school is finally called. The crimson red, thick, velvety curtains are down as they wait to start their section. She quickly gets up and peeks out of the curtains. She looks back and forth, and up and down the rows. Her eyes search and search for the woman.

The woman isn't here. Melissa feels the short pause of disappointment then she shakes it off and sits back down. The curtain rises. She is sitting in front of her group slightly to the side. The audience claps their hands as the group is announced. The announcer walks off the stage and the spotlight is on her. Her heart beats with hard thumps. She's nervous. She closes her eyes. She starts to play the flute. The music tooting from the end of her flute is soothing and enlightening. The notes she plays are fast and jumpy. It sounds like a spring musical portraying happiness and utter joy is in the air. She suddenly feels at ease. Her fear of stage fright fades away as she continues to play. She closes her eyes and plays the flute like she's never played before.

Each notes sounds clean and smooth like soft butter. She makes it look easy. The notes she plays sounds like something that would play in a romantic musical—the lover longs to be loved, but in the end, her heart is broken by love. Melissa closes her eyes and plays the love lullaby song with all of her heart, everything she has in her. Within a few minutes, she flies through each note not ever opening her eyes. She plays the song with no effort at all. The notes slow to a much softer tone. A single tear falls down the left side of her cheek. She feels the single tear slowly roll down her cheek. The tear drips off her chin and falls onto her lap. The very last note vibrates in her blood stream as a whisper and her solo is over. The entire audience claps and stand. The audience's claps and whistles echoes in the Orpheum. She hears the waves of claps and cheers heighten.

She slowly opens her eyes and smiles.

As the audience finishes clapping, the band starts into the next song. She picks up her chair and sits on the end of the front row. She joins the group. Their performance is another seventeen minutes. They finish the performance and clear the stage. An hour later, her group wins second place. They get trophies and ribbons. She's happy. All the practicing was worth it. The other kids celebrate. They go to the movies or go out to eat, but Melissa heads back to the hotel. She takes a shower and goes to sleep. They leave the next morning back to school. As kids wait to be picked up at school, Melissa grabs her bike and rides off into the afternoon. It takes her forty-five long minutes and nearly gets hit by a car that doesn't see her, but she's back at the apartment. She walks past her bedroom and sees that the woman has gone through everything in her room.

Melissa whispers to herself. "What the hell."

She goes to the bathroom and sees yellow, sticky notes crumbled up on the floor. She washes her hands and face and looks at herself in the mirror. She turns the light off and goes into her messy, disarrayed room. She didn't leave any money behind this time. She knows not to. She looks down at the foot of her bed and sees her favorite poster is ripped in half.

Exhausted from the trip. She throws herself on her bed. She looks up at the skylight. She slightly tilts her head to the left looking at the photo of Grandma and Cheíí on the dresser. She gets up and calls Grandma. She tells Grandma about Phoenix. Grandma is very happy to hear her voice. While Grandma praises her, she pauses with silence. Grandma notices something isn't right.

Grandma says in English with a concerning voice, "Are you okay, my baby?"

Melissa hesitantly asks, "Grandma?..."

"Yes, baby?"

"What would you do if you were here?"

Grandma giggles and says. "Why, I would make your favorite, lamb stew, blue corn mush, and fresh frybread, of course. Oh honey, I am so proud of you!"

She ends the conversation with Grandma.

She doesn't get ready for bed. She's exhausted from the trip and maybe just exhausted in general. So, she falls asleep on her bed. She sleeps so hard that her body doesn't move the entire night. She finally gets up with her pillow soaked in drool. Her skin is slightly folded with crinkles. She's a little sore from being in the same spot when she fell asleep. She sits up on the bed. She wipes the drool off the side of her face. She sits up and thinks for a moment. At the end of her thought, she decides she's going to do it.

She gets her purple duffel bag. Packs it with clothes, a book, and her hygiene stuff. She looks at her watch. It's five o'clock. It's still slightly dark outside.

She reaches her destination thirty minutes later. With her single duffel bag and money in her pocket, she locks up her bike on the sidewalk against the provided bike stand.

She goes to the window and points at the chart provided on the booth.

She says, "This one, please. The next one leaving."

The man in a white button-up shirt is working inside the booth.

He replies, "You're in luck. The next one leaves in an hour."

She pays the twenty dollars. He hands her the ticket. She gets something to eat and some snacks for later down the block at a bakery. She notices there is a woman sitting at the city bus station in front of her behind the street. A few cars drive by. She looks down at the woman's shoes. The sole is thin. The laces are dirty. The side of the shoe is torn. The woman looks like she works hard for a living, but not getting very far. Melissa figures she probably has two or three jobs just to stay afloat. Melissa unlocks her bike. She rolls the bike in front of her. A notion she's giving her the bike.

The woman puts a hand on her chest.

The woman hesitantly asks, "Are you sure?"

"Yeah, just please take care of it."

"I will. Thank you little girl."

The woman hugs her and rides off into the city until Melissa can't see her anymore.

Half an hour later, it's time. Her footsteps echo as she steps onto the bus. She finds her seat. Halfway though the trip she eats her blueberry muffin. She slowly chews. The beeper in her bag beeps. She grabs it as she's chewing. It reads, "143". She faintly smiles and puts her beeper back in her bag.

An hour later, she arrives to her destination. She goes inside the station. She dials the number on a payphone. The phone rings a couple times. Someone answers. It's Cheíí. She's a little nervous, but she tells him where she is. He confirms that he'll be there to pick her up in half an hour. Time flies and he arrives. She sees him pull up in a white, single cab, truck. She smiles as he pulls up. Cheíí is always fixing his trucks. It's almost like it's a part of his identity, Cheíí and his truck. Cheíí and his war pony.

Cheíí gets out of the truck, hugs her, and happily yells. "Ahhhh! The Lady!"

He combs her hair with his hand. He kisses the top of her head. They get into the white truck.

Melissa says, "Nice truck, Cheíí."

Cheíí smiles and says, "You like it? My new war pony! Whitey is his name. Grandma named him."

Melissa smiles.

Cheíí asks, "Are you hungry?"

"Yeah, I'm hungry."

"Okay, we go eat, then. How's Flagstaff? How's the weather?"

Melissa smiles, "It's good. It's been raining off and on."

That's Cheíí. When someone is gone from home for a while he always asks how the city is followed by the weather. He asks her the same two questions when she visits. They stop at T & R Market for Cheíí's fix of a mutton sandwich wrapped in a fresh hot handmade tortilla. She feels at ease eating her fresh mutton sandwich in the truck as Cheíí drives. They reach Grandma's. She goes inside and sees Grandma in the kitchen. Grandma is wearing her blood red apron sitting at the table slowly eating her corn meal and drinking her decaf coffee. She puts down her coffee cup. Melissa walks over and gives her a hug.

Grandma cries and says in Navajo. "Ah, my sweet precious baby! You're home. Ah, I missed you. I worry about you all the time. I'm so glad you're home, my baby!"

Melissa closes her eyes and smiles. Her throat tightens. Her chest feels like it's caving in. She can feel the tears building up on the bottom of her eyes. Her nose flares as tears start to form. She wants to cry, but knows she can't. She smiles and feels Grandma's loving vibes wrap around her entire body and soul. It's almost like an electric shock of peace and warmth. Grandma's hugs are always powerful. The high voltage has been powerful since she was a little girl. She still remembers Grandma hugging her and kissing her when she was in diapers. She thinks to herself the one-way ticket was more than worth it. But the question is, does she know where her next destination is and will she be able to adapt like she always has?

Chapter 7. Hey, Arizona!

"You don't understand it now, but know this. The Moon will protect
you, always. The Holy People showed me. It's a beautiful thing."
                                                                -Frank Nez

The next day, Cheíí drops her off at school. The middle school is three
miles south of Grandma's house in the small community of Tohatchi. She goes to
the office, talks to the counselor, and tells her she is a new student. The counselor
tells her she will take care of everything.

The counselor hands her a class schedule. A fellow student is happily
awaiting to give her a tour of the school. She notices he's clearly a nerd. He makes
the lame joke asking if she's had her immunizations since she's been off the Rez
for a while. She doesn't mind the jokes but, she doesn't laugh either. She quickly
interrupts him and asks him if she can cut the tour short so she can go to class. He
hesitates. The upbeat tone in his voice changes.

Disappointed, he replies, "Yeah, sure. Your class is down the hall to the
second left."

He walks off. Melissa waits for him to disappear around the corner back
to the office. She sees the class filled with Navajo kids. She walks pass her
classroom doorway. She goes outside to the back of the building. There are
basketball courts. Between the school and basketball courts there are two khaki
colored portable buildings. The portable buildings are side by side. It looks like
trailers used on city construction job sites. It has no windows. She figures she has
fifteen minutes until lunchtime. She pulls out a joint and starts smoking.

The bell rings. It's lunchtime. Students burst out the double doors around
the corner to her right. They walk up to the cafeteria. The middle school shares the
cafeteria with the high school. It's a hundred yards northwest of the middle school.
She sees students laughing, talking, and even running up to the cafeteria. Years
back she spent less than half a school year in Tohatchi when she was in
kindergarten, first, and second grade. She expects to recognize some friends from
back then. She's finishes the joint, puts the roach into a paper, and folds it. She
starts walking to the cafeteria. As she is walking she recognizes a few kids, but she
doesn't bother to reconnect. She notices they have changed. Like any other school,
there are cliques. She doesn't want any drama or awkwardness, so she decides not

to socialize to any extent.

The school days press on. She knows she's supposed to be annoyed by kids making fun of the way she dresses, but it doesn't bother her. The kids wear jeans and hoodies that are two sizes too big. It seems as though this is the uprising chic of the Rez. The kids back in Flagstaff had a variety of styles much like shopping at a fancy donut shop—there were jelly filled donuts, sugar-powdered donuts, donuts with sprinkles, and even donut holes, but not here. Here, it's merely plain Jane cake donuts—no filling, no coating, no extra toppings, no extra sweetness. She's stuck in the abyss of Pleasantville where indifference is rewarded with foul-mouth badgering and the endless pointer finger.

On her first day she wore her #32 basketball jersey. A few kids spat her way and said, "#32 sucks". She doesn't react. She just blinks a few times normally and keeps walking. It seems as though the Rez is not welcoming to the outside world even though she's from the Rez. She does notice one thing very different about the Rez's middle school that the city middle school didn't have.

She immediately notices all of the kids have a Navajo-English accent. It sounds funny to her. As kids speak, they have a hanging Navajo accent when they speak English—almost like broken English. They don't speak Navajo, but she assumes being around the Navajo language dialect within their families is what makes their English words linger of Navajo pronunciation. She smiles to herself as she overhears different conversations with this broken English-Navajo accent.

This reminds her of her uncle. She wasn't close to her relatives on her dad's side of the family, but she was somewhat close to some of the relatives on her mom's side. One of them is her uncle. She has one uncle. He is the most neutral human being she's ever known. He doesn't get involved in family dilemma. He's as silent as a llama chewing, watching drama unfold from afar. His opinions are like a turkey sandwich filled with humor and mustard is his sarcasm on top. His humor could make Buddha laugh. His appearance is that of his dad, Cheíí—Wrangler's pulled up his waist, tightened with a brown, leather belt, and a buttoned-up, collared, ocean blue, shirt tucked in. He's tall like Cheíí. She can be her complete self around him. He greets her with a hug that squeezes her heart out of her chest. He'll pick her up off the ground, put her back down, squeeze her face cheeks, and say,

"Ahhhhh! It's the little Lady! I missed my whittle kitten! So cute you look like uncle!"

His pinches sting. Her face turns rosy red from isolating the blood firmly between his pointer and thumbs. He lives in Utah. He's non-Morman. She laughs to herself when she thinks about her uncle. The last time she saw him was last summer. He came down to visit for a few weeks. She likes being around him because of the humor he breathes. The entire summer she nearly had to get a prescription for an inhaler from laughing so much. For instance, one evening, Grandma was grumpy. She complained about the cats digging around in her bedroom.

Finally having enough of it, Melissa's uncle put his coffee down, rolled his eyes, clapped his hands together once and said. "Okay, 'nuff of that, time to take your happy pills, and go to bed. Time for bed nnnnnnow-ah!"

Melissa laughed. Grandma rolled her eyes and didn't say a word more as she sipped her tea.

Her uncle often made references about being "john". "John" is the word Navajos use referring to each other the same way White people refer to themselves as rednecks. When the word "john" is spoken, the first part of the word is made with the sound like there's something stuck in the throat. It is not meant to be a put down. Using the word merely points out the Navajo person's Navajo traits that make them look badly. For example, a Navajo family puts on a birthday party. The party identifies just like a White person's birthday—people, food, cake, and sometimes games. There are things a Navajo does to make themselves look badly. White people usually don't take extra plates of food to take home. If a Navajo at a birthday party packs up plates and plates of food, well that is considered what a "john" would do.

Another instance may be a Navajo borrowing money claiming, "I'll pay you back on Friday when I get paid."

As Friday swoops by, the money is never paid back, and that is just "john". The term is taken lightly, funny, and holds a little bit of offensiveness to it, well, at least to the actual "john". Melissa thinks this may be why she is teased so much. She doesn't have a drop of "john" in her.

She goes to her classes. She's interested to see most of the teachers are White and seemingly are miserable. Most of the kids are Navajo there. She only sees one White kid and an African American kid. Melissa expected to be welcomed with open arms, but she was welcomed with just the opposite.

All the times she is called in class to read, stand up to answer a question, or write on the board in front of the class, she is called names. She always has the correct answers and she soon pays for it. Dressing very different doesn't help either. Her wardrobe of drug-money earned, black overalls with white stitching, capped sleeve, body suits with collars, and with loose fitting pants, Adidas, three-striped, track pants and jacket, Lugz boots, and a variety of Tommy Hilfiger shirts, pants, and overalls, was her teen identity she chose. She wears her hair one of three different ways—in a high pony tail with long, curled, side bangs; two braids; or one-sided braid. The name-calling develops in just a few hours—as she's called, "TLC", "City Gangsta", "Brainiac", "City Nerd", "Know-It-All", and the most popular, "Arizona".

One day just as the lunchtime bell rings, she walks out of class. She wants to smoke a joint before she heads up to the cafeteria.

She walks down the covered walkway that connects two separate buildings.

As kids run by they push her.

A boy yells behind her. "Hey! Hey! Hey! Arizona, slow down!"

She stops, turns, and waits for him to walk beside her. He is wearing loose-fitting Anchor blue jeans, black, Lugz boots, and a multi-colored, striped, poncho hoodie with a kangaroo pocket in front. She recognizes him. She has some classes with him. She's shocked he wants to talk, but holds her excitement inside. She ponders what he could possibly want, but she's beside herself because no one has had a conversation with her up until now. She's been smoking solo behind the building. She's been eating lunch by herself since her first day.

The boy asks." We have English, math, and history together, right? I'm Elmoooondo, but you can call me Mondo."

He looks at her, smiles, and asks her, "So, where'd you come from?"

She tucks in her thumbs under her backpack straps near her armpits.

She smiles back and says, "Flagstaff, Arizona."

He says in a deep voice, "Fuh-lag-staff, cool. Cool."

They continue walking across the walkway.

He lightly grabs the ends of her hair, "Did you cut your hair?"

She shyly smiles and answers, "Yeah. Last night."

He smirks and says, "Usually when chicks cut their hair they look ugly, but you look really good. You look like Selenas. I like it. Are you going to grow it back?"

She faintly smiles, "Yeah."

They walk inside the building and exit walking up the hill to the cafeteria. As they are walking, he asks her question after question. She waits for an accent of "john"ness, but it's absent. He asks her if she misses her friends, if she likes it here, and if she knows anyone here. As they are having the conversation, he takes out a joint from his pocket.

As he pats his pants pockets, he exclaims. "Fuck. What the fuck did I do with my

lighter?"

She smiles shyly and gives him her sky blue lighter from her pants pocket.

He grabs it and happily says. "Daaaaaaamn Arizona! You smoke? Cool, cool. That's what's up."

She smiles as she takes hits of the joint with her new friend.

He accidentally drops the lighter when he gives it back to her. She raises her eyebrows and silently checks out his butt when he bends over to pick it up. She blushes. She thinks he's cute with his short fade of a haircut and cute smile. She quickly looks at his butt one last time as he bends back up giving her the lighter. She smiles. She looks at his chest. He's wearing an ebony black colored t-shirt underneath his poncho. They finish the joint and stash the roach in the trees before they get to the cafeteria. He asks her if she if knows anyone he can get a dime bag from. She takes out a sandwich bag that has an ounce of weed.

He laughs and smiles. "Hell yeah, damn that shit smells good, too."

She gets an empty sandwich bag and gives him a dimes' worth of weed. She tells him not to worry about the cash. His face lights up. They continue walking up to the cafeteria. They grab their lunch to go and eat walking back down to the basketball courts. Everyone is busy playing basketball, talking, and laughing. Melissa and Mondo sit on the picnic table next to each other eating their lunch. They talk and have a conversation for the rest of lunch. Just as lunch is coming to an end, there is an announcement on the intercom. The concession stand is open until classes resume.

She doesn't think he likes her. She thinks he is being nice and maybe even being nicer since she has weed. He tells her to follow him to the concession stand. He buys her a pickle and nachos. They smoke off and on together for the next month. During that time she notices teachers are not fond of him in class. Some teachers get so irritated with the sight of him, they tell him to get out their classroom. She asks herself why that is. He doesn't seem like a bad kid. Maybe he's one of those kids that looks naughty, but really isn't. One morning in math class, fourth period, he gets chased out for being ten seconds late to class. She sits at her desk and smiles to herself when he gets kicked out of class.

She doesn't see him for the rest of the morning. During lunchtime, she walks up to the cafeteria by herself smoking a joint. She gets her food and leaves the cafeteria. On her walk down she decides she wants to eat in the science classroom. The classroom is empty. Lunch is over and science is her next class anyway. Class begins. All of a sudden, the intercom comes on. The principal announces a lock down for a drug sweep. He announces drug dogs are in the building and no one is allowed to leave the classrooms. Melissa has an ounce with her, but she doesn't care. The science teacher is White and the hippie type. He tells the class he admires the way of the Native American people. Compared to the other teachers, he's very laid back. He teaches science in a compelling and interesting way. The class laughs about the drug sweep. The science teacher steps up onto a stool. He pushes one of the ceiling panels in. He tells the class to give him whatever weed they have. That was unpredictable. She has no time to waste. She gives him her ounce. Four others give him a bowl, papers, a joint, and a nick bag. He ties it altogether with red yarn and throws it back until the yarn is visible by an inch. He puts the ceiling panel back. He tells the class to finish reading the chapters they are working on since they can't do any lab today.

Moments later, a cop, with superego as his sidekick, bangs on the classroom door. The science teacher opens the door. The dog, the cop, and his superego, come in. The cop is White, in his mid-thirties. He has the classic stoic this-is-police-business facial expression. He wears his uniform tighter than his ego. The cop's demeanor screams he despises brown teenagers. He smiles at the teacher then, turns to the class with a harsh glare.

He sternly says, "Nobody move. Everyone stay in your seat. I won't hesitate to tase you."

Some students raise their eyebrows, but they all remain quiet.

He goes to the back of the room with the German Shepard snitch. The cop dog sniffs around the floor making his way to the cabinets. The cop leads his four-legged partner to backpacks students have next to their feet. The dog sniffs each backpack one-by-one and makes his way to the front of the class. The class is quiet as the dog sniffs. The dog goes to the front of the room. The weed is right on top of the dog now. The dog stops. The class makes a silent gasp trying not to make it obvious. The teacher tells the cop to be careful in that area because butane gas is stored under the cabinets for labs. The dog stops and looks up. The class pauses. The dog takes a few more steps and finishes sniffing around the classroom. The cop tells the teacher to talk with him in the hallway. The double doors have a window on the top half. The cop shakes hands and the teacher comes back inside. The teacher announces he's not supposed to say anything, but there's another drug sweep the last week of school. He tells the class he will give the weed back at the end of the day and hang onto it just in case.

Over the next few months, Melissa waits for Grandma or Cheíí to ask her why she's back and if she's thinking of going back, but they never ask. All the other times she's come to visit Grandma it is as if she's never left. Things go on as usual.

Grandma tends to dirty dishes, cooking heartfelt meals, and cleaning. She never leaves a single dirty spoon in the sink. The kitchen remains orderly. Clean is one of her top and well-known pet peeves. Over the years of being on the Rez, Melissa notices a similar trait in every Rez grandma that she crosses a path with. Every grandma on the Rez has the same pet peeves in their beloved dishware.

Grandma often repeats the phrase. "Don't put eyes in that!"

Which refers to not banging the bowl against a surface making the paint crack or peel off. It's funny to imagine something so little as dishware can make a grandma lose their cool. Even so to make them go searching for their own dishware when it goes missing as if it's their own flesh and blood offspring. She has seen grandmas argue with one another about what dish is their flesh and blood.

Fortunately, Grandma caught on to this dilemma earlier in her ceremony, dance-filled days. She had a simple quick fix.

Grandma makes Melissa paint her initials "R.A.N." with blood-red nail polish on all of her dishware. All of the dishware including forks and spoons were claimed and screamed it belonged to Grandma. Grandma's grandchildren once made fun of her dishware wars. They spray painted "R.A.N." in blood-red paint on all of her sheep. Grandma didn't think it was funny.

Life on the Rez is grand. The usual routine in the morning began with Grandma's cooking. Grandma's food is perfect. For some reason, Cheíí likes his scrambled eggs with extra milk making the eggs sit in yellow milk as it steams in a bowl fresh and hot. He loves his bacon and toast sit with a slight bit of char. Coffee was his drink of choice. On the porch or in his truck before breakfast, he rolls a smoke by hand with loose mountain tobacco. After breakfast, he rolls a smoke again before he sets off on his day. He is retired. He is always fixing something. He stays busy fixing his trucks, tractor, or the sheep corral. Whatever he is working on, he usually has it fixed by lunchtime. She finds it funny when he fixes different components of his truck.

He would come in from outside smelling like tobacco smoke and oil and say happily in English. "There! Done! Got that sum bitch!"

He places a small, cardboard box, or the tray from a 12-pack of Shasta on the table. The cardboard box or tray held the extra parts he didn't put back into the truck's component he was working on.

Then he says in English. "I don't know what these for, but the truck runs good without it!"

She is curious what he works on all the time. She begins to join him when he is working on his truck or tractor. Cheíí treats her just the same as her brothers. He tells her what to do. She doesn't know auto mechanic terminology and is too hesitant to ask what he means. So, she guesses. When she takes apart what she thinks he wants and gets it wrong, Cheíí throws the nearest small tool within reach at her. She ducks down or covers her face when he throws a tool at her. This doesn't scare her. She thinks it's funny.

One of her brothers gets annoyed by her presence often and tells her. "Watch what the hell you're doing!"

This doesn't bother her. She's not close to her brothers. She being the only girl and the youngest, she figures they are stressed with all the work they have to do. She quickly adapts to the daily routine of running four miles with her brothers, dad, and mom in the mornings before school, and then again in the evenings, and of course, on the weekends. They run race competitions every other month.

In addition to running and working on car and tractor parts, she regularly hauls wood, herds sheep, sheers sheep during the summer, fixes things around the house, plants corn, gets propane when it runs out, and hauls water. This is the same routine when she used to visit on weekends, but now it has transformed into her daily life. She doesn't mind any of it. She doesn't even mind staying up all night when they have ceremonies. The songs her dad and Cheíí sing put her at ease. After an all-night ceremony, everyone is running around on adrenaline until his or her energy starts to fade. When the ceremonies are over, she likes driving to the gas station in Tohatchi. She enjoys a suckle pickle, crunchy, spicy-cheesy nachos with jalapeños, and a fresh, fizzing, brisk-cold fountain drink. She's home.

She doesn't mind any of it, well, except for one thing. She dreads the early Saturday mornings. Her dad takes her and her brothers to the base of the middle mountain where they usually go to get wood. A dirt road seven miles north of Grandma's house is the road they take up the middle mountain to get wood. They take that drive every Saturday morning just as the sun is rising. The boys sit in the bed of her dad's 1984, dusty brown, Chevy, ¾ ton truck. She sits in the front with her dad. Her dad drives to the beginning of the road that starts up the mountain. Her dad sits in the truck lighting a huge, Black and Mild cigar as Melissa and her brothers get out of the truck and switch between stretching and shivering from the cold, brisk, morning air. Her dad blasts her pre-recorded, cassette tape mix of the Scorpions, Metallica, and Black Sabbath, in the truck. After a few songs, they are done stretching. Melissa and her brothers take off running up the mountain. The road's dirt is packed down, smooth, but the road is steep. Her brothers being much older than her always take off like a startled deer. She tries to keep up, but she can't. Five miles later, her legs and chest burn. She yearns to walk. Unfortunately, if she walks, her dad will honk the horn and start yelling for her to move, move, move! She hates it when he does that so she runs until her legs and lungs give out. Her running speed is so slow. There is no sight of her brothers. She runs for five hours before she decides to call it quits. She puts her hands on her knees. Her lungs and legs are on fire. She gets into the truck scrambling to catch her breath.

Her dad tells her. "Gooood. Good job. You ran longer this time!"

It's not long before they catch up to her brothers whom are still running up the mountain. They run all the way up to the lake. She hopes one day she will run and make it up to the lake. As time goes on, she get use to the culture of school, but still ends up keeping to herself. She doesn't make any friends as they belong to the Rez cliques. They don't want to associate with the new city kid.

She only sees Mondo a few more times at school and until he suddenly disappears. She never sees him again. Once in a while she wonders what happened to him. The only days she has a good day are the days Cheíí lets her borrow his truck. She takes his truck to school sometimes. She only goes to the store after school before she heads home. She's knows she's home now. She wouldn't know what to do if she had to leave back to the city. She loved being with Grandma and Cheíí. She's not leaving the Rez this time. For what would home be like without Grandma?

Chapter 8. All Systems Down

"The woman in every family is the rock. She is the love, my Lady.
She's strong. She's a warrior, you're a warrior, my Lady. It's in your blood.
Look at grandma. It's in our blood."

-Frank Nez

One day, she wants a pair of new running shoes. Her running shoes are torn on the side. The duck tape on her shoes is no longer holding the sole together either. Her brothers get a monthly sports catalog that have hundreds of running shoes in it. She figures her mom can afford one pair of thirty-dollar running shoes on clearance since she runs so much. She goes into her mom's bedroom with the catalog in hand. Her mom is watching tv lying on the bed.

She asks, "Hey, mom. Can I get a pair of running shoes? It's thirty dollars."

Her mom looks at her, sighs, and answers, "You need to ask your father, okay?"

Her mom goes back to watching tv. She walks out of her mom's bedroom. This is the last time she decides she will ask her mom for anything. Ever since she came back from Flagstaff her mom has been more distant than usual. Whenever she asks her mom for something, her mom always has the same answer, which is to ask her father. She doesn't quite understand this dynamic, but deals with it by other means. She asks Cheíí if she can use his truck to go get some shoes. He smiles gives her the keys and tells her to drive safe. She fills up the tank at the gas station in Tohatchi and heads to the only mall in Gallup. The mall in Gallup is an infant mall compared to the monstrous mall in Flagstaff. She gets her Nikes, gets pizza, a Piña Colada from Orange Julius at the food court, and heads back home.

Once she is home, she goes to the garden. Grandma is getting laundry from the clothesline. She helps Grandma and carries the laundry basket walking behind Grandma with the basket of clothes. Just as Grandma is in the doorway, Grandma slams down onto the floor. It happens so fast. Melissa reacts quickly. She tries to catch her, but Grandma's too heavy.

She yells. "GRANDMA!"

She tries to talk to Grandma trying to keep her conscious.

She remembers the CPR classes she took in Flagstaff. She checks if Grandma has a pulse. She finds it and starts to count her pulses.

She yells as loud as she can. "HELP! HELP ME! GRANDMA FELL!"

Her brothers rush in from the bedroom on the other side of the house. Grandma wakes up startled and in a daze. Her brothers carry Grandma to the bedroom behind the living room and place her on the bed. As soon as they put her on the bed, Grandma starts moaning in pain. Grandma tries to talk but her words are slurred like a toddler. Grandma's disoriented. Melissa grabs Grandma's hand trying to calm her down while her brother runs to get their mom. Melissa's mom tries to ask Grandma's questions, but Grandma doesn't respond. Her mom calls on the house phone to see if an ambulance is available. Melissa stands by Grandma still holding her hand as Grandma lies on the bed.

Grandma looks at Melissa and says in Navajo, "Don't worry, Lady, my baby. I'll be okay. I promise."

Grandma's attempt to smile fails. Grandma starts to drool and can no longer talk. Ten minutes later, the ambulance arrives. Paramedics put Grandma in the ambulance. Melissa and her mom follow the ambulance to the Gallup hospital. After a grueling and nerve-racking few hours, the doctor tells her mom the hospital doesn't have what it needs to help Grandma. So, the hospital flies Grandma to Albuquerque. Grandma is in the hospital for a month before they transfer her to another facility that cares for patients in a coma.

Melissa goes with her mom as often as she can on weekends to go visit Grandma. Since the truck is a single cab, she sits in the bed of the truck. The two-hour drive from Dibé bi tó to Albuquerque is quiet and sad for Melissa. She sits inside the camper of the truck. All she hears is the sound of the wind hitting against the camper. She takes out her CD player from her backpack. Cheíí bought it for her. Every time she takes out her CD player she smiles to herself. She smiles because her CD player reminds her of when he first brought it home. While her dad is often into the new trends in fitness machines, Cheíí is into the new gidgets and gadgets that come out in the nerdy, geek world, the technological advances.

One day Cheíí came home and showed her his new CD player. She was sitting at the kitchen table doodling on her wide-rule notebook when Cheíí came back from town. He told her he wanted to show her something. He sat on his favorite spot in the house—a comfy, fluffy, russet brown, fleece-like, recliner chair by the woodstove in the living room. She walked over curious to see what new gadget he found, and even more curious as to what Grandma will yell at him later for. She stood by him as he took out a portable CD player out of the box. He handed it to her.

Cheíí smiled and asked, "So Lady, what do you think?"

She smiled, nodded her head as she held the CD player, and said, "Cool.

Nice, Cheíí."

Cheíí said, "I got it from the mall. They said this gadget plays the compact discs. You load it like a gun."

She giggled, "Oh yeah? That's really cool, Cheíí."

He told her this music player sounds smoother than the radio and a cassette player combined. After he bought his CD player, he wanted to buy the CD's flat bullets. So, he went to the music store in the mall. He didn't know what CDs to get so he asked the man at the counter what CDs are the most popular. Cheíí is curious to listen to the popular music that teens listen to. The man at the counter gave Cheíí four CDs—Tupac Shakur, Metallica, Lil' Kim, and Notorious B.I.G. Cheíí was very happy showing her how the portable, flat, music gun works. She was beside herself when Cheíí put his earphones on and Tupac's tunes blasted out his eardrums. Later that day, she looked at Grandma. Grandma was sitting at the kitchen. Grandma rolled her eyes and shook her head as she gently slurped her tea. It's been a while since Melissa's had a good laugh because home is not the same without Grandma. Melissa hangs on to her strength as she listens to Tupac.

They arrive at the care facility. Nervous and not sure what to think or expect, there she is—room 103. Grandma is pale and motionless in a bed of white—white sheets, white pillows, white hospital gown, and white blankets. Melissa is overwhelmed with a surrealness of a white blur—A white, fuzzy, blur. It happens every time she visits her. Grandma is lying on the bed with an oxygen tube taped to her mouth. Several wires disappear inside her hospital gown's collar. An IV is taped to her arms and hand. Melissa holds her motionless hand as she sits by Grandma. Grandma's hand is ice—cold, stiff, and not able to retain heat. Her mom and her brothers go in and out of the room for the next few hours. They are hungry and tell Melissa they are going to go get something to eat. Melissa tells them she's going to stay with Grandma. They leave.

An hour later, Cheíí walks into the room. He grabs Grandma's ice-cold hand. Cheíí is wearing his big, diamond rings on two of his fingers. Melissa has never seen Cheíí in turquoise or silver. He just wasn't that type of Cheíí. She only has seen him in gold and diamonds. Cheíí explained to her once, that he would give her gold and diamonds when she gets older. Cheíí admired gold because he said gold was such an important commodity back in the Egyptian days. Cheíí believed the elements of gold weren't of this world. When Cheíí wasn't fixing something at home, he read. Just like Melissa, Cheíí liked reading different books about the military, history, religions, and different cultures of different eras. When he wasn't busy working on something he always wore his diamond rings. She looks at Grandma's hands and thinks about how she used to put on her jewelry when they went to town. She faintly smiles. She wants to cry, but she knows she can't.

Cheíi is still holding Grandma's hand when he smiles, looks at Grandma, and says in English, "Hey there my beautiful Lady. How are you? We miss you at home. It's time for you to come home. You tell that grim reaper sum' bitch that you're not ready to leave yet, okay?"

Melissa's faint giggle transforms into wanting to cry, but knows she can't cry. When Cheíi talks, Melissa hears drops of his heart-being-stabbed emotion. Words can't express how much he missed his little Lady. She walks out of the room. She comes back in the room and hands Cheíi a cup of coffee. She knows exactly how he likes his coffee—two creamers and two sugars. Cheíi sits next to her. He gently slurps his coffee. As evening settles in, it's time to leave. The family goes in and out of the room. The room is silent. The only two that stay in the room the entire time is Melissa and Cheíi. Melissa's mom tells her that it's time to go and everyone follows her mom out of the room. Melissa is the last one out of the room. She kisses the top of Grandma's ice-cold hand and her soft, pale cheek.

She whispers in Grandma's ear, "Hey Grandma, it's the Lady. I love you. Miss you, Grandma. I'll see you later."

After several months, the doctor calls the house and tells her mom Grandma is awake. They rush to go see her. They arrive. Melissa gets out of the back of truck. It's hot today in Albuquerque. The air is slightly sticky and humid. Underneath her long hair sweat makes her hair frizzy. She walks inside the building and overhears the doctor telling her mom Grandma is wide-awake. Melissa is very eager to see her. She runs to Grandma's room. There she is. She is lying on her bed, quiet, calm, and still the very beautiful little Lady that she knows. Melissa smiles and grabs Grandma's hand. It was still cold, but her heart is at ease, finally. Grandma asks her in Navajo how she's doing. She tells her that she is doing well. Since Grandma has been in the hospital, it seemed like home has not been the same. There was often an awkward silence, except when Cheíi was in the room. Melissa is always comfortable with Cheíi's silence. It's never awkward for her. The doctor talks to the adults that are able to legally drive about Grandma's condition and what steps need to be taken before she's released back home. After all the serious, medical talk, things settle down and the tension is broken. The feeling of tension is gone.

Melissa wants to stay and spend as much time with Grandma as she can. She knows visiting hours are over soon and they have to leave.

Grandma asks Cheíi in English, "How's the house?"

Cheíi answers in Navajo, "The house is good."

Grandma replies in Navajo, "Liar. I bet it's all dirty. Dirty dishes piled on the sink. I know because I saw it. When I was asleep my spirit left my body and I went home. I saw the dishes piled up. The Lady is the only one doing dishes. I saw people come visit me, but they don't stay at the house. They do what they always do, they just leave to town and never stay in the house, never take care of the house."

Cheíí laughs and says in English, "Oh yeah? Well we cleaned it. I don't know when you went home, what day, but the house is clean now."

As Cheíí holds Grandma's hand, Melissa's throat locks, her chest stiffens, and she loses her breath. She tries not to cry. Her vision gets blurry. Her bottom eyelid is caressed by the build-up of tears. She realizes at that moment just how much she really missed Grandma.

After months of being in a coma, Grandma makes a full recovery. She has surgery and has a deep cut right underneath her belly button. Grandma is released from the hospital after surgery and back at home. A few of Grandma's daughters come to visit Grandma. Melissa often hears them arguing with her mom about who's turn it is to clean Grandma's wound. Melissa's been watching closely when her mom cleans Grandma's surgery wound. She starts cleaning Grandma herself.

Grandma makes a joke saying, "My arguing daughters have a bigger mouth than the ten-inch mouth on my stomach."

Melissa and her mom help Grandma. They clean her wound, feed her, and help Grandma use a bedpan. She likes giving Grandma a sponge bath. She knows Grandma feels ugly since she's immobile and more so, completely helpless. She washes Grandma the best she can. She's gentle with the washrag and thorough. She takes her time. She changes the water out often and keeps it extra warm. Grandma is like a lizard and gets cold easily. Melissa sings a Navajo corn pollen song as she washes, rinses, dries and brushes Grandma's silver-streaked hair. Grandma falls asleep. The warm water soothes her scalp and heals the wound on her soul. She smiles knowing she's helping Grandma heal. After dressing Grandma, Grandma falls back asleep. She massages her body—clean scalp to numb tippy toes.

Several weeks later, Grandma starts walking. Her wound completely heals. Grandma has not walked for several months. So, she has to go to physical therapy. Melissa goes with whoever takes Grandma to physical therapy. Grandma slowly gains her physical strength back. Grandma's trauma doesn't fade Grandma's stubbornness.

With the exception of the hospital gown, Grandma has always worn skirts or housedresses. Physical therapy is the doctor's orders. It also means Grandma has to accept another change. Melissa's mom gets Grandma the perfect outfit for her recovery stage. Melissa's mom gives Grandma a department store bag with a new fashion statement that screams, "I can do this! Let's do this!" Melissa, her aunts, and mom, are standing between the kitchen and the living room. They try to convince Grandma to try on her new fashion statement. Grandma stands fragile in her sky blue housedress, yet ever so stern, and stubborn to the burning stake in front of her daughters and granddaughter.

As the ladies of the family stand against the strongest colonel they know, Grandma looks in the bag and says sternly in English. "No. I am NOT putting this on!"

She throws the bag back at Melissa's mom. Melissa's mom sternly tells Grandma she has to change her clothes. After a long fifteen minutes of debate between the most stubborn four Navajo women on the reservation, Grandma finally gives in.

Grandma yanks the shopping bag harshly from her daughter's hands and says in English, "Fine!"

She stomps her two little feet into the bedroom. Melissa and ladies wait patiently in the living room. The lady gossip comes to halt as Grandma walks out of the bedroom. Melissa raises her eyebrows as she looks at the colonel. The colonel is the victim of separating her legs through her wardrobe for the very first time. She stands as tall as her little body will let her. It was so quiet she could hear a pin drop on the other side of the reservation. The ladies are in the presence of the colonel. It was shocking. Breathless. The colonel transformed into an over load of softness, comfort, and just a very, very, lilac, purple flower. The colonel, Grandma, a flower? Grandma stands in front of the ladies. She looks down at her feet and up her own legs. No one has ever seen Grandma wear pants, much less have seen Grandma's two legs side-by-side, separated like two divorcees. Grandma's legs are thin-stick skinny. Somehow Grandma's stoic, concrete face cracks with a half smile. Grandma starts to fight the smile. Her mouth twitches.

Melissa's mom tries to hold in her smile and says, "Uh yeah, nice. How does it ffii.."

Unable to complete her sentence, she bursts with laughter. The ladies join the laughing. The laughs become harder and louder. Grandma stands still in her bright lilac sweatpants and matching sweatshirt. This reminds Melissa of the movie, "A Christmas Story". Instead of a cotton-candy pink bunny suit, it's Grandma, drowning in lilac, lavender passion. After a cruel, but entertaining ten minutes of crying laughter, Grandma looks down at herself and starts laughing. Grandma laughs so hard she holds her belly.

Melissa laughs and thinks, "I'm so glad Grandma's home."

Grandma is always here to make things better. Grandma is the Colonel alright. She knows all and sees all.

** ** ** ** **

Chapter 9. WTF

"Sometimes people don't make the smartest choice. You keep going
and remember what *you* want out of this life, my Lady."

-Frank Nez

Melissa is now a sophomore in high school. Everything is as normal as it
can be. This is her world of normal. She's content. She doesn't regret trading her
long ago memory of the city hustle for hauling wood, driving her pick-up trucks to
get propane and groceries and taking Grandma to town to pay her bills, fixing
fences, herding sheep in the sweltering, dry heat, filtering the water in the well in
the mountains, planting and harvesting corn, staying up all night in ceremonies,
literally racing the sunrise and sunset, butchering sheep, being bossed around by
her mother and Grandma, and finally, fixing everything that needs to be fixed.
She's whole, more than she ever has been in her life. It's home and that feeling
never changes.

She kept her five foot, six inches of height, and stopped growing. Unlike
other girls in school worrying about wardrobe and makeup, she spends her time
and money on Grandma and Cheíí. She makes sure they have what they need. She
slowly spends her money she has left from Flagstaff. She doesn't have anything to
worry about. She's matured, but she's still slender and has dark, long, shiny hair.
She dresses like her brothers because she ends up with hand-me-downs. It doesn't
bother her. She knows clothes don't defy her.

Her two oldest brothers have grown out of the house and live in Arizona.
Melissa and her next oldest brother remain. They still share the back bedroom.
Over the past few years, her brother's friends that don't have support from their
own family, come and stay in the house. Just like brothers, they stay in Melissa's
already shared bedroom. They are all related to her through the Navajo clanship.
She sees them as family. They all know Grandma and Cheíí and they love them
just as much. She doesn't bother them. Especially when her brother and his friends
get into the Rez mischief. They party in the middle of nowhere and come back
drunk. When they do this, she gets up and sleeps with Grandma in her bed. Her
brother often takes advantage of her waking her up in the middle of the night to
cook for him and his party cronies. She gets fed up one late night after a long day
of hauling wood. Her brother and two of his friends come back drunken

demanding food. Not wanting to stumble into the kitchen for food, they wake up her up. Annoyed, she gets up. It reminds her of the drunken rants and nonsense she dealt with and left behind in Flagstaff.

She goes to the kitchen, grabs a huge, metal, mixing bowl, three cans of corned beef, and three huge, metal, mixing spoons. She scoops the corned beef into the big metal mixing bowl, gives it to her drunken siblings, and goes to bed by Grandma's side. She goes back to sleep and realizes that she has to keep her distance from her brothers and new brothers in order to not end up distracted from school. There are months and weeks off and on that her brother's friends from school stay with them in the bedroom. Her parents either don't notice or they simply don't care. Grandma, on the other hand, knows every pair of two feet that walks through the front door. She checks up on everyone and greets all the teens with a smile, hug, and a peace of mind. Grandma's bread is waiting when they are hungry.

Melissa never hears Grandma or Cheíí complain about the bills or food being eaten. The teens find solace in Grandma's cooking, hugs, and a clean bed. Grandma and Cheíí doesn't treat any of them any different. When they went back to where they came from, things carried on as usual. She was either outside working on the trucks with Cheíí or in the kitchen cooking and talking with Grandma.

When everything was taken care of, she reads or writes. She grows into writing more and more. She asks Grandma for help learning the Navajo language. Grandma often speaks Navajo to her, but this time she really wants to invest in her language. Her Navajo is rustier than an old warplane deserted at the bottom of the ocean. She once told them her plans for the day is to run after ducks and play in the hot sun. She was trying to say she's going to take a shower and play basketball. She's learning and Grandma and Cheíí are laughing.

It's Saturday afternoon. She's sitting at the kitchen table doing her homework. Grandma's making dough.

The family and Navajo norm uses recycling as a delicacy and not the White people way. White people place reusables in the green bin and it is trusted to be recycled into something else by someone else. Navajos don't do that. Navajos don't rely on anyone else to get it done. Her family is no different. They reuse and repurpose everything. There is no exception to this, especially left overs of bread dough. When Grandma has left over bread dough, she wraps it in clear wrap, puts it in a bowl, and places it in the fridge. It does not see daylight until she's ready to cook it. Once in a while, the family compromises and survives with store bought bread. But in the case of left over dough, it is deemed "no good". So, she recycles it. She makes tortillas or biscuits like she normally does, but it's quadruple in size. It looks like it is for a giant human—the final product is a giant, thick, fluffy tortilla, or a boulder-like in size, super-thick biscuit. Her mission—make sure no food goes to waste.

At this very moment, Grandma is on her recycling mission—on the menu, biscuits for a beast. Melissa's brother is outside practicing basketball. The basketball court is made of compact Rez dirt. The court is on the side of the house behind the hogan. She sits at the table writing her English paper by hand while Grandma takes the huge batch of biscuits out from the oven. She puts it on the stove to cool. Grandma makes another batch of giant biscuits and puts it in the stove to bake and goes outside. Melissa's mom comes in from outside and goes to the kitchen. Her mom checks on the peyote tea she brewed early this morning. The tea is in a used, clear, Ms. Klein's glass pickle jar. Melissa doesn't pay attention to what her mom is doing. She presses her lead pencil against the college-lined loose paper. The tea looks like sun tea—honey-brown in color. Water condensation trickles and slides down the sides of the clear jar. Her mom puts it on the table. Her mom scoops the peyote buttons out of the tea and puts the tea in the back of the fridge. Her mom goes back outside.

Ten minutes later, her brother comes in from outside. Melissa puts on her headband-like earphones and listens to Tupac while she writes her paper. Her brother is behind her. He gets a chunky, bulky, 7-11 Big Gulp cup from the dark chestnut-stained kitchen cabinets. He puts the cup on the table, fills it with ice, and grabs the clear pickle jar from the back of the fridge. The tea 'slooshes' into the cup as he quickly pours. He adds six spoonfuls of sugar. He cuts a fresh lemon in half and squeezes it into the cup. He vigorously stirs it. His stirring comes a halt and his spoon 'clinks' on the kitchen table as he lifts up the cup nearly guzzling down the entire cup's contents. Satisfied, he puts the glass jar back in the fridge.

He walks over to the stove, grabs one of the colossal hot biscuits, and says. "Dang! These are some big ass biscuits!"

He takes a monstrous-teenage-boy bite. She is still writing. She doesn't notice what her brother is doing. Melissa's mom comes in from outside. Her brother is leaning against the kitchen sink eating his prized biscuit and gulping the rest of his tea. Melissa's mom takes the peyote tea out of the fridge. She places the half filled glass jar on the table with an annoyed look on her face. As Melissa feels the vibration of the glass hit across the table to her pencil, she looks up. She takes off her earphones and hears her mom talking.

Her mom asks, "Hey, who took the peyote tea? I need it."

Melissa twirls her pencil, and says, "Not me."

With a mouthful of clumpy biscuits nearly hanging out his bottom lip, Melissa's brother replies, "Ah, shit. Damn, that's peyote? My bad."

Melissa can't help it. She lets out a small chuckle. Her mom laughs, tells him it's okay, and she will make more, and label it. Her mom puts on more buttons to boil. Grandma comes in from outside. She walks across the kitchen. Melissa rests her earphones around her neck and goes back to writing. Her brother goes to the fridge and digs for something else to snack on.

Grandma yells in English. "Haahh! Who took the biscuits from the top of the stove?!"

Her brother answers with a mouthful, "Oh, I did. It's damn dood, too."

Grandma yells in English. "Those are for the dog!"

Melissa laughs. Her brother looks at the half-eaten biscuit, shrugs his shoulders, and takes another bite. Melissa finishes her paper. She's relieved to be finally finished. She takes out her papers she printed from the internet at school earlier that week. It was information of various universities she's interested in. When she was little, Cheíí used to buy her the National Geographic magazines. She grew fond of ocean articles. That interest only grew over the years. So, she thought maybe she could major into something of the ocean. She's never seen the ocean. Maybe it'll be her love-at-first-sight moment. She wants to hear the crashing of the waves. As she sifts through her papers, she reads about each university. Her excitement takes a brief pause as she looks at the cost of tuition, dorm housing, and the estimated expenses. It hits her. She hasn't the slight idea of how she will cover any of the costs. She figures the best she can do is make a to-do list of what resources she needs to apply for college—grants, scholarships, and loans.

As she sits at the table, her mom and brother leave to town. Grandma sits next to her and asks what she's doing. She tells Grandma she's thinking about college and wants to get a degree in something related to the ocean or ocean life. As she listens to herself talk, she smiles inside. She can't believe the words coming out of her mouth. She's been thinking about it since she was little, but to actually hear herself say it and tell someone about it creates a shine and sparkle inside her gut. A sparkle and shine she's never felt before. Grandma smiles and pauses like she wants to say something. Grandma grabs Melissa's hand, softly squeezes it, and tells Melissa she knows she will go to college.

Melissa smiles, squeezes her hand back, and hugs Grandma. She is done making her to-do list and puts her bag away. She is about to go outside and play with the dogs, when Grandma stops her.

Grandma pulls out a chair, pats the seat, and says in English. "Come! Sit here! We talk."

Melissa's silent. She makes a puzzled facial expression. She sits next to Grandma. She waits for Grandma to say something. Grandma looks at the table and then looks at Melissa with a serious facial expression.

Grandma looks into her eyes and says in English, "I am only going to tell you this once so you listen and you listen good."

She nods her head and replies, "Okay, Grandma."

Grandma says, "I know nobody tells you nothing. Your Cheíí and me worry about you all the time. The woman you stayed with in Flagstaff… she's your mother. Your mother and father got a divorce when you were born. Your mother wanted nothing to do with you kids. Your dad try to change her. He say she needs to be with you kids, but she's crazy. She don't want to. All she want to do is go out, drink, drink with strangers, have fun. I tell her that's not fun. You're just making a fool out of yourself. You have kids, be a mom, but she got mad. She doesn't talk to us unless she needs money. I don't know what's wrong with her. She left you here with me so she could go to school."

Melissa is silent. She raises her eyebrows and expands her Chinese eyes. All she can muster is a calm, "What?!"

Grandma puts up her hand up, and says, "That's not all of it."

She looks at Grandma and waits for it. She has no idea what to expect. What else could there be?

Grandma continues in English, "I'm sorry, my baby, but your mom here, is not *just* your stepmom… she's your aunt, your mom's little sister."

She has no idea how to react. She smiles still in quite shock. She raises her eyebrows even higher. She is silent for what seems like ten years. It's like the opposite of winning the lottery. She's won her spot on Jerry Springer, more so. Maybe watching it with Grandma off and on jinxed her?

Grandma grabs her hand and says in English, "I'm sorry, my baby. Are you okay? … Your Cheíí and me were against it from the beginning. That's why your Cheíí and your dad don't really get along. Your dad and mom used to fight a lot. Your dad wanted your mom to be a mom and your mom wanted to go to school and do whatever she wanted. Your mom stayed in the big city and your dad worked and stayed here with you kids. Soon, your dad started being with your aunt. She was having a hard time and he felt bad, I guess. Nobody told you what's going on. I'm sorry, my baby. You went to live with your mom in the city because the judge said so. Your father really fight to have you. Oh my, I worry so much when you left. Your dad called her, but she always say you're at school or out playing. Every month, your dad mailed her checks, child support. I tell your dad to not be giving her money, but he didn't listen. She call here, tells us she needs money for this and that. I know she didn't take care of you. I'm sorry your mom is the way she is. Me and Cheíí are here for you, okay?"

She takes a short pause and says, "What the fuck?"

Grandma laughs.

Grandma puts up her pointer finger, and says, "One last thing, your two grown brothers that are not here *are* your brothers. The brother here now is your cousin. You good, now? Make sense now?"

Grandma releases her hand and says, "Okay, you do what you were going to do now."

Melissa goes into her room. She looks at her basketball motionless on the floor. She opens the bedroom windows and puts the huge stereo speaker cube in the opened-window. She puts in her Black Sabbath cassette tape, pushes 'play', grabs her basketball, and goes outside to the dirt court. She dribbles the ball. She shoots the ball. The music is blasting out the window. She's numb—no anger, confusion, or sadness. As the ball rebounds off the carrot-orange rim, she catches it. She continues shooting the ball. She thinks about everything her mother said to her back in Flagstaff. She makes a shot and it bounces off to the side. She runs to retrieve the ball. She dribbles the ball. The music fades as she thinks more about the woman, her mom, in Flagstaff. She makes another shot and the ball 'whooshes' smoothly into the hoop. The ball bounces, she runs, grabs it, and dribbles some more. For the next few hours, with nothing more to think, she shoots the ball.

The weekend presses by and she can't seem to look her at "mom" the same way anymore nor her dad. She wonders why they've never told her. Maybe her brothers knew since they're much older. She finally makes sense of it all—why her cousin and her dad have tension between them, why he only asks *his* mom and not her dad, and why her "mom", now known stepmom, aunt, tells her to always "go ask your father".

Her high school years are flying by. She is now a junior. Her hair is darker and longer. She still doesn't care how she dresses. She often wears heavy metal and rap t-shirts her uncle sends her. Makeup or fashion still doesn't phase her. She figures people don't care how she looks in her Silvertab jeans, Ozzy t-shirts, midnight black hoodies, and Lugz boots Cheíí buys her. Cheíí always makes sure she has good shoes. She gets up early for her morning run. She smokes weed once in a while. She just smokes to smoke. She doesn't do it to be cool or fit in.

It's Monday morning. She arrives early to school. She goes to the counselor's office. The counselor greets her with a hug. He sways his hands when he talks. He sways his body left to right when he walks. He tells her she's taken all of the high school credits required and she should take college courses at the community college in town. She can take as many classes as she can handle as long as she is back on the bus when it leaves back to school for lunch. Instead of waiting for her counselor to say she can graduate early, he tells her she can take more electives, take college courses in the morning, or be a teacher's aide. She decides to take college courses. She feels like it's the best idea since she can study for the college entrance exam and start applying for scholarships. She wants to get into UCSD. She has a degree in mind—Marine Biology. Now comes the daunting task of trying to figure out how to get in, and more importantly, how she can afford to go.

She still needs to "past the time" when she comes back from the community college so she decides to be a teacher's aide. Even though the desert surrounds her, her heart was getting a degree in ocean life. She takes the college courses in the morning and welcomes the challenge. Not surprised at all, she aces her college courses.

Things adjusted over the past year knowing the truth and who's who. It's the end of her junior year now. The summer in-between high school years she works at a fast food restaurant back in Flagstaff. She uses the paychecks to pay for new school clothes and shoes for school. Her biological mom still lives in Flagstaff and finished college with a doctorate degree, but she hasn't contacted Melissa by any means.

The one time her biological mother did seemingly visit her, she didn't come to see Melissa. She came for something else of interest. Melissa worked all summer long. She dreaded coming back to Flagstaff and she had every reason to. Once her biological mother finds out where Melissa works, her biological utero remains manages to find out when payday is and slithers across town and takes Melissa's paycheck. Melissa is not able to fend for herself, being a minor, she has no say. So, she tries to make sure she works during the shift of payday and when the checks arrive. After the second paycheck is stolen, she confronts her snake of a mother only to deny the accusation. It doesn't take Melissa long to figure out, her biological let-down still gives off the same sting after all these years. Melissa's boss is only able to void out one check. She gets her first paycheck of $750. She can finally buy her school clothes.

While shopping, something dawns on her. She knows once she's back on the Rez she won't be able to have the opportunity to experience anything for a while. So, before her afternoon shift, she goes to the local ticket box office on the university campus. She buys five concert tickets that will happen near the end of the summer in Phoenix. She is excited and keeps the tickets safe all summer long. The day comes and she goes to the concert with one of her brothers and some friends. All she wants is a t-shirt. She finds the perfect concert t-shirt by a seller, pays, puts it on, and walks back to the concert.

She sits on the padded arena seat. The aroma of dampened skunk seep through her nostrils. As the concert begins, she decides to be a part of the madness just for a little while. She walks down into the mosh pit. She is freaked out and excited simultaneously. Beer, sweat, people screaming, and guitar chords blasting through the speakers become her world in that moment. As soon as she enters the wake of the mosh pit, five men pick her up off the floor. She's being carried horizontally over the crowd. She's laughing and screaming. The crowd carry her to the front of the stage. Security personnel grab her and take her to the other side of the concert. She's monkey high from the smoke.

She walks back into the concert. She decides that was enough crazy for her and sits by her brother and friends. She chills for the rest of the concert. The concert comes to a close. They go back to the hotel room. Her friends take out liquor and beer. She tells them she's tired. She falls asleep smiling. Her day couldn't be any more perfect.

It was her first concert. She saw Pantera. She hopes some day she gets to see Ozzy Osbourne, her favorite artist in the universe. Her uncle introduced this beautiful music to her in second grade. One summer day her family was in Salt Lake visiting for a week. Melissa liked being around her uncle. He was laid back and knew how to have good time. He was the opposite of the drama llama. The times his sisters yelled at each other about family affairs, etc., he was the one pulling up a chair, a bag of popcorn, and laughed about it later. He often said, "They're all koo koo." He is the baby of his siblings and the only boy, just like Melissa, the only girl. Just like Melissa, he keeps to himself, and minds his own business. He went to culinary arts school. He kept so much to himself that when he graduated from school, he didn't tell anyone. His place screamed bachelor pad— empty pizza boxes, crushed Pepsi cans, and Hungry-man dinners in the fridge. Piles of records, posters of Ozzy, Scorpions, Jimi Hendrix, and Metallica posters. His apartment barfed acoustic guitars wall to wall. When she was in town, he took her to the movies, showed her real music, and danced in music's history. She always thought he would be a great radio announcer someday since he was a walking music encyclopedia.

She didn't know if her uncle was home, but her aunt said he had the day off and was expecting her. The pretzel thin, long, pigtailed, overall wearing Asian looking seven year old walked the several blocks of crowded city streets and made it to her uncle's place. He was awake. She heard loud music coming out the front screen door. She didn't know what type of music it was. She never heard that type of music before. She was familiar with classical music because she played it. She was familiar with country and oldies because it's Grandma and Cheíí's favorite radio station, KTNN. She was familiar with rap, hip hop, and r&b music because she heard it on the MTV channel, and had underground cassette tapes. But, this music screaming out his screen door was unique to her. The singer's voice was unlike anything she's heard before.

She walked up to the screen door.

She knocked as hard she could and yelled. "Hey, Unc! What's up?!"

Her uncle yelled back. "Hey, who dare?! What'd ya want?! Go away, unless you're Ed McMahon!"

She laughed. Her uncle turned down the music, opened the squeaky screen door, and she walked inside. His apartment had the aroma of Cheíí-oil—An old man stench with a hint of wintergreen flavored gum. She was curious of his piles of records and books. They walked down the street to PJ's, a local diner. They sat at a booth and ordered their food. The server quickly serves coffee and orange juice.

She drank her orange juice and asked, "Who was that? Who were you playing when I walked up to your place?"

Her uncle smiled and answered, "Oh yeah! Yeah! That's Black Sabbath! They're one of my favorite bands, the before the 1978 version, not after because he left Black Sabbath and went solo there, ah, but yeah, Black Sabbath, they broke up like yesterday's Sonny and Cher. The singer you heard, yeah, his name is John Michael Osbourne a.k.a. Ozzy Osbourne. He was born in 1948 from the United Kingdom. Yeah, there's no one like him. All these rappers, R&B, country, pffft, they all sound the same. This guy, Ozzy, is way different than all of it. I'm telling you there is not ever going to be anyone like him. I'll get you his music. Maybe when you get older you can go see him."

She said, "Yeah. I've never heard a voice like that. I was hooked and listened to it for a while before I knocked on your door. I like it. Yeah, I really do. Yeah, maybe one of these days."

She listened to her uncle talk about the history of Mr. Ozzy. She was intrigued. She had fun with her uncle the next few days and soon it was time to leave. It was her last day. She packed the truck up. She fixed her nest of thin mattresses and soft quilted blankets to lay on in the bed of truck. She organized her snacks for later and was ready for the long eight-hour drive back home to Dibé bi tó. Her aunt came to the truck to say good-bye. Minutes came and passed. She waited for her uncle to walk around the corner. She hugged her aunt one last time and got into the back of the truck. The truck started. Just as the truck was put into gear, a familiar voice yelled.

"Hey! Wait! Wait! Wait!"

She gasped in excitement. She climbed out of the back of the truck, ran up to him, and hugged him.

He picked her up off the ground and said. "Awwww! My little kitten. My little Lady."

He put her down, squeezed her face cheeks, and said. "You so cute you look like uncle!"

She yelled. "Ow! Ow! Ouch! Ahh! Okay! Okay! Enough!"

Her uncle laughed.

She got into the back of the truck.

Her uncle came up to the tailgate of the truck, tossed her something, and yelled. "Here! I found this in the trash! You better listen to it!"

She frantically caught three cassette tapes wrapped in cellophane. It was music of Mr. Ozzy Osbourne. She was ecstatic to accept her gift.

She smiled and said, "Thank you!" and the truck drove off.

She listened to it the entire drive back down.

She always remembers that. On the drive back from Phoenix, she thinks about seeing Ozzy Osbourne in concert one of these days as his music helped her through some very tough times. His music helped her forget about the bullshit she dealt with back in Flagstaff. No matter what new artist came out, he remains her absolute favorite music artist of all time.

** ** ** ** **

The summer was long gone. Her junior year in high school seemed like it was going by even faster. It's the middle of the year and homecoming is coming up. She isn't into the basketball and football raves like the rest of the school. It seems like sports is the only reason the community and school come together. She only attends the games her cousin plays. She sometimes sells weed at the games. In the wake of homecoming, her teenage status strikes her like a lightning bolt. She's nominated for junior homecoming princess. She doesn't want to, but is forced by her peers to contend. On the first day of homecoming week, students give away goodie bags of No. 7 pencils, Tootsie Pops, Starburst squares, and small flyers to win popular vote. Evening comes. Melissa asks her stepmother if she can get something to hand out at school for homecoming. Unbeknownst to Melissa, she is slowly getting into the school spirit because of her nomination. It had been a while since Melissa was excited about something. She thinks her stepmom would be, too, but her stepmother hasn't changed over the years. Her stepmother tells her she is busy. Her stepmother is in college. Her stepmother often asks Melissa to help her with her college homework instead. She stoically agrees. Her stepmother goes into the bedroom and closes the door. Melissa's grandparents have been on a casino spree lately. She knows they don't get out much so she doesn't bother to tell them what's going on and possibly ruin their fifth generation of fun. She looks around the entire house trying to find something to give out. She finds a pile of blush pink paper and boxes of cookie mix in Grandma's closet. She makes small bags of baked cookies, but she doesn't feel like that's enough. So, she writes on the pink paper:

VOTE FOR MEL
JUNIOR PRINCESS

It takes her five hours to bake through eleven boxes of cookies—bagging it and stapling on the pink tags. There's a hundred bags. She's happy and ready for tomorrow. It might not be much, but it's something. She wishes she could do something different as she cleans up the flour and greased cookie sheets. Her stepmom takes off into town. She's alone. She has the empty house to brainstorm.

Like a drought, she's all out of ideas. She smiles. She figures she *can* be different, so she will be different. She gets straight to work.

An hour later, she completes her finished product. She puts it in a gallon-size, clear, storage bag, and puts it in her backpack. She goes to Grandma's closet and finds packages of tiny small cups. There must be at least a hundred teeny tiny cups. She thinks the cups are cute and perfect for the job. She grabs it and puts it in her backpack. *Now* she's ready for tomorrow. A few minutes later, Grandma and Cheíí come back. She helps Grandma out of the truck and into the house. She brings in the groceries and puts it away. Grandma goes to the bathroom. Cheíí comes up to her and gives her a crinkly, white and blue Sears shopping bag. She grabs the bag. She smiles and looks at Cheíí.

Cheíí smiles and says in English, "So I hear the Lady gonna be a princess. More like a queen if you ask me. Royalty. Well, what's royalty without a dress? Right?"

Melissa's smile grows into a cheerful grin.

She opens the bag and can't believe it. She hugs Cheíí, gets on her tippy toes, and kisses him on the cheek.

Cheíí smiles, laughs, and says, "Aww! Okay, okay, Lady. You're welcome! Oh, and here. Your Grandma don't like it, but I know you will."

Cheíí turns around and grabs a box off of his chair. He hands her a large, chunky, wide, and heavy shoebox. She lifts the lid. It's a pair of black forest, high ankle, steel-toe, army boots.

She screams, "Oh my God! Cheíí!"

Grandma comes out of the bathroom and walks over to her.

Grandma smiles and asks, "Do like the maroon dress?"

She screams, again and smiles. "Yes! I do! Thank you, Grandma!"

Grandma says annoyingly, "Well, your crazy Cheíí picked it out. If it were up to me, I would of gotten the pretty pink dress and pretty pink shoes."

She laughs.

Cheíí asks Grandma in English, "Well, she like it, doesn't she?"

Grandma answers in English, "Yeah, yeah…she loves it."

Cheíí smiles, claps his hands, and says, "Awwww! That's my Lady. My beautiful Lady."

Then Grandma says, "Ah, yes! One more thing!"

Grandma grabs a bag off the kitchen table and hands it to her. She opens the bag. It's a big box. It's a makeup kit full of hues of lavender, silver, and golden brown color pallets, a bottle of ocean blue nail polish, blinged out bobby pins, and a fitted charcoal black, push-up bra.

She hugs Grandma and Cheíí, jumps up and down, and smiles, "Thank you."

Her excitement went from 0 to 60. She hasn't the slightest idea how to wear makeup. Her stepmom doesn't wear makeup and she doesn't want to ask her. So, she asks Cheíí if she can use his truck so she can go see one of her friends that always wears makeup. Without hesitation, he hands her the keys and tells her to drive safe. Thirty minutes later, she reaches her friend's house. Her friend shows her exactly how much silver eye shadow, rose gold blush, and gold auburn eye shadow to brush on. They have sparks of laughter. For a second, she feels happier than she's ever been.

The next morning, Cheíí tells her she can use his truck since she has stuff to take. She happily takes the truck to school. As she parks, her friends see her and run up to the truck. They hug her and tell her she looks "so pretty", "beautiful", and "fucking awesome". She smiles and says, "Thanks." They walk into the courtyard in front of the school. As she walks in her maroon formal evening gown made of high-quality White people fabric and her clunking combat boots, students stare at her. Most smile at her. Some wave. Others whistle and cat-call at her, "Damn!" Her heart beats through her chest. She finds her breath. She smiles.

One of her friends yell, "Hey, listen up! You better vote for Mel! She's badass and kicks ass! Mel for Junior Homecoming Princess! Yeah!"

Students gather around them. Her friends dig in her bag and start handing out bags of cookies. One of her friends finds the gallon storage bag and laughs.

She says, "What the fuck…Mel? No shit, you wanna hand this out?"

Melissa laughs, "Yeah."

Her friends laugh and giggle and they hand out the small joints that she made. Before lunch they run out of everything. One of her friends offers to hand out jell-o shots. She knew her friends would be crazy enough to bring something for her to hand out. They laugh and secretly hand out shots and jello shots. Every student her friends run into promises to vote for her if they take a shot. She knows it's crazy, but she trusts her friends won't tell.

The day is just about over. Her candidacy day of handing out free shit is coming to a close. She is walking through the courtyard clunking her combats boots on the concrete. She's wearing a sash one of her friends made her in home economics class. One of her friends asks her to wait for him. He was waiting on his ride. She asks him how long it'll be because she needs to go to town. She tells him she can take him home. He agrees. He runs off to the gym to get his backpack. As they walk towards the parking lot, she hands him her last jello shot she was saving for later.

Out of nowhere a security guard yells at them, "Hey! Hey, what's that you're drinking? Is that alcohol?"

They're caught. The little plastic cup is empty, but they have no way to hide the smell.

She thinks she can make a run for it.

She thinks, "Ah, fuck it."

The security guard takes her and her friend to the office. Before they get locked inside the room to be interrogated, her friend manages to run off. She laughs. He makes it and is able to escape. She doesn't chance it. The vice principal tells her she's suspended for three days. She leaves with a pink slip and drives home. There are three trucks waiting for her. It's her friends. They want to go into town with her and buy posters and stuff for tomorrow. She laughs, tells them she's suspended. They laugh, take a drive to the store, smoke, and they all go home. She tries to laugh it off. She knows she felt happy for that brief moment. She knows she probably wouldn't of won, but at least it was fun for a few days.

For the next three days, she spends time helping Grandma and driving her to go do errands in town. While on errands she expects Grandma to be upset with her, but she isn't. Grandma tells her she's glad she's able to be home and help her out. Grandma tells her she is only young once and she needs to have fun once in while. They spend the day paying bills and then going to T&R Market for their freshly cooked mutton ribs and tortilla. After that, she shoots hoops as the hot heat subsides. Later on, she is saddened a little as she finds out news from one of her friends that came by. They told her a lot of people made a homecoming parade float just for her. A lot of people showed up wondering where she was. She laughs.

On the last day of homecoming, her friends come and visit her. She finds out that she did win after all. Her classmates wrote her name on the ballots, drew a box, and checked the box. The officials had to count the next best vote. She's hysterical in laughter. She can't believe it. She wonders what it would have been—winning and being in the spot light.

The next day, she goes with Cheíí into town to get a small needle welded onto a truck part. They get it done and Cheíí asks her if she's hungry. She obliges. He pulls into a local favorite fast food restaurant chain. They sit down.

Cheíí says in Navajo, "I've seen a lot things a moral human isn't suppose to see, stared at death, kids shot, killed, torture. I'm proud I was in the military, but I'm not proud of what I saw and had to do. I saw wide, deep, dirt ditches filled with hundreds of corpses. Things are different nowadays. Navajo way of life is being ripped apart and buried by the White people way. I know education is the only way. Someday you have to leave home. Go find your own way. You are going to have to battle your own people. It's sad, but true. Your own flesh and blood will do anything they can to make you suffer. They don't want you to succeed, but you fight for your education. I know you're smart. It's a beautiful thing. They want you to have a hard time, but you keep going. The Moon will be by your side the entire time. You can and will do it. You will fight with all your might, okay?"

The waitress comes with their tray of Espresso brown colored tray of food. Cheíí stops talking. She thinks about what he said. His kids say he is a crazy man and rants, but she knows otherwise. She knows he sees the future. She also knows it sounds even more in the modern world, but they said the same about Einstein until his findings were later confirmed centuries later. To say he rants makes his wisdom preserved for the intelligent and those whom mature at a more intelligent level. She knows it with all her heart and soul.

She smiles in thought, unwraps her burger, and puts ketchup on it. Cheíí unwraps his burger and pauses.

Strangely, he gets up, grabs his burger in the wrap, and walks up to the counter. She turns around and wonders what is wrong with his burger. The woman in a white apron behind the counter smiles and asks Cheíí in Navajo what he needs.

Cheíí places the wrapped burger on the counter. Melissa stands up and walks up to the counter and stands beside Cheíí. She knows sometimes Cheíí's version of Navajo doesn't mesh with the newer Navajo slang users. Cheíí's Navajo is old school, the genuine, non-polished, ancient times Navajo. Sometimes the younger generation is not used to the ancient words or dialect. She understands Cheíí's old school, gangster slang. So, maybe she can help.

Cheíí points at his burger, then points at the menu, and says in Navajo, "I want this to look like that."

Melissa puts her hand up to her mouth, smiles, and giggles to herself.

The woman behind the counter says in English, "Yes, Cheíí, that is what we made you, a burger."

Cheíí points at the burger and then points at the menu behind the woman again, and says in English, "No. I want this to look like that. Does this, look like that?"

The woman in the white apron looks up at the menu behind her and then looks at the burger and hesitantly smiles. In the middle of the menu is an enlarged photo of a burger—fluffy, shiny top bun, freshly cut, vibrant veggies, and a juicy, mouth-watering, beef patty. The burger is beautifully layered—a work of art. The burger is fit enough to have been handcrafted with a pair of tweezers.

The burger before Cheíí is deflated, flatter than a bald truck tire. The veggies were flatter and deader than road kill. The meat is paper-thin with ragged edges shadowing that of human barf. Melissa contains her smile as the woman annoyingly grabs the burger off the counter and trashes it. She walks back to the counter, sighs, finds her smile, and tells Cheíí in Navajo his food will be ready in a few minutes.

Cheíí nods his head and says in Navajo, "I will wait right here."

Melissa smiles standing next to Cheíí. Cheíí walks back to the table and grabs Melissa's deflated tire and places it on the counter. Another worker smiles, grabs the burger, and starts grilling a new one patty. Melissa stands next to Cheíí and lightly bites the bottom of her lip.

The restaurant is empty, but there is more tension than a pointer finger squeezing a gun's trigger. Cheíí stands up straight with his palms down on the counter. He watches every move of the workers that are changing his tire. After ten minutes, the resurrected deflated tires are ready to roll. The woman in white places the burgers on the Espresso brown, plastic tray, but one question still remains. The plump, shiny work of art is partnered with a new batch of freshly fried, French fries. Both of the burgers are partially wrapped neater than a pressed mailman's collared shirt. The burger's patty and veggies are so vibrant in color it can be seen from the moon with the naked eye. Cheíí looks down at the burgers before him and then brushes a look at the menu. Both of the workers stop what they are doing and hold their breath. Cheíí cringes his left eyebrow at the work of art. He smiles, raises the tray giving props to the chefs, and walks back to the table. The now-true chefs smile, nod their head, and continue what they are doing. Melissa and Cheíí sit down at the table. She grabs her burger and gets lost in its' beauty. She looks up at Cheíí and smiles.

Cheíí preps his burger with ketchup and says, "Don't ever let anyone pee on you and tell you it's raining."

She laughs. They finish their burgers and head home.

Months go by and the homecoming incident is in her rearview mirror. It was a happy moment for her. It's now finals week. She can't miss any of her classes. She's been up late trying to control her fever. She has the flu. Her body aches, grueling and torturous body chills, and exhaustion has yet to subside. She's sweating from the fever. Her body feels like a lifeless, ice-cold, empty tomb. As much as she wants Grandma's homemade chicken noodle soup from scratch, she has to figure how to make it through her first five classes. She digs through Grandma's gold hole in the wall for drugs. She hopes to find some sort of numbing agent to run through her veins so that she can be another body at a desk. She figures if she can get through her morning classes, she can go home at lunch since she already finished the other classes' final exams.

She finds it—Martian green, numbing syrup that makes anyone gag. She puts it on the counter and starts digging in the kitchen cabinets. She looks for the fire-orange, liquid numbing agent that daytime robots use to get through their day. She doesn't find anything better than the Martian green goop. She puts everything back except the green goop. She stares at it. She doesn't want to take it, but she knows it'll numb her body so she can focus on her exams. She does what everyone does. She thinks if 30 ml is the amount a person is staying at home with nothing to do takes, it only makes sense to take half of the suggested amount. That way, she wouldn't be completely zoned out. 15 ml would only take the edge off. She shoots down the 15 ml trying her best to avoid the after taste. Unfortunately, the after taste comes on stronger than a used car salesman. She puts it back in the cabinet and goes to the bathroom to brush her teeth. She comes out of the bathroom. Her stepmom is in the kitchen and asks her if she can help her with her homework later. Melissa's eyes are heavy. Her head feels inflated bigger than a hot air balloon. Her body feels like a hot cup of liquid jello. She nods her head. She doesn't want any human interaction right now. She groggily tells her stepmom she is only going to school half of the day. Her stepmom stares at her. She tells Melissa sternly she's helping her with her homework regardless. Melissa nods her head.

Melissa pours steaming hot Navajo tea in a tall, plastic, Love's, coffee mug. She turns around. Her stepmom has a small, clear cup filled with the Martian green goop, the same green goop Melissa just forced down her esophagus minutes ago.

She says, "I already took some."

Her stepmom says sternly, " Just take it."

Melissa sighs and repeats, "I already took it."

Her stepmom rolls her eyes, harshly places the green goop in the sink, and stomps off with the sudden urge to showcase how heavy her body mass is. She ignores her stepmom as she walks out the front door. She sits down at the table and carefully slurps her hot tea.

She doesn't even feel the urge to be calmed or comforted by tea. She closes her eyes and mentally asks the Creator to take away her achy, ugly, weighed-down feeling. Cheíí honks his truck horn. She looks up at the clock on the wall in front of her. She lost track of time. She gets up and groggily puts on her backpack. Her body aches and pinches with every body move. She slowly bends over, forces oxygen through her mouth inflating her face cheeks with air, stands back up, and grabs her tall coffee travel mug.

Just as she makes it to the front door, Grandma walks with a fast pace into the kitchen and yells in Navajo. "Wait! Wait! Lady!"

Melissa stops at the door and turns around. Grandma has a large shot of Martian green goop in her beautifully aged, sandpaper, wrinkled little hands.

Grandma says in Navajo. "Here take this!"

She sighs and softly says in English, "No, Grandma I already.."

Grandma shoves the small plastic cup full of Martian green, melted, jello shot against her lips. Melissa's words mix in with the gross, green, shot. Her words garble with the enforced shot. She dares not dispute against the Colonel. She squeezes her eyes shut and dares not utter just how bitter the after taste is. She gives Grandma a thumbs up and walks out the front door. She runs behind the truck and tries to throw up the shot. The regurgitation is successful, but the after taste takes over her entire esophagus and lungs like the U.S. troops did in the 1800s. She doesn't regretting throwing up. She slowly gets in the truck. She arrives at school.

Before she gets out to face healthy, human bodies, she tells Cheíí to come back before lunch to pick her up. Cheíí tells her he will be back earlier than that. She nods her head and salutes her Cheíí as she opens the door. She goes straight to class, Navajo language class. She takes her backpack off, puts it on her desk, sits down, and puts her head on her folded arms on top of her backpack. She quickly falls asleep. She wakes up in what seems like five hours later. She thinks to herself why she is so dizzy and why she can't focus.

It's time for the exam. The exam is a standing oral exam. She sits in her desk with heavy eyes, body numb. The room is slowly spinning like a carousel.

For the first time, the Navajo language sounds completely foreign to her. She wonders what possibly could be in the Martian green goop that made her that way even after she threw it up. Her reality is hard to focus on. Her name is called. She can't stand. She tells the teacher in slurred Navajo that she is ill and can't stand the body aches so she will sit. The teacher asks her a question in Navajo. She squeezes her eyes, scrunches her face, and tries to recognize the words. She asks the teacher in Navajo to repeat the question slowly. The Navajo teacher asks her if she's feeling okay and needs to go home. She replies in Navajo that she doesn't feel well and wants to go home now since she is done with the exam now. The teacher laughs and tells her in Navajo to go home and not worry about the rest of her exams. Melissa tells her in Navajo that she thanks her for the baby ducks and she is going to give grandma some cookies. She knows she's not making any sense. She gets up, walks out of the class, and past the office. She doesn't want to check herself out so she walks to the parking lot. Cheíí is sitting in his white, 1996, single cab, war pony, reading his newspaper. Cheíí sees her walking towards the truck, puts his newspaper down, and starts the truck. She gets in, closes the door, and lies down on her side. She immediately falls asleep. It takes her a week to go back to normal.

The sun and moon revolve around the earth enough times to make Melissa a senior. One Friday morning, Cheíí tells her she is not going to school today because she's going with him. They drive towards Gallup. She has no idea where he is going. She doesn't want to ask. She knows it's something important, important enough to miss school. She doesn't have anything going on in school anyway. They enter Gallup. He stops at the first red light.

He says in English, "You know I helped your mother a long time ago, when she was going to school at the university in Flagstaff. She came to me one day and told me she needed prayers to help her get through school. When she told me what she wanted all she kept repeating was her success in school, becoming big in her field, and she wants people to know who she is. I asked her, 'What about being a mother? What happened to that?' Your mother was quiet and didn't know how to answer that. So, I asked her, 'Are you sure that's what you want? You pick school over your family?' Your mother said all she wants to do is finish school. She was having a little bit of a hard time and she said she knows she doesn't have to worry about you. I asked her one final time, 'Are you positive that that's what you want? You be careful what you wish for'. Your mother answered, 'Yes!!!! That's what I want!' So, I shook my head in disappointment and prayed for her. I prayed for what she wanted. I told her that someday it will come back on her. She sacrificed the most important things in her life and she didn't care about it. I'm sorry she did that, but don't ever let anything or anyone hold you back in doing what you want to do. You move forward no matter what. When the time comes for you to be a mother, you be there for them no matter what. Don't do what your crazy mother did. I told her, 'You want to go way up there, go high, and be up there. You want to look down at everyone and you want people to look up at you. You know, when a monkey climbs and climbs, he wants to show off. The monkey wants to show off and say he is the strongest one to climb that high. When he goes that high he feels high and mighty looking down at everyone else, but what that monkey doesn't know is that his ass is showing.' I told that to your mother. She didn't get it. She don't understand that if you wish for things, selfish things, and leave other people behind, karma will come later and it will be your time to pay up. Rising to the top that way is not good. It makes you selfish and greedy. I know you won't do that. I know. I can feel it. After I am gone, when I leave this world, your own flesh and blood will turn on you. They will grow to a scolding hate on you. You will feel like you will lose a lot of people in your life, but you do what you need to get rid of the poison in your life. You don't need that in your life, okay?"

As he finishes talking to Melissa, they arrive at Cheíí's destination. They go inside the building. Cheíí signs in on a clipboard and they sit on the chairs in the waiting room.

She thinks, "He's just doing his usual routine, so why does he want me here, especially on a school day?"

Cheíí looks at the floor and says, "I have been waiting for you for a lonnnng time. I dreamt about you even before I met your Grandma. I dreamt that you help people. I also dreamt of all the obstacles you'll have. Before you were born I wanted to make sure I was prepared for you. Now, everyone is mad at me for doing this, but you are very special. Indeed, very special. I call you, 'The Lady', because that's what you are. You are always heavy in thought and you always push forward. I see the strength you have. You have a fighting spirit just like Grandma. I want you to know that you're special. What I said to you when you were little, it's true. You are not meant to be with anyone, but the Moon. Nobody can handle your demeanor. You're really calm, really smart. Most people see that as a threat. They see it as a hassle. This Moon is very stubborn, says it like it is, but there are some things he still doesn't understand. He has tattoos like me, but more. The Moon is very smart, too. It's almost like he's stuck, can't move forward, then you come and you help him and he help you. I know I sound crazy, 'crazy old man, what does he know?' Your Cheíí, he is really smart. He knows a lot, but he just keep to himself. Your Cheíí, he loves you, Lady. Yes, I love you a great deal. You will be the voice for a lot of people that can't do it. You. You'll feel it in your bones, the love for the Moon. You will have what your Grandma and me have. She feels what I feel. You will argue, disagree with the Moon, but that's him being stubborn. That's okay. He will see what a good Lady you are. So, don't you worry, okay? Trust it. The Moon is not used to someone like you. I am very happy you're here. You are what I live for. I want to see your kids. Don't let anyone put you down, even your own flesh and blood. When the time comes, let it be. You love writing and reading, so that's what you do…"

A woman in her fifties calls Cheíí's name. They follow her to a small office the size of a closet. Melissa starts to put it together; what Cheíí just now told her and where they are. She starts to feel surreal. She is confused, excited, and scared simultaneously. But… she doesn't want to feel excited. She's not used to good news. So far, she's been bombed and sprinkled with disappointment. So, she doesn't hold her breath, but the curiosity does strike her fancy.

The woman 'clicks' with her mouse, and says in English, "How are you Cheíí?"

Cheíí responds with a huge grin on his face, and says in English. "I'm good!"

The woman finishes clicking with her mouse and looks at Cheíí.

She interlocks her fingers, places it on her desk, smiles, and asks in English, "What are we going to do today, Cheíí?

Cheíí tells her in Navajo that he wants to close the special account today. The woman looks at Melissa, smiles, and tells Cheíí it's going to take a few minutes. Cheíí puts his hand on top of Melissa's hand. She looks up at Cheíí and smiles back. Cheíí continues smiling and removes his hand.

The woman says, "The account is ready. Would you like to open an account?"

Melissa realizes the woman is talking to her.

She pauses, and says, "I don't understand what's going on."

The woman smiles and says, "Your Cheíí got a CD in your name before you were born. It's been sitting here at the bank waiting to mature. What does that mean? Well, this money is yours. You can put the CD back and let it mature for another four more years, eight more years, or even ten more years. You can take the money out, open an account here today, or you can open another CD, and let it mature. What would you like to do?"

Melissa is speechless. She cannot find one word to speak. Her words are tripping over themselves as she opens her mouth and nothing comes out. She raises her eyebrows and thinks quickly. She knows she needs to be smart. She tells the woman she wants to open an account. She is completely shocked and looks at Cheíí. Cheíí tells her he is very proud of her and wants her to succeed. Her new checking and savings is now active. She's never had a bank account before.

The woman smiles, hands Melissa her new bankcard, and says, "Okay, you have one-thousand dollars in your checking account and you have seventeen-thousand in your savings account. Would you like to do anything else today?"

She smiles, and replies, "No. I'm good."

Melissa and Cheíí walk out of the bank back to the truck.

Before they part ways to get inside the truck, she runs up to Cheíí, hugs him, and says happily, "Thank you, Cheíí. Thank you."

Cheíí squeezes back, pats her back, laughs and says, "Ohhhkay Lady. I know. It's for you, okay? You use it for school."

She starts to feel tears forming on her eyelids.

She chokes out the single word, "Yeah."

They get into the truck.

Cheíí starts up the truck, revs it three times, and says, "Okay. We go eat."

Ten minutes and five stoplights later, they walk through the double glass doors of a popular fast food restaurant that sells fried chicken. She usually gets the two-piece drumstick meal with mashed potatoes, macaroni and cheese, and a biscuit. Just as she gets the same thing every time they go, Cheíí gets the same thing, too. Except what he wants is not an easy task. It's more complicated to order than the pickiest Anglo, New Yorker supporting child-slave labor sticking up their nose for a half caff, skinny, double-foam, double shot, 140 degree exact, cup of caffeine-kick in the veins.

The chicken place is deader than Mussolini's suspenders. They walk up to the counter. The food service worker greets them.

The worker says in English, "Hi. Welcome. What would you like?"

Melissa looks at Cheíí, then at the worker and says, "I would like the two-piece meal, please, with mashed potatoes, mac and cheese, and a drink, please."

The worker presses buttons on the register. The worker looks at Cheíí.

She asks, "What would you like, Sir?"

Cheíí puts up his pointer finger, and says, "I want one wing."

The worker nods her head and says, "Okay, the one-piece meal, what sides do you want?"

Cheíí says, "No. No meal. I just want one wing."

The worker makes a confused and hesitant face and asks, "Sir, a wing?"

Cheíí puts up his pointer finger, again and repeats, "I just want one wing."

The worker looks behind her. Melissa giggles and thinks she can maybe help this time before the worker panics.

Melissa says, "You can charge him for the cheapest meal. Separate all the food from the one wing and then just put the rest of the meal onto my plate."

The worker hesitantly smiles at Cheíí. She presses the buttons on the register. Cheíí pays for the food and they sit down and eat. Melissa is still completely shocked how the day has been. She thinks about what he said earlier. She wonders what else he dreamed about. She takes her time and finishes the meal. She can barely contain her excitement. She wants to scream and jump up and down, but with Cheíí that may be a bit awkward. They clean up their table and walk out of the restaurant. She gives in. She runs after Cheíí, hugs him, and jumps up and down as she's still hugging him screaming in happiness. Cheíí looks down at her and laughs. He squeezes her before they part ways and get back into the truck.

They arrive home. Her "mom", dad, and "brother" are not home. She gets out of the truck and runs inside the house. Grandma is making fresh tortillas. She runs to Grandma, hugs her, jumps up and down, and screams. Grandma laughs. She realizes Grandma has a visitor. One of Grandma's best friends is another grandma, her distant cousin. But through the vines of the Navajo clans, the other grandma is Grandma's sister. She comes over every so often to chit chat and see how Grandma is doing. Melissa likes it when she comes over. The other grandma is always happy, upbeat, and gives Melissa ten dollars. Every visit since she could walk, the other grandma tells her it's for good luck. Melissa puts it away with the rest of her money. She hides her money in the attic.

As the ladies talk, a sugar cookie colored truck pulls up to the woodpile. Someone gets out of the truck and sits next to Cheíí. They sit on upright logs. Melissa recognizes the truck. It's Cheíí's friend that occasionally visits.

Melissa thinks, "It must be visiting day."

She grabs a tortilla and starts eating it as the Grandmas talk. Curiosity strikes the other grandma.

The other grandma walks to the door and asks Grandma in Navajo, "Who's that woman sitting next to your man?"

Grandma replies in Navajo, "Ah, don't pay them no mind."

As Cheíí and the woman talk at the woodpile, the other Grandma stands at the screen door, silent, and watching them like a hawk. Grandma looks at Melissa. Melissa slowly chews her tortilla and shrugs her shoulders.

Cheíí and his friend remain in conversation sitting on the wooden logs at the woodpile.

The other Grandma continues to look out the screen door.

She yells through the screen door in Navajo. "Hey! You're too close!"

Melissa wonders why she's yelling. Melissa walks up to the screen door standing next to the other Grandma trying to figure out what all the fuss is about.

The other Grandma grabs the broom against the fridge, goes back to commanding watch, and says sternly in Navajo, "Who do they think they are? She better not..."

Melissa squints her eyes. She now sees why the other Grandma is on such high alert. Cheíí's visitor has long hair. It's curly and permed like Shirley Temple, but much longer. Melissa chuckles and is about say something, but the other Grandma has had enough. She marches out with broom in hand. She starts yelling in Navajo raising the broom up in the air.

Melissa and Grandma scramble after her trying to tell her to wait in both English and Navajo.

As they stride to the woodpile, they see the visitor place their hand on Cheíí's knee. Cheíí and his visitor are sharing a laugh.

Melissa thinks to herself, "Oh my God, this Grandma is fast and raging!"

The other Grandma makes it to the woodpile. She starts hitting the bristles of the broom against the suspicious-no-respect-woman with long curly hair. Clouds of dust surround the frisky, poor, "other woman" as the other Grandma strikes the broom in a Navajo woman rage. The "other woman" puts up her arms in defense from the broom-whisking blows. Grandma, Cheíí, and Melissa are yelling in English and Navajo telling the other Grandma to stop and get a hold of herself. The other Grandma, out of breath, finally stops. As the dust settles, the other Grandma hones in on Cheíí's visitor. She realizes the suspicious woman is none other than a man—a Navajo man that for some eccentric reason wanted to not only grow his hair, but get it proudly curly-fry permed. The other Grandma pauses in disbelief. She's speechless and Melissa doesn't blame her.

Melissa starts laughing building up to a raging laugh. She is ready to fall onto the ground. She hasn't laughed so hard in a long time.

The other Grandma, obviously still upset, points the poor, worn-out, bristled broom towards the long, curly-haired, man, and says in Navajo, "And you stay away from him!"

Grandma looks at Cheíí and shakes her head. Cheíí looks at Grandma smiles and shrugs his shoulders. The other Grandma stomps off back to the house still mesmerized in a rage. Grandma smacks Cheíí on the left arm and covering her laughter. Melissa still laughing leans up against Cheíí laughing and practically ready to surrender to the funniest thing she's seen in her teenage life. After a five-minute laughing session, the ladies walk back to the house to accompany the other Grandma and talk about why a man would never consider to tie up his hair.

*** *** ***

Today is Melissa's high school graduation. She is not in particularly excited, but it's an appreciative milestone. After the ceremony she doesn't take off to party like the rest of her graduating class. Instead, she gets a freshly dispensed, 40 oz., Cherry Pepsi, cheesy nachos with jalapeños, and a perfect pickle at the gas station. She goes back to Grandma's house. She got into UCSD, but she can't afford to go. She was denied scholarships because they didn't support her major. She doesn't know anyone in California. Maybe it just wasn't her path to take.

She seriously doesn't want a boyfriend, but she know she'll experience it anyway. So, during her last semester in high school, a boy asks her out. He's average. They've only been going out for a few months. She could use the money given to her to go to UCSD, but that's not enough to cover the first year. She researches several resources, but she can't find any loopholes to save her life.

Because of the tension between UCSD and her boyfriend, she breaks up with him. He doesn't support the idea of her education much less her leaving. So, that makes it a tie-breaker for her. She needs to concentrate on her future and nothing less.

The summer settles in. She takes a job at the local gas station. Fortunately, she attends the local college in town. She manages to save money and buy a car. She is ecstatic, but she will soon hit unforeseeable potholes and take detours that are all in her lane.

** ** ** ** **

Chapter 10. Beauty in Chaos

"I love that you're strong. You're a strong lady, my Lady. I say to
myself, 'G, that Lady is strong' and that makes me proud."
-Frank Nez

High school is a distant memory. The local community college doesn't
have her major. So, she changes her plan. She compromises and takes courses for
a degree in auto technology. Time doesn't fly and it's been a grueling, dragging
year. It's her third semester. She ends up on the same boat, just a different end of
the boat. The teacher, even classmates, constantly make sexual remarks. They give
her a hard time making her perform unnecessary steps to rebuild a transmission,
which in turn, takes her much longer to complete such class, hands-on,
assignments. They enjoy her frustration. She often tries to file a complaint, but that
goes nowhere fast. It's useless. She finds out the chair of the department is related
to the teacher. No matter how many letters she writes, she ends up at a dead-end.
It's as useless as the piece of paper the U.S. government forced her ancestors to
sign hundreds of years ago.

It's gotten to the point where someone exchanged her medium, musky
blue, Michael Myers, bodysuit for an extra small on exam day. The exam is
entirely hands-on and no one is allowed in the work area in street clothes. Staring
at the scarlet red, brick wall, she decides she's had enough. As the class giggles
amongst themselves, she walks out of class and goes to the closet version of a
student union. She orders green chile cheese fries and annoyingly sits down. On
the table next to her she sees a university catalog book. She grabs the catalog and
flips to the degree section. She grabs the entire section with her fingers and starts
flipping. As she flips the pages, she stops her pointer finger on a page. Her finger
falls on the page. It's pointing at "Medical Laboratory Technician".

She shrugs her shoulders, and says, "Fuck it."

She takes her green chile cheese fries with her to registration and registers
for the classes for next semester. She makes it to the last semester of school. She
only has three more classes to graduate. It's not her strongest area—biology and
two advanced chemistry classes.

She understands the material. It's even confirmed by the grad students at
tutoring as they tell her she knows the material, but in class, the teacher tells her

otherwise. The teacher is quicker than a bolt of lightning striking a tree shutting down her every attempt to pass. No matter how many hours she studies, goes to tutoring, or joins study groups, she gets the disappointing and unrelenting "F" on every tree-killing footprint. She refuses to gives up and takes the same classes two more times.

She decides to give it one very last encore. She knows it could be possible, but then, it happens. The worst comes to worst. It's mid-semester.

One afternoon after class, the teacher tells her, "You know, you shouldn't throw such a bitch fit. I'm aware of the complaint you're trying to get attention for. You won't be anything, but a waste like the rest of the people here. You better not submit another complaint."

She knows his behavior is wrong. She felt it after her very first day of class when the teacher undermined her educated guesses in front of the entire class calling her "a wanna-be science major prune". The feeling stayed with her. She felt it as soon as she got up in the morning listening to her coffee percolate. Ever since the first day of class, she knows she had to do something.

A few weeks before the final exam, she finally confronts the teacher.

She says, "I don't care what you have against me, but someday you'll understand your own fear."

He smirks and unrelentingly says, "I'm going to fail you on the final exam, so you shouldn't bothering coming."

She smiles and replies, "Your people tried to exterminate me and my people, but you didn't succeed. All you have left are words and the very little power you have here. You don't have any power over me. You can't take away my education."

Without a word left to muster, he's silent. His facial expression mirror that of a dunce. She walks away from his desk.

She shows up and finishes the final. She knows she aced it. All semester she studied smarter, but sadly, it's not enough. A few days after the final, she finds out two other female students are going through the same dilemma. They, too, are Navajo. After sending a fifth and final complaint letter, she receives a response indicating that if she can prove the allegations, she will be granted her degree.

The next obstacle is convincing the two students to help bring weight making her anchor more concrete. They are too overwhelmed by it and tell her the teacher threatened them. They were satisfied in just changing their major. They don't want anything to do with the complaint. Melissa has found herself in what seems like wasted time towards a small degree she will never get.

Meanwhile, she gets promoted to assistant manager at the gas station she's been working at. Since the promotion, she has a hard time gaining respect since she is nearly two decades younger than her coworker counterparts. The sun is about to set on her being 19. Her sunrise of waking up a 20 year old is soon coming. Still, she presses on. She tries to show her worth in unclogging toilets, scrubbing greasy, gas islands, and painting over graffiti on the outside of the building. Once in a while she is tempted to steal gas, the fresh, plump, two-dollar bananas, and the fresh, cheesy pizza she fires up, but she quickly shakes that evil conscious off. She makes a close friend with the manager. It's clockwork—own the royal blue smock, spray, sweep, mop, wipe, scribble some nonsense on a clipboard, eat bologna and ice burg leaves, poor people lettuce, between eighty-eight cent wheat bread and drink a can of Sunkist for lunch. She wrapped up her double shift bumping heads with smashed customers at 2am. Her royal blue smock echoes how messy her life feels—paint and gasoline stains, worn, and armpit holes.

Fortunately, she had one thing in her life to really live for. But even that, was a semi-mess that she made into a beautiful part of life and to ultimately keep going. We have to back up to see what happened there, when she broke up with her now ex.

So, going back to the break-up, it was a horrible day for her really. It wasn't the closure she was expecting. She just wasn't ready for a relationship. She was trying to figure out her future and how to initially get it started. To her that was college and noting less. He made his stand as an asshole when he told her he didn't want her in college because she's leaving him behind. In her mind, that wasn't her problem. The day she broke up with him was the first and only apathetic human being she allowed in her life and it was time to move on. He was plastered, of course. She told him whatever they had was over. Unaccepting to this, he became belligerently combative. He made sure she'd anguish to ever have accepted his offer of being his confidante.

Fueled with the anger and an unwanted state of rejection, he grabbed a handgun pointed it at her head, and forced himself on her. She fought as much as she could, but she wasn't about to bleed out to her death or die over something as small as a break-up. The pillage is quick and animal-like. He spits on the side of her face. He gets off as quickly and forcefully as he got on top of her. It crushed her. Not the break-up. Not the penetration of his enraged member. Her mind was injured more than its' ever been in her entire life. It pierced her heart like a sword. Her soul felt lost. She could feel it. She wasn't herself. It was like she died. She felt dead. She slowly got up and pulled up her pants. With his back turned she ran outside to the truck and drove back home.

She drove the long way home. She took the back roads and tried to shake it off. She eventually told herself she should of saw it coming. She should of kept her distance and never saw him again. She told herself she can't change it. It's too late. She can't take it back. She made it home. She sits in the truck in front of

Grandma's house. She wants to tell Grandma and Cheíí what happened, but she didn't. Taking a shower never felt like an excruciating pain she's never felt before. She couldn't seem to get the disgust off of her. She got out of the shower and rolled the biggest and tightest mountain smoke she has ever rolled. Her Cheíí told he if she ever goes through something overwhelming, she always has the mountain tobacco to roll, smoke, and pray. All she has to do is give it to the smoke. If she does that, she doesn't have that weight with her anymore.

With wet, unbrushed hair, she walks out in front of Grandma's house. She held her rolled smoke, a small red metal container of kerosene, a plastic pitcher of water, and the clothes she wore. She walked just past the woodpile. She stopped. She bent down and placed the rolled smoke, clothes and shoes, plastic pitcher, and kerosene on the dirt. She got on her knees, pulled weeds from the ground, and drew a circle in the dirt with a near by thin, cedar branch. She poured water in the circle and dug a hole with her right hand. The dirt was cool, soft, and soothing against the back of her hand. She poured the rest of the water into the circle and dug up more dirt creating a hole deep enough for her shoes and clothes. She rolled her clothes around her shoes. She placed it inside the dug circle. She poured the kerosene onto the pile of clothes and shoes. She strikes a single match and threw it onto the clothes. She puts both of hands in front of the fire palms down. She starts to pray in Navajo. She acknowledges just how badly and violent of a trauma she's just been through. She asks the Creator to take the anguish and pain she feels in her soul. She requests to prosper in strength.

She completed her prayer. She watched in silence as her the clothes she once wore crackles in the orange-red flames. After a while, there is nothing but smoke and ash. She scrapes the ash together and placed more dirt over it using her hands. She leveled it out with the rest of the original mother earth before she dug a hole. She didn't repress the memory. She chose to move forward towards her goal. With the help of the Creator and Holy People, she pushed herself through it. She told herself to focus on school. She doesn't have time to be caught up in the emotional tidal wave that will sweep her away and eventually drown her.

Nine months pass and she is with-child. She accepted her son. She loves him with everything she has in her. She doesn't care about the grapevine whispers. Her son is three years old and perfect. She changed her major twice. Even after the rude hiccups, she persists. Grandma watches her son while she works and goes to school. Melissa treats time preciously. She isn't at work until just a few minutes before her shift and she isn't at school longer than she needs to be. She gives Grandma half of her paychecks.

It's another day trying to gasp for air. She hates leaving her son, but her Grandma adores him. She kisses her son good-bye and heads to work. She hugs Grandma and drives down the dirt road with a long, cloud of dust following her.

She moves into the employee trailer next door to the gas station. It's temporary until she quits. She knows there is something in store for her. When she finally has a day off, she takes her son and Grandma out to eat at Earl's, a local, popular restaurant. Grandma is adamant about the bill. She sure can't say "no" to the Colonel.

The semester ends. She is trying to figure what to major in next. One day the manager, her friend at work, tells her the armored guard that stops at the store asked for her. He always hesitated to say something to her. She ignored his verbal advances thinking about how to handle her college career. After two months of verbal freezing, he becomes brave and asks her out on a date. She refuses.

Months later, she goes into work on her day off. She's going to pick up her paycheck. She sees someone she long forgot about and doesn't want to see. She ignores the person and walks to the office in the back. The manager, her friend, grabs her arm and pushes her into the walk-in freezer. Melissa asks her what's going on. The manager screams and tells her that person has been waiting for a while and wants to talk to her. Melissa gets upset. She tells the manager she has no interest in getting involved. The manager convinces her to say something. She grabs her paycheck, leaves the office, and walks up to the guy. She tells him she doesn't have time for him and for whatever he wants. She doesn't wait for his answer. She walks out of the gas station and into her car. The guy runs out to her car and asks her to roll down her window. She annoyingly rolls it down an inch and tells him she has no problem moving him out of the way with her car. He moves back and she drives off. She spends the rest of her day off with her son and Grandma. Later in the evening, they go for a walk down the half-mile long dirt road. The dogs happily wag their tails and pant around them as they walk.

Over the past three months, she's gone on two dates with him. On the last date she severed the tie and moved on. The two dates led up to the unexpected visit that day, and that was just about be her next pothole. Her mind and her heart argued when she saw him. Her heart wanted to prove to her mind she was right, but her mind told her she doesn't have time to find out.

After the surprised and unwelcomed visit, he came to her work every other day for three weeks. He tries to convince her he's not a loser. She repeatedly tells him school and her son is all she has room for, but he remains unconvinced. He tells her he wants her to finish school and she could attend the university in Flagstaff. His persistence pays his ticket to a three-month relationship with her. She moves to Flagstaff only to find another bottom dweller of the sea. She finds out sooner than later this time. Just when she decides that he may be "the one", everything takes a mild turn for the slight worse. She finds out this bottom dweller is an egotistical slosh and adores the attention from different vaginas. Within a month of moving in with him she lands a job at a coffeehouse, but, he gets fired from his benefit-plus job and lands a shitty job at a bar. He's gone every night of the week.

On the morning of his birthday, he promises her a night of movies and dinner since he's getting off work early. That's the normalcy she craved and longed for— simplicity. After being stood up, she goes to his work. It's empty. A bartender is behind the bar cleaning. She asks the bartender where her *now* ex-boyfriend is. The bartender smiles. He tells her where her ex-boyfriend is at and for her to wish him a 'happy birthday' for him.

She finds the bar and heads inside. She ignores the cover charge sign. The bouncer urges her she needs to pay the cover charge.

She says, "I am here to break-up with my boyfriend and of course, tell him, 'have a happy fucking birthday'".

The bouncer smiles and lets her in. She walks up to the bar looking around for him. The bouncer follows her, walks behind the bar, and whispers something in the bartender's ear.

The bartender places a shot on the bar and says, "It's on the house, hun."

She tells the bouncer she will be right back. She doesn't see him. There are naked girls occupying every vertical log made of shiny metal. The strip club is occupied with men smiling, talking, and grasping their glass bottles. Some are proudly groping naked girls. The blue, purple, and red stage lights rotate from the floor to the wall. The place is filled a gross humidity of groin sweat. The aroma of I-just-got-off-work-so-I'm-going-to-take-a-load-off-here-and-enjoy-my-drink-since-I've-had-a-long-day's-work fills the air.

She walks past the bar, side stage, and tables of seafloor dwellers. She stops at a dark, blood red, velvet curtain. She opens it. There he is. He is holding his drink as a girl puts her "baby exit" in his face. His friends laugh, cheer, and touch the girl. The girl sees her and stops. She stands up and moves over. His buzzed erotica quickly dissolves into reality.

She looks at him and says, "You will always be a fucking loser. Peace, you fuck, I'm out."

She walks through the velvet curtains. She ignores him yelling after her. She walks up to the bar and takes the shot. The bartender gives her a smile and a knuckle-to-knuckle ovation. She walks out of the bar to her car. He runs in front of her car. He waves his arms in the air begging her to stop. She rolls down the window and tells him to move. He tells her he loves her. Just as she was going to tell him to move out of the way again, a drunk girl staggers out of the club asking him to come back inside. He ignores the drunk bottom dweller. He moves out from the front of her car and argues with the girl.

She drives in silence back to the apartment. She doesn't feel like crying nor is she hurt.

She stops in front of the apartment. She closes her eyes and takes a deep breath. She goes inside. She packs three large duffel bags. Her son is asleep. She calls her friend and tells her what happened. Her friend tells her to stay at her place until she figures it out.

The next morning, she drops her son off at daycare and heads to work. When she arrives at work, her friend tells her she can't stay with her because her and her boyfriend need to figure out some problems they've been having. As her shift presses on, she slowly starts to mentally panic. She finishes her shift and picks up her son. Her son's caretaker asks her if she's okay. She tells the caretakers she's just tired. They end up sleeping in her car outside a department store.

The next day, she takes a shower with her son at the local truck stop. As she drops her son off, she holds him and wants to cry, but knows she can't. She drives across town in silence. She usually blasts Ozzy to help her think, but right now she wants to feel. She tells herself it's not worth crying over. She parks. She sees happy people walking into the building. She grabs her apron and hat and walks inside. Her boss and coworkers greet her, but she doesn't take the bait. She doesn't want to be happy today. She has to think about where she is going to sleep.

Her boss notices her silence and asks her what's wrong. She tells her she has a small hiccup to figure out. Throughout the shift she feels uneasy. She sells her guitar at a pawn shop and stays in a crack motel for a month. Things are not looking so bad. She applied to the university months ago, but never found out if she got in because the university would of mailed the letter to her ex's place.

After work, she visits the university she was just at a decade ago. As she walks through the campus holding her son's hand, the tall new buildings awe her. Students roam the landscaped trees and well-kept grounds in their backpacks. She was accepted, but decides not to enroll. She didn't have the money for books, much less a roof over her head.

She calls home from her cellphone, but no one picks up. She calls a second time. Her stepmom answers. Her stepmom asks how she's doing. She quickly interrupts and asks her if she could send some money, just enough to get through to her next paycheck. Her stepmother annoyingly tells her they are leaving to Laughlin. She knows it was a mistake to call. Maybe someday her parents will genuinely care for her. With her cell phone minutes running low, she ends the conversation and turns it off.

The next five months drag. It feels like it won't change for her. She slept with her ex-boyfriend but once and the condom she used proves it's 0.01% defectiveness. She's pregnant. When she calls home, her stepmom always answers the phone insisting her grandparents are busy or not home. She feels her life fall into a surreal life as she is forced to sleep in her car. Her belly gets closer to the steering wheel. She knows it's hormones, but late at night when the city sleeps, she cries as her son sleeps in the backseat.

She's running out of time and money. She takes her son to work with her off and on. Her coworkers are happy entertaining her son and even go as far as often bringing him food. She's happy to be pregnant and have a healthy son, but with everything else, she's numb.

One morning at work, she calls home.

Grandma answers, "Hello?"

She rubs her belly and quietly says, "Grandma?"

Grandma answers, "Yes? Hello?"

She says, "Grandma, can I come home? I…"

Grandma shouts, "The Lady, oh, my beautiful Lady how are you?"

She replies, "What would you say if I told you I'm pregnant?"

Grandma laughs and muffles over the phone, "A baby? That's wonderful. Cheíí! Cheíí! The Lady is going to have a baby! Your Cheíí is smiling, clapping his hands, and says he's happy and wants you home. So, when are you coming?"

She didn't think it was odd that Grandma didn't ask for her ex-boyfriend. In a way it felt like Grandma already knew.

Grandma said happily, "We are here for you all three of you. Come home. Don't worry about anything. Just come home. We want to see you! I want to see my great-grandbabies! Now me and Cheíí have an excuse to go shopping! Oh, I can't wait!"

She finishes her conversation and hangs up the phone.

She tells her boss she's quitting in a few weeks. On her last day, her boss and coworkers surprise her with a baby shower. The entire coffee shop is decorated with bright yellow, rose pink, and sky blue ribbons and balloons. She gets six boxes of Huggies, ten pairs of baby clothes, and three bottles of baby wash. She accepts the White people baby shower with open arms. It's time to go. She hugs everyone and they cry as they say good-bye to her son they've grown to love. Her boss hands her a sky blue envelope. She pulls out a card enclosed with five hundred dollars.

She's shocked and says, "I'm sorry, but I can't this."

Her boss says, "I knows exactly what you're going through. I'm a single mom of three. You come to work everyday and I know you're exhausted, but I see a fire in you. I know the fire in you will never burn out. So, don't let it, okay? You fight for your dreams."

Her boss cry as they hug. They help her load up her car. She buckles her son in his car seat and they drive off.

She makes the three-hour drive. She's finally home. Her father and stepmother live in their own house an eighth of a mile before Grandma's. She drives past their house and drives up to Grandma's. Before Melissa and her son get out of the car, Grandma runs out to the car and greets her. She gets out of the car and then gets her son out of the car seat. Grandma cries as soon as she touches Melissa's bursting, hard, belly.

Grandma cries and says, "My Lady, my sweet, sweet baby is home."

Throughout the rest of the pregnancy, Grandma and Cheíí are there for every carrot with chocolate sauce, barfing session, and kick the baby makes. They coincide with her and only see it as a blessing. They take her to a medicine man. The medicine man sings sacred songs and prayers to welcome the new baby.

*** *** ***

Her brand new baby boy is now a year old. She gets her old job back at the gas station. She's worn out her presence at the gas station. She feels odd as her biological mother starts to come by to visit. Maybe her mother really means to patch things up between them, but she'll need more than the biggest band-aid she can find to "fix" this.

Her mother insists to come visit her. Her mother now lives in a city two hours away. She invites Melissa and her boys for a week. She cautiously agrees.

She's reading to her boys in her mother's living room. Before her mother races out the door, Melissa stops and asks her mother to watch the boys after work so she can look up some information on the internet at the library. Her mother insists to use her laptop in the bedroom. Her mom changes her mind, takes the day off work, and takes her boys to go eat. Her mother tells her to go take some time and see a movie alone. She agrees.

Instead, she heads across town to check out a private college. It's everything she assumes. It's expensive, but it offers free daycare for full-time students, financial aid, and assistance with a job after graduation. Being on campus feels good, but she realizes she's back at square one. She still would have no place to live.

She does have two thousand dollars saved up, but that's not enough rent for the entire year. Could she possibly work and go to school? Where does that leave daycare? She wasn't about to touch her savings account. It still has another year to mature. Even with tough mud, she did manage to put three thousand dollars away for her boys' college.

She leaves the college leaving the admission process open. Her mother and boys pull up at the apartment just as she does.

During dinner, her mom asks what's bothering her. She wants to blurt it out, but she knows her mother doesn't have the answer. Even if her mother wanted to help in some way, her mom would want something in return. It was predictable as much as a cow eats grass. She doesn't respond to her mother. She eats a few more bites of her Pizza Hut slice. She stops eating. She can't take another bite knowing she's stuck. She's stuck in a dead end job with school out of reach. Her mother casually mentions she is moving to Flagstaff next month. Her mother tells her if she is serious about wanting to finish school, she could go to school there and take over the apartment lease. She doesn't think much into it, but feels it will somehow work out, so she agrees.

The next morning, she leaves her boys with her mother and goes to the private college to complete the admission process. After a few hours, she is enrolled and scheduled to start classes within the next month. They give her all the resources she needs to apply for scholarships and grants. She already feels accomplished.

Later that afternoon, she heads back to the Rez with her boys. She has to work tomorrow and put in her two weeks. She finishes out her two weeks. She packs three duffel bags into her wolf gray, four-door, ford Taurus. It's been a while since she's had a good drive. She tells herself nothing is going to get in her way this time, absolutely nothing.

*** *** ***

Moving to a new place is exciting for most. Most young adults adore the city lights, the people, and popular spots to hang out, but not Melissa. Adjusting to Albuquerque is not her blithe. She just wants to be a role model to her boys and finish school. Her oldest son is in kindergarten. Her new baby boy is a toddler and is in daycare while she's in class all day. She works and goes to school full-time, Monday through Friday. She gets up at 5am, gets ready, gets her boys ready, and leaves the apartment. She drops off her son at kindergarten and then heads off to school. Once at school, she takes her son to the campus daycare and heads to class. Mid-day, she checks in on her son in daycare and eats her lunch in an empty classroom. Late afternoon, she rushes to pick up her son from kindergarten, takes him to the school daycare, and goes to her next two classes.

Two years later, her life remains the same. However, she is starting to fall behind in rent. She tries not to panic. The landlord visits wanting to know why she's falling behind. She tells the landlord she's waiting on a scholarship. The scholarship is enough to pay for five months rent. A week later, just as her landlord serves her an eviction notice, her scholarship check arrives. She pays five month's rent. To make the money last, she buys in bulk—diapers, hygiene supplies, cleaning supplies, school supplies, and food.

With housing, the kids, and food covered, there is one last thing she has to take care of before graduation, an internship. She gets lands an unpaid internship at the biggest attorney's office in the state. She must fulfill hundreds of hours interning. She decides to spend those hours in every division. Everyday, she starts to get much more interested in criminal law. Every other day she goes to a different division ranging from misdemeanor cases to felony cases.

Half way through her internship, she learns there are some things that no humane person should ever see. She gets out of the elevator and tries to familiar herself with the division's floor. She notices everyone in the division is crying— from the receptionist to paralegals to attorneys to the victim advocates. She doesn't understand what is going on. She thinks maybe they lost someone that worked in the division.

A Hispanic woman in her 50s comes up to her. The woman is wearing a scarlet red blazer with a blush pink blouse tucked into her black pencil skirt. Her tummy hangs out a little. The woman's neck is complimented with a long, fake, pearl necklace. The woman has curly, shoulder length, gray hair. She notices the woman's eyelids are puffy and swollen. The woman's eyes are blood shot red. Her nose is runny from crying. There is more smeared, black mascara on the woman's cheeks than around her eyes. The woman is holding an overused tissue in her right hand. The woman introduces herself and starts elaborating on the purpose of the division. She explains to Melissa what she will be doing there. As they walk into one of the rooms, the woman grabs two-dozen files from a shelf and shows her where her cubicle is.

The woman tells her to make copies of each file and organize the file. She grabs the files and sits at her closed cubicle. She goes to the copy machine and starts copying each piece of paper. While it's copying, she reads each document carefully. The copy machine makes time fly. It's lunchtime. The floor is deserted. She sits at her cubicle. She gets her lunch box out from her backpack. She sees a violet, tabbed, file sitting on top of the next pile of files she has to do. She grabs it and places it next to her food. As she slowly chews her bologna sandwich, she opens the file. There is a pile of photos paper clipped together. She slowly takes off the paper clip and looks at the photos. She's not sure what she's looking at. It looks like a pile of old clothes and an old, very worn shoe. After she's done with the photos, she flips the page and carefully reads. A few pages later, she stops chewing her bologna sandwich.

She puts the rest of her sandwich back in her lunch box. She dashes to the bathroom. She doesn't make it to the toilet. Chunks of undigested, chewed bologna, and wet, wheat bread spew from her contracting stomach into the large, grey, wide, garbage between the twin, white porcelain sinks. Her face flushes. Her heart beats through her ears. She lurches forward over the sink. She grabs a dusty brown, paper towel and swipes her mouth. The paper towel lightly scratches her cheeks and chin as she wipes of the excess. She controls her heavy heaves from the abrupt ralphing session. She washes her hands with cold water and Dial soap. She slurps cold water from her cupped hand and spits it into the sink. She makes her hands soapy and washes her mouth and around her mouth. She rinses the soap off. She dries her hands and face with two paper towels and heads outside for fresh air.

Once outside, she walks to the end of the building. At the corner, there is a group of formally dressed smokers. One of them comes over and asks her if she's okay.

She answers, "I just read something I probably shouldn't of read."

The older, Hispanic woman, puffs her cigarette and asks, "Are you an intern?"

She answers, "Yeah."

The woman asks, "Which division are you in?"

She replies, "Violent Crimes Against Chil…"

The woman opens her gaudy purse and hands her a cigarette, "Girl, you're gonna need one of these. So, what are you interning for?"

The woman hands her a lighter. She lights the cigarette.

She replies, "Brook Creek. Interning for my paralegal degree. 120 hours to go."

They puff their cancer sticks. The woman asks what made her freak out. She tells the woman what she read and saw. They smoke and talk before heading back into the building. They separate at the elevator getting off different floors.

She walks back to her cubicle. She puts her uneaten sandwich away. She grabs the next stack of files and makes her way to the copy machine. She finishes the stack and sits back at her cubicle. She stirs the courage to finish reading the file. Her chest feels like it's being squeezed by a vice. She can't help, but to cry. The older, Hispanic woman with the red blazer and pearls comes to check on her. The woman looks at Melissa. The woman tells her that is the case that broke the entire division as soon as it they got it. The woman hugs her and tells her that it's hard seeing cases like that, but they have to stick together to get through it.

Later, Melissa leaves work. She's numb. She can't believe something so evil could happen like that. The photos she thought were a pile of old clothes and an old, worn shoe was actually the remains of a little boy. He was buried in a shallow grave. Because of the hot summer temperatures, his little body quickly decomposed. It made her think of her boys. How little they are. Her youngest is around the same age of the little boy. She's hit with a tidal wave of emotion. She can't imagine what that beautiful baby went through.

She drives back to school to pick up the boys from daycare. The boys see her and run to her. She gets down on her knees and wraps her arms around them. She holds onto him for what seems like an eternity. She doesn't hold back her tears, she can't.

She looks at her boys and says, "I love you so much."

For the next few weeks, she wakes up in cold sweats at 2am. She can still hear sounds of a little boy giggling. In her dream, she sees a little boy skipping then it fades to someone snapping a camera of a crime scene and an unrecognizable woman screaming in rage throwing sand up into the air in the background. It's the same dream every night. With very little sleep, she finishes her week in the division. She's transfers to another division, the gang division. It's her first day in the division. She sits in on a gang-related trial in court. A man killed his little brother because of territory. It's between two gangs. The two gangs sever a family in half. From babies to grandparents, they are fully invested. The courtroom is divided. One side wears marshmallow white, oversized t-shirts, baggy pants, and clean white bandanas and the other side is occupied by royal blue, button-up smocks, baggy blue jeans, and the girls are murdered in obscene, royal blue lipstick and eye shadow fit for a circus. She's intrigued. Each family member is branded with a single bandana and a slew of permanent body ink. All of the men wear suspenders. All of the women wear dark black eyeliner, black lip liner, and aren't interested in remaining silent as they quietly chatter amongst themselves. The courtroom feels like it's about to turn into a violent cock fight. The tension turns surreal. She decides to sit on the ocean blue side of the family since it's near the doors.

The trial lasts for an hour. She listens in on testimony from both sides. Two family members testify. They are dressed normally, non-gang attire, and sternly say the gang life is ridiculous and shouldn't have taken a life. The tension remains steady. Finally, it's over. She waits for the courtroom to clear. The crowding, pushing, and shoving reminds her of sheep eager to get out of the corral. Moments later, a fight breaks out in the hallway. Bailiffs break up the fight. She squeezes past the pushing and yelling and heads back. She talks with the attorney handling the case. He is an old, African American in his late 50s ready to retire. He explains to her he has been in the gang division for over twenty years. It is his passion.

Over the next few months, she observes the courtroom and learns the paper process of the system. She remains intrigued.

She completes her internship and classes with a stunning 3.9 GPA. Her hard work finally pays off. She makes a call home and invites the family to her graduation in the next few weeks. Her stepmother tells her they will definitely be there.

** ** **

One of her friend's mothers from school offers to watch her boys as the graduation ceremony begins. As other graduates in royal blue gowns find their seats, she turns to scan the bleachers. She doesn't see anyone. An hour goes by. She stands up and gets in line next to the stage. With nine people in front of her, she knows they won't show up. Her heart starts to sink for a second, but she quickly forgets about it as she spots her boys in the crowd. Her boys wave to her smiling and give her a thumbs up. She smiles and waves back. Her name is called, she walks to the stage, and shakes the director's and teachers' hands. She proudly grabs her degree, waves to her boys, and blows them kisses. It doesn't take long for the graduation to be over. She doesn't take photos like everyone else. She just wants to spend time with her boys. They go back to the apartment and she makes Navajo tacos.

A few hours later, just as they were about to eat, the doorbell rings. It's Grandma and Cheíí. She invites them in. She serves them. Just as she sits down, her doorbell rings again. It's her dad and stepmom. She smiles, invites them in, and hugs them. She asks why they are so late. Her dad blames her stepmom saying they got the time wrong and then got lost on the other side of town. Grandma and Cheíí said they were told the graduation wasn't until later. They all apologize to her as they ate.

After dinner, they leave. Grandma and Cheíí don't like leaving the house empty. Her dad and stepmom like hitting the casinos. She offers them to stay and maybe they could go to the movies to celebrate. They all decline. She doesn't say anything further.

She pays rent for another two months then has to move out to a cheaper apartment. She ends up moving into a one-bedroom apartment. She only has enough money to pay rent for three months. She's been putting in job applications since she's had three months of school left. She hasn't heard any good news yet. Not wanting to feel overwhelmed, she goes home for a few weeks. Just as she is unloading wood with the boys, her Grandma yells from the house. Someone on the phone is asking for her. She dashes to the phone. Out of breath, she hangs up the phone screaming. She happily tells Grandma she got a new job and starts in just a few weeks. The two weeks fly by. It's summer. The school offers free daycare up to six months after graduation. She is grateful. She plans to save her paychecks for rent and for daycare.

She goes to work, has her own cubicle, computer, and a court docket to maintain. She is assigned a judge. She falls into her work duties and falls prey to her jealous coworkers even quicker. Regardless, she keeps to herself and just works. One day her assigned attorney changes courtrooms. She gets assigned a new attorney to work with. He is just another pushy, arrogant, Anglo and uses it to his advantage. She's heard of him making his former paralegals turn sour before. She jinxed herself wondering how they could be stressed out.

He's apparently having a bad day—his norm. He calls her on the desk phone. He tells her he's late, forgot the case docket in his cubicle, and needs her to run it him at the courthouse. She is confused. Her coworkers certainly don't run frantically to the courthouse to fetch dockets. The only time she goes to the courthouse is to file motions or get a last-minute motion signed by a judge. She hangs up the phone telling him she'll be right down. She twirls around in her office chair, gets up, walks over to his cubicle, and grabs the rubber banded docket off his desk.

One of her coworkers pokes her head over the cubicle, and says, "Don't do it."

She makes a puzzled face and looks at her coworker. Her coworker is in her late forties. The woman has curly, chestnut brown, shoulder length hair, Hispanic, glasses, stands taller than her at 5'11", and always wears a white gold, Tiffany, heart charm, heavy-gauged necklace and bracelet. Her attitude is sharper than any quick blade. She's seen this woman refuse to be bossed around by anyone, much less, any attorney. She decides to take Bryanna's advice. She places the docket back on the cubicle and walks back to her desk. She calls her attorney and tells him she doesn't have time to fetch his docket. Bryanna walks back over to her cubicle. Bryanna gives her a crash course of work do's and hell no's and how to handle the attorneys. Melissa is finally able to clarify what her job duties are. Bryanna only talks to Melissa and another woman the same age as Bryanna. The three talk about office drama during breaks and lunch. They help her maneuver the office flaws. The older women and Melissa stick out like sore thumbs, but they don't care and just work. Melissa flies through her probation period and gets a raise. She's happy about the promotion, but comes to realize she hates her job.

After a few weeks of making calls, she finds a new routine. Three times a week, she drops off her boys with a fellow student that has classes on different nights. She leaves work at 5pm sharp. Even with rush hour traffic, she is able to make it to her evening classes. After nine months of sleepless nights and dragging workdays, she starts to feel the weight of work and school pounce on her. She is starting to fall behind at work. She has to get to work an hour earlier so she can catch up. She doesn't want to risk a possible promotion. It pays off and gets the promotion making two dollars more an hour, but it's not much of a break from the chaos of school.

Even with her new promotion, she can't keep up on rent and daycare payments. Out of the blue her mother invites her to dinner. Her mother has since moved back into town and bought a house. Her mother asks her to move in with her. Her mother travels often and needs someone to watch her house. She despises the idea, but has no choice. She moves in. Soon after, her brother moves in. He's a chef and a slave to the bottle. She feels bad for him and thinks maybe he just can't catch a break. So, she helps him. She pays for his phone, gives him rides, and tries to be the little sister she would want to have. She is barely able to afford to pay for her classes, so has to take out more student loans. She's starting to hurt in bills. She's not able to save any money. Her paycheck is gone before she's even paid.

She finds the strength from her boys. She's struggling, but feels it inside her soul there is a way out. She doesn't feel stuck in the poverty quick sand. Instead, she feels like she needs to see through the darkness. In her time of chaos the city brings, she goes outside to the dawn sun. She wakes up her boys early. She blesses them with water and the sunrise. She remembers what Cheíí told her all those years ago. She prays with all her might. All she needs is the help of the moon. The moon will get her out of the dark paycheck spent abyss and out of the loneliness.

At work, Bryanna takes her under her wing. Bryanna makes sure the attorneys don't take advantage of Melissa. A few attorneys ask her out on a date, but she adamantly refuses. She didn't want be in the dating world. At this point, she knows she has the potential to find her purpose in life.

She only makes a friend from school-Saniya. Saniya is a little younger and smaller than her. Saniya has dark, midnight black, shiny hair, and is Hispanic. Saniya is intelligent, funny, warming, and she felt like she knew her from another life. Melissa is shocked to find out Saniya has four boys. Saniya invites Melissa and her boys over to her house to work on an assignment.

Saniya's boys happily invite her boys to play Monopoly in the bedroom. Saniya's family is a fresh breath of air. Saniya's husband is a trucker and hardly home. She thinks, even though Saniya has a husband, she is a single mom, too. Just as they wrap up the assignment, Saniya mentions ordering pizza. She tells her she wishes she could, but she doesn't have the means to. Saniya happily tells her not to worry about it. Her heart perks with happiness. She can't believe there are still nice people left in the universe. They finish the assignment, pizza, and part ways with a hug. It may have just been homework and pizza to Saniya, but to her, it was showing that there still is love and compassion left on Earth. She puts the moment in her back pocket.

In five months, she'll have her degree. Unfortunately, her exhaustion was spent mentally and financially. It's too much. She doesn't want to burn the bridge at work and school so she quits. She figures she can regain her strength and energy and return to work and school later. She gets hired as a full-time nanny caring for newborn twins. Surprisingly, she makes triple the amount she made at the attorney's office. She is stoked. Not only does she get ahead of her bills, but her stress melts away faster than a snowflake in Phoenix. She puts money in her savings account. She moves out of her mother's house into a two-bedroom apartment. She trades her old, Ford Taurus in for a mom-pride, baby SUV. Just as things start to look up, she crosses an unexpected path that turns her world upside down and inside out.

Chapter 11. Morphine Memory

"It's not too long now. The Moon awaits, My Lady."
-Frank Nez

The mother of the twins trusts her so much she's able to take the babies with her on errands. Within six months she's refreshed. She has enough money saved to return to school and work. But, something out of the norm happens. She's been running into the same guy periodically and each time he hits on her. She dismisses every advance. She has better things to worry and wonder about.

The fourth encounter is at a local car wash. She just finished rinsing suds off the SUV. Just as she closes the driver door, there's a knock on the window. Startled, she turns and laughs. Embarrassed, she places her left hand onto her forehead. She smiles. She opens her door. She doesn't recognize him until he points out the other three times luck has been on his side. He hands her his number on a small piece of receipt paper. With her door propped open with her left foot, she refuses his advance for the fourth time. He grins, encourages to take the small receipt paper. She obliges. He tells her to have a good one and walks off.

She looks at his number and says, "Sure. Yeah, right."

She crumbles up the receipt paper and flicks it towards the passenger floorboard.

Preparing to find a part job and returning to classes, she continues to be an extreme piggy bank hoarder for the next two months. One day while cleaning out her SUV, she finds the balled up receipt paper. She flattens it out. She tries to remember whose number it is. She doesn't recognize the handwriting. It's not hers. She dials it.

She makes the one phone call she will truly regret. It's him. His charm hooks her faster than chumming a shark. They text back and forth for the next month. He says all the right things and gives her the impression that he has the right head on his shoulders. He convinces her to move out of state with him. Maybe he is a good guy. Maybe this is her chance. She figures she can finish school as soon as she gets there—a fresh start.

Her new place is nothing like the city she left behind.

She settles in and lands a job with a local attorney's office. She can't wait to finish school. She grows to love her job and gets an unexpected promotion. Her promotion helps her trade in her little SUV for a stunning, royal blue, Silverado truck. She pays off her truck quickly. Her new boyfriend, not having a vehicle, asks her to buy another truck he can use for work. He tells her he will eventually save up money for his own. She is happy to help and buys a second truck. With the substantial income from work, she pays off the first truck rather quickly and pays off half of the second.

One peculiar day, her boyfriend comes back to the apartment rather early. While she's reading Judy Paternak's, "Yellow Dirt: A Poisoned Land and the Betrayal of the Navajos", he asks her to be his wife. She slowly puts the book down and hesitantly agrees. They blatantly set off to the local clerk's office. Three signatures and a state seal on a regular piece of paper later, it's distastefully official. The rest of the day doesn't seem too much out of then norm. She figures it's suppose to feel that way on your wedding day. Maybe all the hype of happiness in the movies is just that, hype.

That night, he wants to celebrate and have sex, but she just isn't into it. He gets upset and leaves slamming the front door. They haven't had sex, yet. She told him when she moved they will when the time is right. She doesn't understand why it's such a big deal as it never was before. Now, she doesn't feel too proud being married. His demeanor changes like day and night. When he returns, he is distant. He ignores her boys. He doesn't acknowledge them and walks past them. She regrets marrying him even more. Her brain becomes overwhelmed screaming to get an annulment or divorce. She tries to figure out how to tell him she just wasn't ready.

Two weeks later on her day off, her new husband doesn't return home. He doesn't call or text her back. She thinks it's military business and isn't worried. He finally comes back late one night and says he's tired. He falls onto the bed and is dead asleep.

The next morning, she's in the kitchen. It's her day off. The boys are reading in the living room waiting for her to drink her coffee so she can take them to school. She hears his phone ringing. It's under a pillow next to him. The phone rings four more times. She thinks it might be his boss, so she walks to the bedroom and grabs his phone. A photo of a woman with barely-covered nipples covers the screen as it rings. Her heart sinks. She goes to the bathroom and locks the door behind her. She takes a breath. She answers it on the next ring. She talks to the woman. She finds out her new husband cheated on her.

Trying to control her distraught, she takes the boys to school and runs at the local track. As the sweat drips down her back, she thinks how she will confront him, and furthermore, leave.

She returns to the apartment. He's frying eggs and bacon in a skillet. He's texting on his phone as they stand in the kitchen. She takes a breath and tells him what happened earlier. He fires denial at her. She calmly asks to see his phone. He refuses. His best friend unexpectedly shows up. Wanting to help, her husband's best friend yanks the phone from him and hands it to her. Just as she grabs the phone, a text comes in. It's a photo of another naked woman. Her husband lunges at her trying to attack her. His best friend pulls him back. She goes to the bedroom and starts packing her clothes and boys' clothes. With nothing more than annoyance, she leaves with her duffel bags.

For the next week, Holiday Inn is her home. She comes back to the apartment with her youngest son the next morning. She pulls into the parking lot just behind the apartment building. She doesn't see her new ex's best friend's truck. She enters into the apartment slowly. Closing the front door behind her, she pauses and listens. There's silence. She tells her son to go to his room to pack.

She puts her keys and phone on the table. As she walks to her bedroom, her husband dashes out of the bathroom. They scuffle. He slams her against the wall. She tries to fight back. She yells to her son to close the bedroom door and lock it. Her husband slaps her. She punches him with all the strength she has in her. As they scrap, she tries to reach for her phone on the corner of the table. Just as she is about to grab it, he trips her, and starts kicking her. She grabs his foot and kicks him in the groin with her right foot. He falls to the floor and curls up like a wilted, dry, dead bug. She slowly gets up. Her face and head feel wet. In a slight daze, she yells for her son to get the keys.

Her son grabs the keys and heads for the front door.

As he opens the front door, his little voice yells. "Mom!"

She's still in the hallway. She's leaning up against the wall in a daze. Her soon-to-be ex-husband is still curled up a few feet away from her. She staggers to the front door. Behind her, she hears him grunt and struggle to get up. She frantically locks the front door behind them. She grabs her son's hand and tells him to run.

What seems like seconds later, the front door rattles. He yells her name behind the door. With no time to run outside the building and make it to the truck, she picks up her son. She runs one flight of stairs downstairs at the end of the hallway. They hide behind the stairs. The hallway light is broken making it pitch black behind the stairs. She quiets her breathing. She puts her hand over her son's mouth. She looks at her son and puts her pointer finger to her sweaty lips cuing him to be quiet. He nods his little head. She hears him walk down the opposite side of the hallway. She hears the hallway door open and slam shut. She thinks in a haste if she should make a run for it. Her instincts tell her not to. Seconds later, the door down the hallway opens and slams shut, again. She hears his fast paced footsteps coming down the hallway. He stops in front of the stairs. He is feet away from her and her son. Through the opening between the stairs she sees his side profile. His hand is shaking. Its' grasping a handgun. She covers her son's eyes. He walks to the right of the stairs and out the front of the building. Through the front of the building's windows, she sees his best friend run up to him. She hears him tell his best friend to check the exit in the back.

He walks down the sidewalk and down the street with the gun at his side. He crosses the street. She sees someone walk out of the office to her left. Scared for her life, she runs to the office and locks the door behind her. She tells the office staff to call the police. On the side of the office doors are tall, narrow windows. She sees him come inside the building. He starts walking towards the office. She picks up her son and runs to a back closet behind the desk. She quickly puts her son in the corner. She frantically closes the closet's accordion doors. She covers up with trench coat-like jackets. The closet door doesn't close all the way. She can see through the crack of the adjoining accordion doors. One woman gets on the phone with the police. Melissa can faintly hear the operator ask where the emergency is. The woman remains calm and tells the operator the address of the apartments and quickly tells the operation they need to send police to a possible domestic violence situation. Through the narrow, office side windows, she sees her husband quickly tuck his gun into the back of his pants. The office doors rattle. He tries to open the door, but it's locked. He knocks on the door. Not wanting to alarm him, the other woman standing in front of the desk unlocks the door. She quickly tells him that the office is on lunch. He pushes his way around her. He walks in and smiles. The woman asks him what she can help him with. The other woman is on the phone. He asks them if they've seen a woman with a little boy. They tell him they haven't seen anyone. He quickly scans the room with his eyes and tells them to have a good day. He walks out of the office and out of sight. The woman immediately locks the office door. Through the office window and the crack of the closet door, she sees her new ex-husband and his best friend walk back into the apartment. She stays in the closet until the police arrive.

She tells them she doesn't want to come out of the office until he is sitting in back of the unit. She hears a swoon of cops yelling followed by a huge thud, then more yelling. Minutes later, cops walk past the front office. He's in cuffs and is forced into the back of the police car. His nose is bleeding. He bangs his head on the car window shouting something she can't understand. More police units show up. They lamely give her a domestic violence packet and have her write a statement. The officer tells her the paramedics should check her out. She refuses. She thinks she has more important things to worry about. She knows he will post bail and be out in a couple of days or even the very next morning. She quickly thinks what her next move should be. She gets as many bags packed as she can and drives to a different hotel across town. She takes out $500 from the bank and pays for the hotel for another night.

She picks up her oldest son when he is out of school. She calls into work for the next two days. That evening, she orders pizza and figures out what she needs to do. She doesn't know anyone there besides her boss and she's already called into work for the week. She doesn't want to bother her boss with more grief.

As the boys are eating, she hears a knock at the door. The boys stop chewing and look at the door then look at her. She puts her finger over her lips telling them to be quiet. She slowly goes to the door and puts her left eye to the keyhole. She tries to control her breathing. Through the keyhole she sees five people, maybe six, dressed in olive green, camouflage, military wear. She doesn't see her new ex, but asks them what they want through the door. They assure her he is not with them. They plead with her to open the door. She finally opens the door. The superior officers greet her.

They introduce themselves. They take off their hats as they walk inside the hotel room. She closes the door behind them. They tell her they are aware of the situation. They plead with her to go to the hospital to get checked out. They tell her he's posted bond and is out of jail. He is restricted to the barracks on base and military officers are watching him. They continue to say his weapons are taken away along with his rank. The highest-ranking officer is an Asian, maybe in his fifties. He has a slight Asian accent that blends into the English he's speaking.

He says, "Your ah-boys would be safe at my home. You need to go to hospital. We worry about you, you know. My home and hospital are on base. Come. Get your things. We can escort you to the hospital and your boys can come with me at my home. It's time for you to be safe. Come."

She replies, "I don't want to leave my boys with people I don't know."

He smiles and says, "Some of the officer's wives will be there, too. For your support. You will be escorted everywhere you go. You and your boys will be safe. I promise."

She sighs. Feeling like she has no choice, she agrees. She packs her bags and they leave. She parts ways with her boys with hugs and kisses. She sets off with the other officers. One officer is by her side asking if she needs anything every ten minutes. She tells him she doesn't need anything.

It starts to sprinkle as they arrive to the hospital. She gets out of the very black, GMC fully loaded Yukon. She stops and looks out into the distance. She sees fog hug the mountaintop, she can't help, but to think of home. Followed by an officer, she limps and nearly falls just as she reaches the hospital. The officer lends a hand and helps her walk into the hospital. The sliding doors open to the emergency room. She limps up to the receptionist desk and sees a sign that reads, "Please sign-in. We'll be right with you." She grabs the white, smooth, BIC pen. Her right hand shakes as she scribbles her name on the paper clipped to the clipboard. The officer leads her to an almost empty hospital waiting room. She finds an ocean blue colored, cushioned, polyester chair to rest on.

With the officer just inches of her, she sits in silence. CNN echoes through the room as nosey military wives stare at her like she has a tail. Her left cheek and forearms are bruised, purple plums. Her long hair is tied up in a messy bun. She has a large, square, band-aid covering the left side of her head. Some blood managed to stain through the band-aid making a dark impression through the beige strip. After an annoyed fifteen minutes of stare downs, she's called to the back. She feels like she's walking the plank of shame. With a sore butt, legs, back, stomach, and side, she slowly struggles to sit on the cold, hard, thin mattress of a hospital twin bed.

A woman comes in. She's wearing a black blazer with black slacks fit for a social worker's salary. A worn ID tag with her photo dangles around her neck. For the next fifteen minutes, she feels like a freak on display—a mere foreign matter being examined, a subspecies. The woman takes dozens of pictures and asks her double the questions. The woman asks for a statement. She tells her she's not in the mood to write. The woman offers a recorded verbal statement. She agrees. Moments after, the real pain and soreness sets in—it's all over her body. Her left side screams in excruciating pain with every move. The white-coated doctor enters the room.

He fit the bill of the white doctor in every hospital as he asks, "So, what do we have here?"

She wanted to say, "Ignorance. Blind common sense. Sprinkled with a dash of stupidity."

Instead, she answers, "The wonderless result of domestic violence. Small abrasions, some scrapes, and possibly more."

He asks her questions and performs some physical tests that makes her feel less of a dominant woman and more of a dog that's been kicked relentlessly by its' owner. After the physical examination, he confirms she has a slight concussion and two cracked ribs. She is restricted to bed rest. Just as the doctor walks out of the room, her phone rings. It's him. She looks at her phone screen and ignores it. It stops and the notification of "missed call" screams on the phone's screen. It rings, again. The officer by her side grabs her phone and answers it. He tells her new ex not to call again and hangs up the phone.

Feeling much like an old, tattered, forgotten stuffed animal in the attic, she sees several military officers and military police walk back and forth in front of her room staring at her as they walk by. She is on display for another torturing four hours. They finally give her enough pain killers fit for a horse and tell her to rest.

Suddenly, it hits her.

She feels surreal.

She feels the floor lift up off the ground and up towards the ceiling.

Why does it feel like a dream? A bad dream.

Is this really happening?

How could of this happened?

The white ceiling, white floors, white walls, and white lights of the hospital makes her feel woozy. It's so bright. So white.

The officer helps her back into the SUV.

The officer takes her back to the superior officer's house where her boys are.

She is greeted with a gentle hug and tea at the kitchen island. The household doesn't have kids, but they have guest rooms that are more welcoming than a hotel room. They set up sweet and sour pork with white rice on a large tray for her, but she isn't hungry. The officer's wife helps her into the shower and gives her painkillers after. The officer's wife helps her into the guest bedroom upstairs and tells her to rest. Her muscles pinch all over as she slowly lies down on the bed.

It's not too long before she enters the painkiller's utopia. She feels like she's floating. The once stabbing pinches and head throbbing turns into a numbing silence. She hears her boys' giggles in the living room. She faintly smiles and closes her eyes. The tension in her body and brain turns into cotton candy and she falls asleep.

Late into the night, her meds wear off. She hears a tap at the window. She opens her eyes and hopes she's just hearing things. A few seconds later, a red brick clashes through the bedroom window making her fall out of bed. She screams from the pain of falling on her side of where her cracked ribs are. The officer's wife runs into the guest bedroom and drags her into the hallway and into the master bedroom. She sees the superior officer run downstairs to check on the boys. He then runs out the front door. She hears car tires screech against the pavement. The superior officer is too late. He comes back inside and makes a phone call.

Seconds later, the military police drive up. She realizes she's not safe anywhere. She stays with them for a few days, but knows she can't stay there for long. She doesn't want to be an inconvenience to them.

The officers take her and the boys back to the apartment. They assure her he is not anywhere near. She knows she needs to get the boys away from there, so she calls her father and stepmother. They don't offer any solutions and don't want to make the long drive. She has no choice. She then begs her mother to keep the boys until the divorce is final.

Her mother arrives that evening. She then begs her mother to take her belongings back down in a rented storage truck. Her mother refuses. Her can feel her eyes accumulate tears on the bottom of her eyelid as she kneels down on the paved sidewalk. She kisses and hugs her boys. She tells them she loves them and she'll be home soon. She watches the car drive off until they disappear around the corner.

After they leave, she rents a truck. The officers load up everything and unload it in a local storage. The apartment is now like her, empty, cold, and no sense of home written anywhere. A few bags of rice, beans, and mac and cheese occupy the cupboards. Five cherry-red apples and a box of Cheerios accompany the kitchen counter. A couple of pots and pans are on the stovetop. One plate, one spoon, fork and a knife are all that's left within the kitchen. A purple sleeping bag, a duffel bag's worth of clothes, and a few bottled hygiene liquids is the rest of her divorce-survival gear.

She decides to stay at the apartment stressing she doesn't want to place anyone else in danger. The officers beg her to stay with them until the divorce is final. She adamantly declines. They leave and tell her a few officers will be outside the complex. Evening sets in slowly and painfully. She sleeps in her bedroom on the floor. She can't sleep. She blinks her eyes open with every sound she hears and voices she hears in the hallway. After a few hours and telling herself he's not going to show up, she finally falls asleep.

For two weeks there is blissful silence. She's eating her pasta one day and suddenly hears a bang at the door. Frightened by the loud bang, she grabs her phone and dials 9-1-1, but doesn't press the 'call' button. She goes to the door. With her eye wide open, she looks through the peephole. No one is there. She looks back and forth straining her eye trying to see if someone is hiding down the hallway. She figures it's someone that maybe ended up on the wrong floor.

She turns on the gas burner under a tea kettle full of water. She sits back at the built-in counter keeping an eye on the flame hugging the tea kettle. She sees small amounts of steam coming out of the spout.

She flinches as a loud bang hits against the door. Then another. Steam starts to blow softly out of the tea kettle's spout. She grabs the phone, dials 9-1-1, runs to the bedroom and tries to lock the bedroom door, but the lock is stuck and doesn't turn.

The operator picks up, "9-1-1, what is your emergency?"

She presses the side button of the phone to turn the volume all the way down.

She faintly hears the operator repeat, "Hello? Are there?"

She opens the closet door and closes it.

She hears two more loud bangs at the front door.

The operator asks, "What's that noise? Hello? Are you there?"

She quietly and frantically says, "Oak, Oakwood Apartments, B1202, please hurry."

The operator replies, "Ma'am, tell me what's happening. Ma'am?"

She quietly says, "Shhhh..."

The operator says, "Ma'am stay on the line with me."

She hears the front door burst open. She hears heavy footsteps 'kush' on the beige carpet. The tea kettle is whistling in the kitchen. The footsteps go to the boys' bedroom.

Her heart is beating through her chest.

Her forehead and the palms of her hands begin to heavily perspire.

The operator says, "Ma'am, units are on their way. Please stay on the line with me."

The footsteps stop then start walking towards the bedroom where she is. A different set of footsteps turns off the screaming tea kettle on the stove. She hears three male voices. She quickly recognizes her ex's voice.

She hears one man say, "Hey, man what the hell are you doing? Are you crazy? I thought all you wanted to do was talk. Dude, you broke the door, you're nuts."

She hears him say, "Shut up."

He slowly opens the bedroom door. He slowly walks to the closet door. She puts the phone in her back pocket. He slowly opens the closet door.

He looks down at her and asks, "Why are you hiding?"

She doesn't answer him.

He asks her sternly, "Why are you leaving me?"

He puts his hands on his head and starts to scream and cry. She doesn't want to look at him. Suddenly, he grabs her by the hair. She tries to punch him in the face. She misses and punches him in the neck. The two other men come running in. They yell at him that he's crazy and needs to stop. They grab him and hold him back. She's in a daze and stands up against the wall in the hallway. It feels like a knife is puncturing her side.

His friends push him into the other bedroom. She limps and grabs her already packed duffel bag and runs out the door. She limps to her truck, but the tires are slashed. She limps into the street and keeps running as fast she can. She groans in pain as she runs with a limp. She hears him screaming her name in the distance behind her. The yelling turns into him arguing with the other two men.

She runs three blocks. The street curves and there is a gas station at the end of the block. She crosses the street and runs to the gas station. She spots a large garbage bin next to the store. She hides behind the trash bin. A homeless woman sitting behind the store looks at her and realizes what she's running from. The old woman grabs a worn hoodie and jacket out of her tarnished, metal, shopping cart. She hears screeching of tires in the distance. They're coming.

The homeless woman runs to her and frantically tells her, "Here! Give me your bag. Put this on!"

She hysterically puts the hoodie and jacket on. Slightly groaning in pain, she pulls the hoodie up over her head. Her heart is pulsating with an uncontrollable frenzy. Her side is wildly pulsating in a sharp pinching pain. She takes a deep breath and tries to slow her breathing down. She wants to gasp in pain and to the very least, react due to the pain, but she knows she can't. She keeps her head down. She can barely see the gas pumps and the parking lot. She sees a red truck turn off into the store's parking lot and circle around the gas six gas pumps. The windows of the trucks are down.

She hears him yell to his friends, "I know I saw her run this way."

One of the men replies, "Nah, she didn't come this way."

The other man says, "She's not here, man! Just some homeless bitches. Let's go, man, fuck!"

The red truck makes a full screeching turn. She slowly looks up. The truck's red break lights flicker as they do a rolling stop and peel out back onto the main road. She takes a deep breath. Her hands shake, she gasps, and holds her side.

The homeless woman looks at her and says, "You can't keep running."

She slowly takes off the hoodie and jacket. She gives it back to the homeless woman. The homeless woman gives her a black and white, striped, plastic, shopping bag. She looks inside and takes out a brand new, black hoodie with the tags still attached. The woman tells her to take it. She thanks the homeless woman and reaches into her pocket. The money she had in her pocket is gone.

She says, "Fuck!"

She limps back through the gas station parking lot, sidewalk, and road where she was just moments ago. She thinks she must of dropped it when she was running. She's begging herself hoping to find a wad of money. She crosses the street. She runs with a slight limp and makes it back to the apartment. When she reaches the apartment building she sees military police cars parked out front. She starts to limp away from the building. She runs back towards the gas station. She walks past the store.

She gets lost in the city and finds herself sitting in a rigid, metal tunnel under a freeway. She squats in the tunnel trying to catch her breath. She stands up and digs in her pockets. She only has eleven dollars and fifteen cent. Her phone is gone. Her phone must of fallen out of her pocket along with the money. She wonders if it would be smart to go back to the apartment. She decides to turn back and starts walking back towards the apartment. She stops around the corner. The military police are gone. She sees a truck she doesn't recognize parked in front of the apartment building. A man in a military uniform gets out of the driver's side.

He's on the phone. He leans up against the grill of the truck. She can't hear what he's saying. Now she knows she can't go back to the apartment, well at least for now.

She goes back to the gas station and asks the homeless woman if she knows where she can go for the night. The homeless woman tells her the shelter is full by now and on the other side of town. She tells her she can stay with her at a shed she sleeps in a few blocks away. The woman tells her it's safe and she padlocks the gate behind her. The shed she sleeps in is out of sight. She is scared, but feels like she has no choice. The woman seems like a normal woman just down on her luck. The woman lets her sleep on a brand new sleeping she's been saving. She's finally able to get a good night's sleep.

The next morning, she buys the woman breakfast at the gas station. She thanks the woman for everything she's done for her and walks to the apartment manager's office.

The manager tells her the rent is paid up for the next two months. The manager tells her she didn't tell her husband about the rent being paid that far in advance. The manager explains that her husband signed the forms reassuring he's moved out and off the lease. The manager tells her the apartment is solely in her name, but she didn't tell him that. The manager urges her to change the locks.

She's still in quite a haze about everything, but also knows, at this point, she has little to no avenues. The manager offers to stay with her and she can borrow some extra furniture at no charge until she moves out. She tells the manager she has no place to go until the divorce is final, so she agrees. The manager stays with her and only leaves the apartment to go to the office and take care of the property.

The next morning, her boss shows up at the apartment. They drink tea and she tells her boss exactly what's going on. For the next few hours, they talk about what her plan is. Her boss wants to help her. Her boss takes her to the bank to take out the rest of the money, but discovers it's all gone. Her checking account, savings account, her special savings account, and shockingly, her boys' college fund accounts, are all cleaned out and closed. She talks to the bank manager. He informs her that her husband came in an hour ago and emptied the accounts. Her boss talks to the manager and tries to reason with the bank to try and get any of the money back. The bank manager refuses and tells them the account was a joint account. There's nothing the bank can do. She feels her heart drop to her feet and shatter into tiny pieces on the floor. She slowly walks towards the door. She is so overwhelmed with exhaustion, anger, hurt, and stupidity that she hits the plastic bin full of bank brochures off the island table.

She yells. "Fuck!"

Her boss walks over to her.

With tears ready to fall from her bottom eyelids, she says, "I need to figure out how to get myself out of this hole."

Her boss hugs her and calmly says, "I'll give you an advance."

She replies, "I think I have to quit."

Her boss says, "Well, I'm not going to let you. You work and you are going to do what you need to do. I will help as much as I can. I'm not going to let you give up."

She replies, "He slashed my tires."

Her boss answers calmly, "We'll get you tires. Come on. You must be tired and hungry. Let's get some food in your system and get you some rest."

Two days go by and she goes back to work. Her boss ensures her a light work load due to her injuries and needing rest. She's nervous, but feels more and more at ease as the sand funnels through the glass.

It's a good day so far. The good day stretches to two weeks. Payday is coming up. She doesn't expect a large paycheck because of her advance. She goes to lunch with her bosses. She notices a guy dressed in army attire eating across the restaurant. She tries not to be paranoid and tells herself that it is, after all, a military town. Soon, she notices the guy texting on his phone. Seconds later, the guy is on the phone trying not to look at her. She tries to keep calm. Her bosses catch on to her nervous demeanor and stop mid-conversation. She tells her bosses what she thinks is happening. Two of her bosses don't hesitate to call the cops.

Ten minutes later, he shows up. Before he can spot her, the cops show up and he is arrested. She loses her appetite and doesn't even touch her food when it comes. Even though he'll be back in jail, she knows she's only safe for a week, and it doesn't stop.

One evening while shopping with her boss at the grocery store, a man dressed in dark blue from head to toe pushes her.

He says, "We are watching you, bitch. You can't hide."

She pushes him back and yells for her boss. Her boss calls the cops, but it's too late, the man leaves before the cops get there. They both know the cops won't do anything. She goes to the base. She goes straight to the platoon unit's main office. She tells the superior officers exactly what is going on. She doesn't feel justified and she sure as hell doesn't feel any safer. She feels like a tattletale and soon the bully's friends will come at her with full force with their name-calling and rock throwing tactics. She fights the urge of feeling vulnerable.

That evening, while she's eating Chinese take out with her roommate, the apartment office manager, there is a knock at the door. She quietly gets up, goes to the door, and looks through the peephole. Looking through the peephole, she doesn't recognize the man. It's a man wearing a highly decorated formal uniform. She knows it's important and he doesn't look like he's one of his friends. Her roommate tells her to make sure it's not him. She tells her she's pretty sure it's not him. Her roommate tells her she has 9-1-1 on standby and ready for her to answer the door. She answers the door and instantly recognizes the man's face. It's her older cousin from her dad's side. He hugs her and smiles. He tells her he's sorry for not coming sooner. She's surprised and relieved to see him. He explains to her that her mother reached out to him through a message on social media. Since then, he's been trying to find where she is. He tells her he found the address of the apartment listed after he contacted her husband's superior officers.

The next day, she moves in with her cousin and his family across town. She becomes very close with his family and a few of the neighbors that live in the same apartment complex. She makes close friends with Dakota and Ruth, sisters that live just across from her cousin's apartment. She hangs out with them. They know her story. Dakota and Ruth come over often. Soon, she quits her job at the attorney's office. She tells her boss that she doesn't want to be a burden to their office. She gets another job where she knows he won't find her. Her cousin helps her to make the divorce move forward, but her husband is contesting the divorce. She decides she has to move back to the city where she came from, if the divorce doesn't go anywhere soon.

She lands a job at a Mexican bar that military soldiers don't ever come to. The traffic that comes to the bar is Spanish speakers and an older crowd. She begins to learn the language and starts to feel like she can move forward. She slowly starts to save money, again. With her truck fixed, she doesn't have any problems going to and from work. Ever since the day of the brick being thrown through the window, she's been trying to find her other truck. She didn't give her husband the truck. She paid off the truck and it's solely in her name. She's been trying to figure out where he could of hidden it. Both of her trucks are paid off and are in her name. She consults with her boss a few times for legal advice, but there is really nothing she can do until she knows where the truck is. The very least she can do is report the truck stolen.

One day before shift change at work, she's down in the basement stocking up the bar before she leaves. The bar back tells her there is a man waiting for her. She automatically thinks it's her cousin checking up on her. She leaves what she's doing and goes back upstairs. The bar is empty. The bar back tells her the man went outside. She goes outside. As soon as she goes outside two men put a black pillowcase over her head and throw her in the back of the truck. She tries to kick the men and scream, but they are too fast and pick her up like she's a small helpless puppy. She can barely see through the black pillowcase. She asks the men where they are taking her. The men don't say anything. They drive for about ten minutes and they end up at a park that is secluded and empty. They tell her they know where her cousin lives and that they will start getting his family involved if she doesn't leave his place. They hit her with their fists and tell her she needs to withdraw her attempt for divorce and if she doesn't they'll be back. They throw her out of the truck into the grass at the park. The truck tires squeal as they leave.

She has no idea where she is. She's never been on this side of town before. She has no phone, no money, and no truck. She left it all at work. She runs to the only building she sees nearby, a hotel. She runs inside and tells the manager to call the cops because she was kidnapped and hit several times. The manager calls the cops for her. After three hours, and still no cops, she's ready to give up. She's tired of the drama and not able to sleep at night. As she sits in the hotel lobby, a happy family walks by her. The kids are happy with their parents. She automatically smiles and thinks of her boys. She misses her boys.

She looks outside and whispers to herself, "Fuck it."

She decides to hitch hike back to the city where her beloved boys are. She starts walking onto the freeway. She didn't do much today, but she feels exhausted.

Minutes later, a car pulls over and someone picks her up. It's an older woman, maybe in her fifties. They talk as the older woman drives. She also just got off work and is headed down to the grocery store. The woman tells her she is not driving far. She asks why she would want to leave the city to another city that's out of state and over a six hour drive with nothing but the clothes on her back.

They arrive at the grocery store. As the woman pushes the grocery cart, the woman tells her she went through the same thing ten years ago. The woman tells her she had to move out of state, too. The woman says the cops won't do much besides tell her to report it. At this point, she needs to be smart about how to get the divorce.

The woman finishes grocery shopping and takes Melissa back to the bar. Her truck is gone. Her boss tells her the truck was towed. He urged to pay the tow truck driver, but the driver refused. She goes to the back to find her phone gone. She confronts her coworker. Her coworker denies stealing it. Frustrated with it all she goes to the back. She uses the landline and calls home. Her stepmother answers.

"Hello?"

"Hey mom, look, I'm going through a lot right now. Is there anyway you and dad could pick me up and take me to the boys?"

The other line sighs.

"Well, I'm really busy, but I'll let your father know. See what he says."

Before she can say another word, her stepmother hangs up.

The only other number she knows by heart is her mother's. She calls her, but it goes to voicemail. Eager to leave a voicemail and not knowing what to say, the voicemail prompt tells her the voicemail inbox is full. She sighs and hangs up.

Not knowing her cousin's phone number or anyone else's for that matter, she grabs the money she made from her shift and starts walking.

She's at her breaking point. She just wants her life back. She walks for forty minutes. She sees a Wendy's. She orders a number two and walks across the street. She arrives to her destination. She feels almost relieved. She hopes no one will recognize her as she walks through the glass doors of the building. She finds a seat and sits down.

Across from her she sees a little girl. The little girl is staring at her and her bag of fast food. The little girl looks hungry. The little girl is wearing a faded Hello Kitty shirt, has a soiled face, and her Reeboks look like it's seen ten miles of harsh road. Her mother is sitting next to her asleep. The little girl wakes up her mother and asks if she can sit by the lady with the brown bag. Her mother tells her she can. Melissa refrains from taking out the food from the bag. She folds the opening of the bag. She looks at the bag and then looks at the little girl. She smiles and gives the little girl the bag.

The little girl's mother says in a stern voice. "Get back over here! Let the lady eat! Leave that lady alone!"

Melissa faintly smiles and says, "She's fine. Is it okay if I give her some food? I didn't touch it. I just got it a few minutes ago."

The mother smiles.

The mother presses her lips together and mouths, "Thank you".

The little girl happily grabs the bag. The little girl opens it and gives Melissa a flattened cheeseburger. The little girl grabs the other smashed cheeseburger, unwraps it, looks at her, smiles, and takes a bite. She gives the little girl a dollar and tells her to buy a drink from the vending machine.

For the next hour they enjoy each other's company. It comes to an end as the little girl's destination city is called over the intercom. She hugs the little girl and gives her fifty dollars. She tells her to make sure she eats and drinks something. The little girl tells her thank you. The mother walks over and tells her that she can't take the money. She tells the mother the money is for food and drinks. The mother hugs her. Before they get on the bus the mother orders food at the snack bar. Melissa smiles. She sits back down, grabs the brown bag under her sat, and starts to eat soggy French fries.

She hears the double glass doors swing open, but doesn't pay attention to who's coming inside the building. She looks at the floor slowly eating her cold, limp, soggy fries. A pair of black and purple Nikes stop in front of her. She looks up. She can't believe what she sees. She doesn't know whether to get up or stay in her seat. She puts her fries back in the brown bag. Her chest tightens. For a second, she holds her breath. She puts the paper bag on the seat next to her and stands up.

She says. "What the fuck? What are you doing here?"

She smiles and puts her arms out. Ruth smiles and hugs her. Ruth squeezes her. She squeezes her back. Dakota joins in on the hug.

Dakota cries and says, "Oh my God, girl. We were so worried about you!"

Two tears roll down Melissa's face as she closes her eyes.

Melissa pulls back from the big hug.

Melissa asks them, "How the hell did you find me?"

Dakota says, "Well Beck talked to your boss. Your boss told us what happened with the truck, your phone calls home, and what direction you started walking. So, Beck figured you'd be here."

Ready to cry, she says, "I have to leave."

Dakota says, "You can't leave, yet. You have to fight her husband all the way through the divorce."

She replies, "I don't give a shit about alimony. I just want to go home."

Dakota says, "Mel, you're not alone anymore. I promise. You have us now."

Melissa says, "I'm fucking exhausted."

Dakota laughs and says, "Shit girl I would be dead now if I've been through half of the shit you've been through. Hey, the toughest and shittiest part is over, okay? You know Beck has your back and we do, too, girl."

Ruth grabs her bag of food. They get in Ruth's car and drive off. She asks Dakota to use her phone. She talks to her boys for a few minutes. She tells them she has some things to take care of before she comes home and she will be home soon. She felt her heart tear at the tip as she hung up the phone. They get some take-out and go back to her cousin's apartment.

Beck reassures her nobody knows where he lives and he has officers he trusts on standby. The sun seems brighter for once. Her cousin is able to locate her truck and happily brings it back to the apartment. Day in and out, he becomes her rock. He helps her maneuver the military legal mumbo jumbo since she's completely numb and on auto-pilot. Unfortunately as far as divorce and stalking goes, she hits a dead end. The legal services on base inform her since her husband is already using the services, she can't use it.

One day, Beck returns from work. He tells her his superior officers are coming over tomorrow to talk about what her plans and options are. The officers come over the next day and suggest a proposal weaker than a three-inch nail being hammered through lime green jello. She knows they are not interested in helping. She only knows they want the situation to disappear and covered up as soon as possible.

They only suggest marriage counseling and his rank to be taken away. It's her turn to take the floor. She tells them they are not looking out for her best interest. They hardly took course of action to make her safe and let alone feel safe. She tells them if they were concerned for her safety, they would know how to handle the stalking. She tells them the police reports, military reports, all of it, is just paper. It's paper that can be easily overridden and destroyed and nothing will stick.

She explains the real problem is her marriage. That single piece of paper that makes her still attached to him. She tells them all she wants is the divorce to be final. That is all she wants. They apologize that "she feels that way" and have nothing further to say except that divorce is not the answer. They leave.

Being with Beck, Dakota, and Ruth, she finally feels the heavy weight come off of her shoulders. Beck leaves early in the morning to work and comes straight back to the apartment. He calls to check up on her during the day. Dakota comes over and watches cable with her. She doesn't remember when the last time she watched tv.

One evening, Beck goes to his bedroom and tells her if anything happens he is just fifteen feet away. After a change of clothes, he walks into the living room. He tells her there is no way around the money. He continues to say they could not locate the money her husband withdrew from the accounts. He got a hold of the bank. He found out her unofficial ex-husband took out a total of $71,233.10. Beck is shocked and tells her he knows she worked hard to save up every penny. She sighs and continues watching tv.

She knows she messed up. She thinks nothing could ever take that feeling away, that feeling of failure and let down. It shook her dignity and soul more than any earthquake could. The money Cheíi gave her, the money she saved from scholarships from school, and the money she saved from work was all gone, all of it.

She only has $100 left from the last time she worked. She goes back to the Mexican bar with Beck to get her last paycheck, but it's not much. Her boss asks her if she wants to work one last night, she refuses, and they leave the bar. She is very careful with what she buys. Eventually, she hits the dreaded money drought.

One afternoon, she decides she doesn't have a choice and goes back to the bar and talks to the owner. The owner tells her he has another bar she can work at and no one knows he owns it. He doesn't even share that information with his staff. He tells her to work there starting tonight and work as long as she needs to. He gives her the address and she thanks him.

She only works three nights a week, but it's enough to keep her tummy full, get her what she needs, and money wired to her boys. She's been using

Beck's truck to go places.

One evening at work, she gets a phone call. It's Beck. Her tells her that her truck is gone and he will talk to her husband's superior officers about locating her truck.

Her truck is gone and she feels it in her gut.

She won't ever see it again.

It's gone.

With nothing else to reach and completely exhausted from it all, she faintly laughs and tells Beck, "Fuck it."

Beck starts to tell her what she can do to put the debt on him as part of the divorce.

She interrupts him and says, "Nah, man. Fuck it. I don't give a fuck about alimony, lost assets, debt. I don't care about any of that shit. I just want the divorce, bro. No more and no less. Once I get that divorce I can move on and figure out shit after."

Beck says, "Okay. Okay. I understand. Hey, don't worry, it'll be okay, but in the meantime, you need to eat, and get more sleep. I know you want to feel better, but I promise you, you're safe."

He pauses for a brief moment.

He tells her he saw the hospital photos. He read all of the reports from the fight to the stalking and his friends throwing a brick through the window on base. Beck tells her that her husband was disciplined and the respect he once had is all gone now and he deserves what he got.

She doesn't say anything.

She doesn't need to say anything.

Beck quickly changes the subject.

He asks, "Hey, you want barbecue for dinner?"

She answers, "Yeah, sure. Doesn't matter."

Beck says, "Don't worry, cuz. It'll be okay. Everything will be taken of. Well, I have to get back to work. I'll see you at home. I love you, cuz."

Before she hangs up, she pauses and says, "Thanks, bro."

Beck, "I'm sorry I wasn't here for you sooner."

She smiles and says, "I know."

She hangs up the phone.

A guy from Beck's platoon drops off a bag of food for her at work. She tells the guy thanks. He tells her it's no problem. She eats her food, finishes her shift, and goes back to the apartment after work and goes to sleep.

She gets up early the next morning. She takes a shower and turns on the tv and slowly eats a bowl of cereal. It's her day off. She is expecting Dakota to come over soon.

It's now late afternoon.

She goes out onto the balcony. The balcony is attached to the living room. She is looking out the balcony with a blank stare. She sees Beck walking down the sidewalk, up the stairs, and hears him rattle the keys as he comes into the apartment.

He comes out to the balcony, pulls out a cigarette, and says, "I know this ain't no mountain tobacco shit, but it's close enough. It will help. It's helped me through many tours, bro."

She doesn't say anything.

She feels too exhausted to muster a thought much less a single word.

He gives her a pack of cigarettes, a pack of skinny black and milds, and a blue lighter. She smokes a cigarette while Beck talks. He talks and she listens. He cracks jokes and talks about the good old days. She just smokes and smiles. They finish their cigarettes and head back inside.

She goes to the kitchen and grabs a bottle of water. She sits back down and flips the channels to find something to watch. She's not really in the mood to watch anything. So, she goes to the computer on a small desk between the kitchen and living room. She logs into a social media website. She sees twenty-two, unread, personal messages. She stares at the teal blue circled number "22". She fights with herself mentally to 'click' on it. She already knows it's her unofficial husband. She clicks on it and reads an array of threatening messages from him telling her he will kill her if she leaves him. She takes a screen shot and emails it to Beck.

Seconds later, Beck yells from his bedroom, "I'll take care of it! You can delete it. Now block that loser!"

She does just that. She decides she wants to deactivate her account for now, just until everything is straightened out.

Just as she is about to hit the 'deactivate' button, she receives two more messages.

She looks at the number "2" in a blue circle in the corner of the computer's screen. She slowly scrolls the arrow over the number "2". She takes a deep breath as she 'clicks' on it. The message opens up on her screen. The two messages are from a long time friend from high school.

The message reads, "What's up Melly? Just wanted to say hey. I just got off work. Bored. Hope all is good with you. Take care and talk to you later."

The second message reads, "Don't make it too long that I don't hear from you, homie."

She gives a faint smile and decides to write back.

Her fingertips hit the keys as she punches the keyboard to type out the response, "I'm okay. I'm just going through some shit. It'll be all goody two shoes sooner than later. No worries. How's work? Ttyl. Melly."

She deactivates her profile and smiles.

For the next couple of hours she googles on the computer "how to get rid of a stalker", "how to deal with a stalker", and local jobs she can apply for that wouldn't allow her unofficial ex-husband to know where she is. Beck slides a small box from his bedroom towards the desk. She gets up, grabs the box, and sits back down at the desk.

From his bedroom, Beck yells, "It's yours. Got it earlier today. It's activated, cuz."

She opens the box. It's a brand new cell phone.

She smiles as she holds her new phone.

It dings and vibrates notifying her of a text. It's Beck.

His text read, "Ordered pizza. Should be here in a few."

She texts him, "Thanks, cuz."

He texts back, "Of course! Sorry it took so long."

Five minutes later, the doorbell rings. She grabs the pizza, gives the pizza guy a tip, puts the box on the kitchen counter, grabs a slice with a thick, white printed paper towel with flowers on it, and sits back at the computer. She realizes she wants fizzy bubbles of Coke in her mouth so she grabs a vibrant, red, shiny can of Coke out of the fridge. She sits back at the computer. She stops typing and looks at the tv. She finally decides she wants to watch something on tv. She logs off the computer and sits at the couch. Beck joins her with a soda and a slice. They watch, Schwarzenegger's "Predator."

Over then next month, she goes to work on the weekends, and doesn't want to do anything else. She feels drained and just wants to go home to her boys. She will have to start over from scratch once she's home. For now, she just wants to go to work and come back to the apartment and push the rest of her energy to get the divorce finalized and figure out how to start over.

Her new friends, Dakota and Ruth, have been her pillows to scream in when she starts to feel overwhelmed. She tells them she feels stupid and should of known better. They reassure her that shit happens and when it does, that she needs to not back down and that she will get through it. Soon, she becomes all talked out and doesn't have anything else to vent about. She accepts her mistake and moves on.

One day while at the apartment by herself, she looks at the photos of her boys in her phone and wonders that they are doing. She calls them but can't seem to get a hold of them. She texts her mother to tell her boys she misses them and will call later. She then calls and leaves a voicemail.

After she hangs up, she goes out into the balcony and smokes a cigarette. It's colder than a bitter witch's heart outside. She puts her hoodie on over her faded Ozzy t-shirt. She's wearing washed, thrift store, dark blue, jeans and worn, laced, Nikes. Her long, black, hair is tied up in a ponytail.

Dakota comes out of her apartment and yells. "Mel! Melly Mel!"

She ignores her.

She knows Dakota is coming over.

Dakota walks up the stairs and comes into the apartment. Dakota goes to the balcony. Dakota tries to convince her to go somewhere with her. She puts out her cigarette.

She whispers to herself, "Fuck it, what else could happen?"

She tells Dakota she'll go. Dakota is screams in excitement.

They leave for the movies. Dakota's sister Ruth goes outside and is about to smoke. They all end up getting in the car and going to the movies. Dakota drives while her sister Ruth sits next to her. Melissa sits in the back. She plays a game on her phone. Her seatbelt doesn't work. It doesn't bother her.

They arrive at the movies too late and miss the movie. They decide to get ice cream until the next show. On the way, a man in a pick-up truck doesn't know how to drive through a six-way intersection.

His truck slams into the car the ladies are in.

Before the collision, the last thing she hears and clearly sees are the pick-up truck's headlights and the screams of Dakota and Ruth.

The aftermath of the car accident leaves Melissa in a shatter of glass and her breath taken from her. She struggles to breathe as bystanders get her out of the back of the car. Her vision and hearing becomes blurred and hazy. She knows she stopped breathing.

As she's lying on the street covered in blood, she hears the voice of beloved Cheíí.

She feels a single tear drop run down the side of her eye and drip into her ear. Her arm is stretched out.

She feels Cheíí's hand on top of hers.

As paramedics are on their knees surrounding her, she hears Cheíí say, "Ah, My Lady," he says, "my sweet, beautiful Lady, you're home."

She feels a burning sensation in her chest.

Then she feels nothing. Nothing, but Cheíí's hand on top of hers.

She closes her eyes.

** ** ** ** **

She hears voices. She hears medical terminology. She can't open her eyes. She feels like she's sucked in a deep, deep dream.

She hears someone talking to her but she doesn't know what they are saying. It sounds like they're talking under a pillow. She slowly opens her eyes. She still feels like she's in a dream. She's weak, dizzy, and feels like she's floating in mid-air.

Moments later she feels someone carrying her dead weight. She looks to her right to see who's carrying her. She sees a man, he's a blurry figure, but she knows it's a man. He has short, dark hair. She closes her eyes and fall back into a deep slumber.

In her dream, she sees the openness that she's at all too familiar with. The sky is as blue as ever. The sun is bright and she feels the overwhelming nostalgia she's been craving. She's back at the Rez. It looks like she's at Grandma's. She's overlooking the open, field-like land. The hills are as far as she can see. The hills are covered with sagebrush, sparingly cedar trees, and there he is to her left. He's still wearing his dark blue Wrangler's and sky blue button-up, collared shirt. His sleeves are rolled three-quarters up his forearms. She sees his cross tattoo on his hand, his moon tattoo on his forearm.

He's just feet away from her.

He's still as tall as she remembers.

She feels his warmth as he smiles at her.

He grabs her left hand, smiles, and says, "The Moon awaits, My Lady. My sweet, beautiful Lady. It's time for you to leave here and meet your Moon."

Just as she is about to say a word, the wind starts to howl.

The wind blows her hair over her face.

He lets go of her hand.

She's confused.

He walks off in front of her and stops with his back to her.

She sees his hands cup around his mouth.

She hears his voice yell. "Clear!"

Confused she looks around.

The brightness of the sky turns into a deep, dark abyss.

She hears an array of voices. She hears a police siren and then she hears an ambulance siren.

She hears an unfamiliar woman's voice say, "Be strong, hang in there, you're a strong Lady."

Then the noises fade out.

She can feel it in her mind that she is dreaming.

She talks to herself in the dream, "Yes, I am dreaming. I know I am, but where am I?"

She hears the sound of a crackling fire. She is standing in the kitchen at Grandma's. Stew bubbles on the stove as Grandma claps her hands with dough. She's making tortillas. She stops clapping the tortilla dough in between her hands for a few moments and with one hand turns over the hot tortilla being grilled on the stovetop. Mists of white surround her as she walks through Grandma's house.

She walks to her bedroom and crouches down on white tiled floor. She ties her black shoelaces.

She looks around and says, "Why am I stuck in this dream? How can I wake up and get out of it? I just want to go home."

She gets up off the floor after she ties her shoelaces. She walks pass her parents' bedroom, makes a left and passes the bathroom, and walks down the two steps entering the kitchen where she sees Grandma cooking. She walks past the light green, retro, kitchen table and light green, marble swirled, swivel chairs.

She can feel her feet inside her shoes as she switches her weight from her left to her right as she walks. As she walks, time slows down. She is stuck in this dream as if someone pressed the 'slow x5' option on the VCR. She keeps walking, but with each step it's harder to push each footstep. She passes the black, iron cast, stove filled with the echoes of a crackling fire inside. She walks out the front door.

She hears the brown, front door of the house, close behind her, then she hears the white screen door slam shut.

The crisp, cold, brisk air burns against her face. She can feel the frozen, misty air touch her lips as she inhales with a deep slow breath. It feels like she is drinking through a frosted glass full of slushy, ice cold, water.

Her throat feels ice cold like it's coated with icicles. It makes her gasp as the freezing sensation stings her lungs. It's so cold where she is standing. She can see her breath against the outside air. The sun is slowly rising in the east. She hears dogs happily barking as they know exactly what's going to happen next. She feels their large paws press up again her thighs and the side of her legs as they jump up and down wagging their tails. She pulls her hood up over her head.

She begins to move her body into a slow jog. Her breath is slow, long, and deep as her body tries to find comfort in the freezing air. She sees her arms moving back and forth as she runs. As she is running towards the sunrise, she hears Cheíí voice in the distance.

With no bodily form of Cheíí and only his voice, she hears him say in Navajo, "Lady, I see you, I know exactly where you are. It's time to wake up and live, live your life. It's going to be hard, but through the darkness, through the evil, the Moon will guide you."

She runs faster and faster down the dirt road. Behind her she hears a horse running. She hears the hooves running catching up to her. She looks behind her as she is running and she sees nothing but a dark abyss. The dogs that were running by her side are gone. She hears coyotes howling in the distance.

All of a sudden she stops at the end of the dirt road and comes into path with a very large, bullhead snake. The snake is coiled up and talks to her in Navajo. She covers her ears and starts to pray. The snake slithers off in the opposite direction. She uncovers her ears. She hears a woman scream in the distance. Startled, she starts walking and she only hears the hissing of snakes at her feet.

She comes to a narrow bridge. The bridge is brittle about to break. The moon shines bright enough showing her what steps to take. She hears snakes hissing and slithering all around her. She is sure there are snakes floating next to her on the side of the bridge. She doesn't want to look down. She doesn't want to see the evil creatures. She walks across the bridge and steps off.

The moon's light shines on an area in the distance. She walks towards it and walks to a construction site. There, just the steel frame of the building is exposed. She sees a Navajo man wearing an orange, long-sleeved shirt, a brown, fully-brimmed hard hat, worn Wrangler, blue, work jeans, and long ankle boots. His pants are tucked into his long laced up light brown boots. He's walking quickly across the steel frame of the building.

It's nighttime and the moon is shining like a spotlight on this man walking across the steel plank. The man laughs and yells at the other guys working. He is hard at work.

She looks up at the man. The man stops, waves to her, and blows her a kiss. He then does a strange dance of moving his body in-between his arms while he moves his hips left to right. She feels weird at this moment. She feels the surrealness of being happy watching this man work. She then remembers what she's going through back on earth, in reality, and stops smiling. Not wanting the man to lose concentration she turns to start walking away. She starts to walk off and the man yells her name.

He cups his hands beside his mouth and yells. "Mel! Melly! Melissa! I'm waiting. I'll be here for you. Just be patient. Okay? Can you hear me? Mel! I'm right here, waiting…"

She hears his voice trail off into the distance. She dreams the same dream a few more times.

** ** ** ** **

She slowly opens her eyes. Everything is a blur. She breathes in the unfamiliar scents of fresh paint, new carpet, and cigarette smoke. She looks to her right and sees a white wall. She realizes she's lying down on a twin mattress. She feels a sting on her left arm. She pulls it up her head to see what it is. She sees an IV attached to her inner forearm. Her lips are chapped and cracked. Her mouth and tongue are dry.

She faintly whispers, "fuck."

She feels like she's going to faint as she lifts up her head. She feels woozy. She tries to sit up, but falls over. She hears voices. She lies back down as fast as she can without making noise. She hears male voices. There's a knock on the door. The male voices are coming from the room further down the hallway.

She thinks perhaps the voices are coming from the living room. It's male voices, maybe two or three different voices. She recognizes one of the voices.

Someone knocks on the door again. This time the knocks are harder and louder.

She hears a man's voice from outside the front door, "El Paso County Police. Open the door!"

The men run into the other bedroom. She can hear them panic.

A male voice says in a panic. "Fuck! Fuck! Fuck! What should we do?!"

A second male voice says, "Just play it cool. Calm the fuck down. I'll answer the door. You go make sure her door is closed. Go!"

She quickly closes her eyes. She's familiar with one voice.

It's him.

He says. "Okay, coming hold the fuck up! Hold up. Hold up."

She hears two clicks then the front door squeak open.

"El Paso County Police Department. Why didn't you open up when I first knocked, sir?"

He laughs, "Oh yeah, sorry. I couldn't hear you I had the tv on too loud. What can I help you with?"

The male cop says, "Are you Demetri Keres?"

He replies, "Yes, I am."

The male cops says, "When was the last time you saw your wife, Melissa Keres?"

He replies, "Wow, it's been a while. We're actually getting a divorce, so, I just leave her be until the divorce is final."

The male cop says, "Well, we have reason to believe that she is here. May we come in and have a look around? I see that there's a protection order in place, Sir. We would like to see if she's here."

He scoffs and says, "Oh well, see I know my rights. I know that you need a search warrant, mister officer, sir."

The male cop says, "Well we sure would like to have a look see. Other wise, you'll be sure to hear more and more from us. Why don't you let us look around? It will just take a few minutes and then we can be on our way."

Her anxiety fills with hope as she internally pleads inside.

She thinks, "What would happen if I scream?"

She thinks about what they would do to her if she screams and the cops don't hear her or find her.

Another thought inside her head pushes her to say, "Just do it! Scream! Scream! Now! Come on!"

She yells out. "Help me! I'm in here! Please help me!"

But it doesn't come out strong and loud as she pictured in her mind. In her mind she is screaming and screaming. She quickly realizes that she is weaker than she feels. Two blinks later, she feels herself breathing through her chest. She feels an ice-cold hand on her arm.

As she looks to her left, she sees a blurred, pale, white man holding something in his hands.

He tells her quietly, "Shhhh. There now. There won't be any of that. Go back to sleep."

The conversation between the cop and her husband quickly fades out and it feels like she's dreaming again. Her mind is screaming to snap out of it. She's begging to get out of there, but she can't. She feels a hot sensation going through her arm. The hot sensation turns into a cold sensation. She feels frozen. Her mind tells her she's frozen in time with no way out. She's stuck in a deep, frozen, dream on repeat.

The last thing she hears is the cops asking her husband at the door, "What was that? Tv, huh? Better turn that down."

** ** ** ** **

She slowly opens her eyes. All she sees are fuzzy figures. She's woozy. It's a heavy and damp feeling within her body and it feels gross. She closes her eyes as soon as she hears voices coming from the next room. Then she hears footsteps creak on a wooden floor. The footsteps are coming to the room. She lies as still as she can. She can feel her heartbeat radiate from her chest down to her toes. He comes in. He yells to the other room if he should give her more morphine.

The man yells back, "Grab that fork right there. Poke her. If she moves her toes give her a little more, if she doesn't move, she's good."

At this moment, she's screaming at herself inside her head. She tells herself to stay calm, keep her breath steady. She pictures her boys' smiles. She thinks how badly she wants to get back to them. She relaxes her body and there it is. She feels a dull stab of metal prongs into her ankle bone. She doesn't move more than the fork pushing against her skin. She feels the pressure of the prongs let up. She hears the 'clank' of the fork being placed on a small table next to her. She doesn't dare flinch.

He laughs and says, "Oh shit this is a trip, man. My wife is doped up!"

She feels his presence on the left side of her. He's standing. He kneels down next to her. He gets so close she can feel his body heat. His breathing is coming closer.

She can feel him starting to lean on top of her left arm and then her chest.

She feels his breath on her left cheek. She wishes she could grab that fork and stab him. She feels like a kitten, fragile and helpless. Her anger starts to build like a raging fire. For now, in this very moment, there's nothing she can do. She knows if she moves, he will give her more morphine and she might not ever wake up. Her thoughts cleared as she takes small breaths and waits. Still. Dead still. Her anger turns into a type of anger she's never felt before. She can feel his lips press onto her dry, cracked lips.

She feels his lips move in front of her nose and lips as he whispers, "No one can have you. You're mine."

There is silence. She can feel him staring at her. It's sickening to her. She focuses on her relaxing breath. She still feels his light heaving and sickening breath blown onto her face.

The other men yell from the other room, "Hey man, are you coming or what?!"

He stands up and walks out of the bedroom. She hears the bedroom door close, but remains very still. After she hears the front door slam, she hears the a deadbolt being locked. She slowly opens her eyes. Everything she sees is a blur, a surreal, faint, white blur.

She thinks, "So, this is hell."

She squints her eyes as she looks around and tries to snap out of the daze. She feels high, but with a twist of the sourest lemon.

She thinks to herself, "Well, ain't this the shittiest pitcher of bitch lemons anyone could ever drink?"

She realizes she's been there a while. Her body feels out of place, almost like it's not her body. The cute fat she once knew in her around her belly button, that cupped her voluptuous butt cheeks, the beautiful meat in her arms, and made up her perfectly thick thighs is gone.

From her neck down, she is sore. Her body feels like it was used as a punching bag. She felt like a cookie dipped in milk, soft, and ready to dissolve. She looks to her left. She can see a parking lot through the bedroom window. She see's her unofficially ex-husband's best friend's beat up truck in the parking lot.

She uses all the strength she has in her and sits up. She looks down at her arm. She screams angrily and rips out the needles from her left hand and left inner arm. She throws it all on the ground. She slowly stands up. She slowly falls on her side and onto the bed. She grunts in pain. She wants to moan, but holds it in. She rolls her lips inward instead. It helps her endure the soreness and piercing pain all over her body. She forces herself to stand up, again. Her body feels like a small turkey being held up with softened butter. She manages to limp to the bedroom door and open it.

She squints and two pairs of keys come into focus on the table. She grabs it, opens the front door, and runs down the stairs to the car in the parking lot. Her heart starts to pound through her chest.

She scrambles to open the door. Her hands shake as she tries every key. She feels the weakness in her body. Her strength is gone. She finally finds the correct key and opens the driver's side door.

As she gets into the truck she nearly falls out.

She hears a male voice yell behind her. "Hey! Are you okay?!"

She panics. She uses the every bit of strength she has and forces herself in and closes the slams the door. Her hands shake as she puts the keys in the ignition. She starts the truck. Her hands tremble as she puts her seatbelt on and drives out of the parking lot into the road. She has no idea where she is. Her vision is blurry and she can only see ten to fifteen feet in front of her. All of a sudden a huge weight builds onto her body. She feels her body's exhaustion just from going from the bed to the truck in the matter of minutes.

Her heart is beating faster through her chest, down her legs, and into her bare, feet then back up through her legs into her arms and hands. Her entire body was throbbing and pulsating. The coldness of her bare feet felt good. Even though her feet were freezing, she felt like it was a bonus since the cold would shake her out of the tiredness she felt in her body.

She mentally tells herself, "Come on focus! Stay with me! You can do this! You can do this! Snap out of it! Snap the fuck out!"

She squints as she drives. She drives through three stop signs and gets onto the main street into the city. She recognizes a big building. She knows where she is now. Seeing the building, she knows it will take at least ten minutes to drive there. She stops at a stoplight. A very blue, tall, Monte Carlo with its' windows down pulls up next to her. The car's vibrating speakers blasts Tupac's, "Changes". The people in the car start yelling at her. Seconds later, the traffic light blinks green.

All of a sudden, she gets a jolting pain in her right leg. Her leg stiffens faster than a lightning bolt. She can't move it. She screams in pain holding her right thigh. The cars behind her honk in jumping tones. The cars drive around passing her in the right lane honking and yelling at her. Her leg muscle tissue finally loosens up. Her right foot slowly pushes against the gas pedal.

As she drives through the intersection, she feels a sharp, stabbing pain in the left of her side. She remembers her ribs were cracked. The pain abruptly shoots a stabbing blow. She drives the truck off the road crashing into a white, wooden, picket fence. The fence surrounds a business.

She gets opens the truck door and falls onto dampened, vibrant green, plush grass. The plush grass feels sharp and stiff under her cold, bare feet. She panics and runs into the street. Cars honk at her as she runs through traffic and nearly gets hit. She holds her side as she limps on her bare feet. Her feet running below her feel like it's not attached to her. She limps through an alley way occupied by homeless people. They stare at her. A homeless man starts to follow her asking her if she needs help. She waves her arms around and screams for him to get away. He puts his hands up and backs away.

Only paying attention to the fact that she needs to move, she limps out of the alley back into the street. Just as she stops to catch her breath, her body is abruptly thrown into a grassy area just pass the sidewalk. As she lies on the grass, she screams in pain. She gets up and before the driver of the car gets out, she slowly off.

Behind her, she hears a woman ask, "Oh my God, are you okay? You're hurt, don't move."

She ignores the woman. She continues running off into the blur of a distance as fast as her body can take her. She almost feels like her body is dragging itself. Her feet start to pound with pulsation, but she ignores it. She can't take it anymore. It's too much. She gets woozy and weak and falls to the ground.

She looks to her left and squints. She sees the side exit to the apartment complex.

As she lies in the grass, she screams. "AAAAGGGHHHHHHHHH!"

The grass is cold and stiff under her weak body. Her entire body is throbbing with a sharp sensation. The sharp sensation moves up and down her entire body. She closes her eyes and takes three deep breaths. She sees him. She pictures his smile. She pictures his voice. She imagines his voice.

She hears him say, "Get up, Lady. You're almost there. Come on, get up."

She gets up onto her knees and then onto her feet. She starts walking. She makes it.

She knocks on the door using the rest of her energy. No one answers the door. There is only stillness in the air. She hears car driving in the distance. She hears an airplane flying in the blue sky. Her legs and hands begin to shake. The little field trip from the other side of town was too much for her body. She knows the drugs are still in her veins. With nothing else to do, but wait, she passes out.

Hours later, she wakes up lying on the soft, yet firm, beige couch she's come to know. She recognizes the aroma of burning sagebrush and sweet grass. She opens her eyes. It's Beck.

He says, "The ambulance is on its' way. It's okay, I'm here."

She softly says, "No. No. I…"

She blacks out.

She wakes up with a jolt and a heavily beating heart beat. She takes a deep breath. Beck hears her and immediately walks into the bedroom.

He asks, "Hey. How are you feeling?"

She replies, "Dizzy and exhausted, but glad to.."

Beck interrupts her and says, "It's okay. You're safe."

The military police show up moments later. They want to talk to her, but she is still very-not-in-this-world. She lies on Beck's fluffy, soft, yet firm, Tide-smelling bed. She falls into a deep slumber listening to Beck's voice.

The next morning, Beck's wife and Dakota help her take a bath. The luke warm water brings out the soreness in her body. It's everywhere. Shockingly, she feels an uncomfortable soreness in her hipbones, pelvis, and vagina. Her bath is a calming moment that she wants to hold onto forever. She feels relaxed, safe. Every muscle in her body pinches when she stands up. She wonders if her husband would do such a thing or even worse, if he would let someone else do something to her when she was drugged up. Beck's wife and Dakota hold her and wrap a towel around her. They help her dry off and put a long, soft, comfy, cotton sky blue t-shirt on her. They help her step into clean, cotton, sky blue, panties, and finally help her put a thin, light grey, cotton robe on her. They help her lie on the bed.

Falling prey to her body's exhaustion, she falls asleep on the bed. She wakes up to Dakota brushing her hair watching, "American Horror Story" on tv. She looks up at Dakota and closes her eyes. She feels dizzy. The room is spinning, but she doesn't panic. She lets it spin. She falls dead asleep.

She wakes up to unfamiliar female voices, but listens again and immediately recognizes the voices. She can't believe it. She's in the front seat of her mother's SUV. She doesn't react other than telling her mother she needs the bathroom.

Her mother replies, "We'll make a quick stop first. Then I'll take you."

She falls in and out of sleep only to wake up at a storage garage she recognizes. Her mother backs up the SUV to her storage unit, which is already opened.

The second voice is her aunt.

Her aunt asks, "What important stuff do you have?"

She softly begs her mother and aunt, "Rent a small trailer. I want to take everything back."

Her mother replies, "No. We have to leave now."

She hears her aunt whimper and say, "I'm so sorry, Mel, but you have to leave everything behind. Someday you will rebuild what you have."

Her mother grabs two duffel bags full of clothes from the storage unit. Her aunt grabs a big, plastic, blue bin of toys. She slowly gets out of the SUV's passenger seat and walks over to the storage unit. She looks at the couches, brown boxes, bookshelves, kitchen table and chairs. She slowly walks back to the SUV. Her aunt and mother help her back into the SUV. She hears the storage unit's sliding, metal door slide shut and they drive off.

She drifts in and out of a daze.

She hears her aunt on the phone, "Yes, we got her. She's safe. We're taking her home. We should be back tonight. Thank god we found her..."

Her aunt's voice fades out along with her vision. She passes out.

She awakes to the sound of feet running up and down a wooden floor hallway. She slowly sits up in the bed.

The bedroom door swings opens. Her heart sinks with fear.

She hears a familiar voice.

She can't believe it.

She's feels the ache in her heart and starts to cry.

It's her boys. They come up to her and hug her. She hugs them back with as much strength as she can muster.

Her boys say happily, "Mommy! We missed you. I'm so glad you're home."

An hour later, her mother and aunt leave the house with the boys. There are cops parked just outside the house. She limps into the living room. She can't believe who she sees.

Grandma.

Grandma is sitting on the couch softly slurping her tea.

Grandma gently puts her tea down and calmly tells her in Navajo, "Come here, my baby."

She completely ignores the pain in her body. Her body feels so frail and weak. As she kneels down she sees purple bruises on her wrists, arms, and her ankles. She kneels down onto her knees in front of Grandma. She wraps her sore, weak arms around Grandma's petite body.

Grandma sobs and hollers holding her. Grandma's arms are warm and very soft.

Grandma's tears fall onto Melissa's face.

Grandma holds her tight and sobs to her in English. "I'm sorry! I'm sorry I wasn't there for you, my baby. My grandbaby, my sweet, sweet grandbaby, my Lady. We knew you'd make it back home alive. You're home. Me and Cheíí knew you'd be strong. We prayed to the Holy People for you to come home and to give you strength. We pray with everything we have in us. Oh, sweetheart. You're going to get your life back. I know you lost it all, your nice trucks, your job, and all the money you've been saving over the years. I'm so sorry, my precious baby, but I promise it's going to be okay. Cheíí is back at home. He wanted to put down cinders for you to protect you. He told me to tell you, 'You're a strong Lady, My Lady, I love you. I won't let anything happen to you. I'm here'."

She finally feels her entire self. Her soul, her spirit, her mind, her heart, her mind, and her body, it aches in pain. But she was still very happy. She's finally home. Now, she thinks about how to get her life together. She knows time won't wait for her to heal. She has to keep moving. This time she tells herself that she is not going to let anyone convince her otherwise. She tells herself she is going to find the drive to finish what she started, even if she has to start over, from scratch.

Chapter 12. Fuck-it

"You do what you have to do to finish. I know you can do it. Keep
going, Lady, you keep going."
-Frank Nez

She doesn't waste any time. She decides to quickly enroll back to college.
It doesn't take her long to figure out she wants to go to law school. Of course,
without a doubt, there's a baby hiccup. The university she attended before was a
private university. Which means the credits accumulated from her associate's
degree won't transfer. Not letting that stop her, she gets into the fuck-it-stage of
her life.

She does something she never thought of herself doing. She knows it's
the only way to get to her goal. She has to start all over, from the bottom. She
enrolls into the local community college. She knows it will take her just a little
less than forever, but she has to start college all over again and enroll as a
freshman. Thankfully, she gets accepted into the local community college. She
goes back to college in full swing taking on a full-time class schedule.

She asks her mother if she can stay with her until she's able to afford her
own place. Her mother annoyingly agrees. Her mother tells her she has to help pay
the bills, if she's going to be staying there. Without hesitation, she happily agrees.
Before she is able to get her student loan and grant money from school, her mother
starts to indirectly complain about bills and more so her presence.

She is unable to work because she has no means for daycare. So, she
decides to donate plasma. It's not much money, but she manages to make enough
money to make her mother get off her back.

Three months later, she finds out she is pregnant. She has more "fuck it"
running through her veins these days, so she embraces the pregnancy. She stops
donating plasma. Fortunately, donating plasma doesn't affect the baby. However,
it does affect her body's white blood cell count resulting in her becoming anemic.
She tells her doctor she just wants the baby to be healthy. She does her research
and finds out her diet must drastically change. She must concentrate on foods that
are high in iron. This becomes a little of a challenge because she can rarely chew
her food. Her nightmare with her *now* ex-husband left her with a troublesome jaw
that developed into TMJ. There are days when her jaw locks so tightly she can't

even slurp soup.

Still, she embraces it with open arms. Having a baby doesn't tarnish her plans in any way. She sees her new baby only as a bonus and someone else on her team and by her side. Together they will grow into a beautiful person.

It's only a few and very rare times that she doesn't how to feel since she now knows what happened when she was passed out on drugs at her ex-husband's hands. She accepts the fact she has to keep going. That's her only choice. She can't give up. She can't listen to all the whispers or have people feel sorry for her. She doesn't care how it looks. Yes, she now has three babies for three different people, but she has no problem embracing the fuck out it. She refuses to allow the world to tell her that she is labeled as a slut or a waste.

She knows she has a greater purpose, a greater purpose than gossip, and judgment. She's never judged people she's met that have slept around, had one-night stands, and have slept with more people than they can count on both hands. All she needs to know is that she knows who she is and that's all that matters. She just wants to finish school and be one hell of a mother, a teacher to her boys and now a brand new baby. She tells herself that no one can take that away from her. She looks at her brand new baby just the same as she does her boys—they are a blessing.

Living with her mother just as she years ago doesn't change by much. It's still a crazy roller coaster. Her mother is somewhat sympathetic for her up until she realizes that her bills are one hundred dollars than normal and her definition of a peaceful house is now no more as kids are loud and annoying. Now that the hype of her missing "daughter" is over, her mother quickly goes back to *her* normal.

Melissa's big belly presence and her two boys are nothing but a bunch mosquito bites in her mother's life. Her mother's nice demeanor changes faster than the seasons changing. Her mother complains about her only "daughter" being too loud in the living room with her highlighter and textbook or the boys at "home" doing their homework in the bedroom laughing taking up space.

There are only two things that help her mother not feel so agitated, Melissa and her boys gone and away from the house and wine. Her mother lets her borrow her SUV to do "errands", but really she leaves to finds another place, any place, where they feel comfortable. Often times it's the mall, the park, the community college campus, or the library. No matter how much her mother nags about everything from throwing paper into the trash rather than the recycling bin to using up the toilet paper that Melissa bought to having the fridge filled of food, Melissa wants to be away from her mother just as much as she does. Wine often does the trick for her mother as it numbs her ability to care about her daughter's presence. Melissa knows exactly how her mother is. Her mother has two different personalities and two different versions of herself. One is for the professional, scholastic, white people side. That side is nice and sane. The other side is the solid quid pro quo fueled with frustration and displays of child-like realms of slamming doors, stomping feet, and loud sighs.

Melissa knows she's nothing more than a show horse. Her mother organizes get togethers at the house. That is the only time she is nice with a glass of red, spoiled, cured, liquid grapes in hand. Her mother's liquid courage transforms into her mother showcasing just how much heart she has to help out her only daughter. Melissa and her boys never mingle. Melissa and her boys stay in their bedrooms doing their homework.

The second semester flies by and she not only has good grades, but she has a beautiful little girl. She has her brand new baby girl in the middle of winter semester. Her instructors happily allow her to complete the rest of the semester from home. Between the frequent breast feedings, laundry, cooking, and cleaning, she reads, writes, and takes her tests online. More than eager to spend time with her beautiful brand new baby, her aunt brings Grandma to visit off and on. Her aunt offers to help take care of the baby a few times during the semester. She is more than grateful even when it is only an hour or two a few times a week. She manages to buy what the baby needs as her scholarship, grant, and student loan money pours in at the beginning of the next semester.

She hasn't been able to save any money, until her third semester. She invests her left over grant and scholarship money into an older model SUV—a Dodge Durango. She can't be any happier. Her new-to-her war pony is 4x4, has leather seats, and with a little love will be able to take care of Melissa and her family. Her boys change the oil, filters, do a tune-up, and change the brakes. She buys four new tires and replaces the shocks. She replaces the cracked windshield, too. She is very happy and most of all, she paid for the pretty white war pony upfront in cash. It's hers free and clear. She doesn't tell anyone of her accomplishments. She just keeps going. She is very proud of herself.

Soon, the baby hiccups start, again, but this time it's more personal. She regrettably gained weight from the pregnancy making her back often giving out. Exhausted and tired of her back going out, she decides to take a stand. She buys a popular workout routine that has over ten CDs. It's a two-month program. She takes it one day at a time. During the first week, she cries. She's surprisingly still in an emotional anguish from her past. As the CD plays, she fights through it. She's on her knees sweating. Her palms are flat on the floor in front of her. Her body hurts all over. She hears the man working out on the tv say, "I know this hurts. I know. But get up. Get up and dig deep. Get up."

So, she does. She fights off that anxiety and emotional pain she just felt and completes the workout.

The everyday soreness in her butt, hips, arms, and tummy starts to pay off. It takes her two months, but she works vigorously with every molecule of energy in her. She goes from a size 18 to a size 7. She was once 190 pounds and now she's 127 pounds.. She teaches her little family to eat less bread, less fatty meats, and eat more fiber and iron.

She only makes a few friends in some of her college courses. One is a Navajo man, he's a military veteran and the other is an older woman. She studies with them often. They lean on each other when the assignments or life gets tough. Satisfied with her grades, she decides to take on more classes the following semester. Her friends think she's crazy. She takes on seven classes in a single semester. With her mom, workout, and study routines down, she aces all of her classes. She has two semesters left.

In one of her last classes she has to fulfill 100 internship hours before the semester is over. Everyone in the class picks a number out of a bowl. The number is attached to a specific internship site. She gets the number '7'. She is assigned to do an internship with the local police department. She gets started right away. She does her background check and gets her internship schedule. She asks her aunt to watch the kids for two weeks at her mother's house while she fulfills her hours. She does her hours during graveyard shift.

She looks at her planner. It's scribbled to death in red, blue, and purple ink. In red are study hours and when bills are due, in purple are the kid's parent-teacher conferences, and written in blue is her class schedule, and now, internship hours.

She sighs and says, "Fuck it, I'll sleep when I'm dead."

They schedule ride-alongs with police officer as her internship hours. She doesn't know what to expect.

A few days later, she drives across town to a tiny of a box police substation. She parks in the small lot behind it. An officer pulls up next to her mother's SUV. She grabs her backpack and gets into the unit. The officer is an older Hispanic male. His bags under his eyes have bags. He introduces himself and they set off. The sun is still out. It's a beautiful evening. She quickly texts her aunt her shift is starting and will text her later. She asks her aunt to kiss the boys and sweet baby girl for her. Her aunt texts back telling her not to worry and to be safe. She puts her phone away in her back pocket.

The first notification pops up on the silver, chunky, laptop screen next to her. It leads them just outside of a run down apartment complex. Five other units arrive. The officer tells her it's a daily cop meeting. The officers stand in a circle. They go over some small details before every shift. Before they leave one of the officers hands her a cavalier, bulletproof vest. She puts it on over her shirt and puts her black hoodie on top if it. The vest is stiff and heavy. The vest reminds her just how fragile her human existence really is. They part ways.

Melissa and the officer get back into the unit. The officer taps on the laptop keyboard. He explains how to read calls coming in from dispatch. Surprisingly, he explains majority of the time, the calls are up to the officer and whom would "like" to respond the call. He tells her if he's in the area of the call, he responds to the most important calls first.

He uses his best discretion and they drive to the first call. It's at a popular breakfast restaurant chain. He flips on the sirens and goes ninety down a heavily crowded street. Vehicles quickly clear a path for them. They make it to a plaza. In the middle of the plaza is the breakfast restaurant. As they drive up, she sees an ambulance parked just outside the entrance of the restaurant. There are a dozen people standing on the sidewalk watching.

A woman in her early 20s is lying on her back in the parking lot in front of the entrance behind two parked cars. Melissa and the officer walk up to the paramedics that are standing watching the other paramedics. The paramedics are performing CPR on the woman. Off to the side, the woman's 20-ish year old boyfriend is standing in between the two cars with his hands on top of his head. He's pacing back and forth in-between the two cars. He's distraught and crying. The officer gets information from the paramedic and walks over to the young woman's boyfriend. He pulls him to the side where he can't see his lifeless girlfriend on the rough paved lot. The boyfriend pleads to be with his girlfriend. Melissa walks towards the entrance of the restaurant watching in horror. She's speechless.

Seconds later, the boyfriend yells to be by his girlfriend's side. Two more officers run up and hold him back. Some of the restaurant workers come out of the restaurant and stand next to Melissa. The restaurant manager tells her the boyfriend proposed to the girlfriend just last week. She further explains the restaurant is where they had their first date two years ago and the entire staff knows the couple. The couple is active and seemingly healthy as they go on hikes and enjoy life together. Both are in their freshman year in college. The manager tells her things went on as usual that day. The couple ate, left, and suddenly, the boyfriend runs inside the restaurant yelling to call an ambulance. The ambulance came and immediately started CPR on the young woman. Melissa doesn't say anything. She stands in silence and feels the worst is about to come.

45 minutes flies by. The paramedics are unable to get a heartbeat.

She hears one say, "call it".

The paramedics put their equipment away and cover the body with a white sheet.

The boyfriend yells. "Wait, what?! What do you mean 'call it'?! What are you doing?! Why did you stop?! She's going to get up. Baby? Baby! Get up! I'm right here! Get up! No, please, get up!"

He starts to scream her name. The young woman lies there with a white sheet on top of her body. She's motionless, breathless. Melissa has seen the aftermath of death before. A motionless life of a sheep, a dog, and a small kitten, but she has never seen a person die before. The restaurant staff cover their mouths and start crying. A tear from each eye streams down Melissa's eyes. She wipes her tears with her sleeve. Conversations come to a halt as a blanket of silence covers everyone's speech. She can't imagine what the man is going through. One moment, he is planning to spend the rest of his life with the love of his life, and the next moment, he's yelling at her to wake up, but she can't because she's dead. There was no warning. No good-bye. The love of his life is taken from him. Melissa's throat tightens. Her chest feels constricted to breathe. A few more tears stream down her face. She has nothing to say.

She walks over to the parked police unit, opens the door, sits in the seat, and pulls out her phone. She keeps the door open. She looks at a photo of her kids on her phone. She texts her aunt to kiss her babies for her. Her heartbeats slow down into a bursting, slow beat. She takes a deep breath. She feels her heartbeats deepening with every exhale. Later on, the officer gets into the unit. There are no words. The officer is just as choked up as she is. The unit is filled with silence.

The only words he says is, "We're headed to the next call, aggravated assault."

She wipes the tears off her face, nods her head, and responds, "Okay."

The next call is in a very run down apartment complex that has more potholes than landscaping. There is more trash outside a brown, metal, dumpster bin than in it. People drink on the stairs at the end of the complex. There are kids running around the complex wearing worn clothes and some with no shoes.

The alleged suspect of the assault left the scene and other officers are in pursuit. The officer and Melissa are the first to arrive at the scene to take a statement from the alleged victim.

They find the upstairs apartment and knock on the door. A woman in her early twenties answers the door. The woman looks like she is stuck in the 80s. Her fake, hot pink nails are longer than her fingers. She is wearing a slum of large, bulky, 80s costume jewelry—large, fake gold, chunky, triangle-shaped earrings, an array of neon yellow, thick, plastic, bangle bracelets, semi-worn, high-top basketball shoes, dark purple MC Hammer-like pants, a cherry, bright red, off-shoulder blouse and wild, lime green lipstick and eye shadow. The woman invites the officer in the apartment. Melissa follows the officer and closes the door behind her. There are three kids, the oldest no older than three years old. They are about a year apart. They sit on the small kitchen floor eating fried chicken drumsticks. The toddlers and baby are wearing an old, thin, frayed, stained t-shirt. Their diapers are full, plump, and sagging in a huge bulk between their little legs.

There is a tiny, green, frayed couch in the living room and a small, ten inch tv on the stained, dark brown, flattened, carpet floor. Melissa can feel the soiled dampness under her soles as she walks. There are no photos, works of art, or posters on the poorly painted, custard yellow walls. The apartment looks poorly constructed. The uneven carpet creates bubbles and lag in different areas of the floor. The all of the doors look like it's from the '70s. The doors are stained an ugly dark brown and are thin and narrow.

She looks at the kids eating on the floor. She can't help, but to say in her mind, "Damn, that's so fucked up."

Another toddler walks out from the back bedroom crying. The young mother picks up the crying baby places the baby on her no-hip hip. The woman begins to tell the officer her ex-boyfriend "busted up [her] windows after he pull outta strap, and blazed out."

The woman continues to say, "he jus' a jealous busta 'cuz he don't like ma new flava I be into."

Melissa walks over to the kids. She kneels down and talks to them. The oldest toddler runs to the back of the room and hands her a diaper. Melissa smiles. She grabs the diaper from the toddler's little hands and looks at the officer. The officer looks at the woman.

The woman says, "Yeh, sho', you can change da lil' ma ther' ha, I don't mind. I been too damn busy messin' wit diss foo to be changin' dem diapers."

Melissa picks up the toddler, lays her on the couch, and changes her diaper. She asks the woman if she can use her bathroom. The woman points to the back as she talks to the officer. She goes to the bathroom, throws the diaper in the trash, and washes her hands. As she washes her hands, she looks up at her reflection in the cracked mirror. The facet squeaks as she turns it off. She opens the bathroom door slowly. She sees the babies standing just outside the door. She looks down and smiles. The toddler's have the dirty face a baby gets when he or she eats something messy, but it looks like the babies haven't had a bath in awhile. Their skin has dried food caked on their chins, chest, and arms. Melissa sees two clean washcloths folded on top of a metal shelf on the bathroom wall. She grabs a washcloth, pumps soap on it, then runs the water until it turns warm. She runs warm water onto the washcloth and rings out the excess water.

The toddlers walk up to her. She steps inside the bathroom with the door still wide open. One by one, she wipes down their tiny little faces, hands, chest, under their neck, and arms with the warm washcloth. Soon, the washcloth is soiled with food and grease matter. She grabs the baby lotion on the sink and puts it on the toddlers. They look cleaner. Melissa knows they feel much better, too. As soon as she's done, the toddlers reach up to her. She kneels down and they all give her a big hug. She gets up and walks back towards the living room with the toddlers.

The officer finishes talking to the woman and they leave the apartment.

Melissa gets into the unit. She wants to ask why he didn't call child welfare services or why he didn't intervene on the care and hygiene of the toddlers. As she is about to mouth something, she stops herself. He answers her silent question.

He sighs and says, "There are thousands of kids living in a similar condition. I've seen worse. The kids weren't in danger at that moment, but I know exactly what you're thinking."

It's dark out now. The sun has long set. They take a quick a break and fill the stereotype of getting donuts and coffee miles down the road. They go inside the coffee shop. Surprisingly, the donuts and coffee are free. She enjoys a few freshly made donuts and coffee. She saw them make the donuts and freshly brew the hot coffee. She wants to ask if the officer has ever come across someone ever spitting in his food or drink, but she resists from asking.

As they head out the door, her dumbfounded curiosity intervenes and she just has to know. She runs to the coffee and donut masterpiece maker and asks if indeed the food and drinks were spat in. The worker smiles. He reassures her he never has. In fact, his father and grandfather were cops and he has nothing, but respect for law enforcement. The worker shows her a photo on the wall of him as a kid with his grandfather in uniform. He refills her cup and throws her another donut. She smiles and thanks him. He tells her to be safe out there. She runs back out to the unit. They take a few minutes to slurp and take bites before they leave to the next call.

With the sun out of sight, the cold of the dark night settles in. The temperature drops to a very cold 42 degrees Fahrenheit. She knows the average temperature of a fridge is exactly 42 degrees Fahrenheit. She gets her long sleeve, thermal shirt out of her backpack and puts it on.

The next call is a trespassing call at a large department store. They make the ten-minute dash and arrive at the location. The police unit slowly drives around the building. The officer asks her to use the spotlight on her side to look around the property.

As she scans back and forth with the spotlight, she notices a figure sitting and slumped over. It's sitting on the end of a metal bench. She points and tells the officer there is someone sitting on the bench. The officer drives as close as he can and puts the unit in park.

They shine the spotlight onto the mysterious person sitting on the end of the metal bench.

She says, "That's some freaky shit out of a scary movie."

The officer squints at the person on the bench, and says, "This ain't no scary movie, kid."

The officer slowly gets out of the unit. The slumped over figure looks it's holding something in its' arms. He or she has long hair covering what he or she is holding. Melissa makes the assumption that it's a woman because of how long her hair is and the fact that she's wearing a long skirt.

The officer slowly walks up to the strange woman.

He cautiously asks, "Ma'am? I'm a police officer. Ma'am, are you okay?"

Without taking his eyes off of her, he talks on the radio on his left shoulder.

He says, "Ma'am, do you need help? I'm Officer Morris. I am here to help you. I need you to look at me. Ma'am?"

Melissa quickly realizes what she is holding and gently opens the door and gets out. The officer slowly reaches for the gun on his belt and continues to talk to the woman. The woman slowly lifts up her head. Her eyes are slightly open.

The officer says, "Ma'am, give me what you have in your hands. Give me what you are holding. You need help. Ma'am, I am here to help you."

The woman slowly looks down at what looks like a pile of rags rolled up. The woman starts to mutter a jumble of words under her breath. The woman starts to slowly rock back and forth. Melissa slowly walks closer to the woman. The officer puts his gun back into his belt holster and shines his flashlight on the woman's lap.

The officer puts his flashlight back into his belt holster and says, "Ma'am, I need you to give me the baby."

The officer walks closer to the woman. He slowly opens his arms. The woman slowly looks up and starts to sob. She slowly hands the wrapped baby to the officer. The officer slowly grabs the baby, requests a medical unit, and back up to their location. Melissa walks to the officer and gently grabs the wrapped baby from him. The baby is so light almost as if she's only holding a pile of dirty clothes. The officer tells Melissa there is a small box of infant formula and a bottle in the back seat. She nods her head, rushes to the back seat of the unit, grabs the premade, liquid formula, and goes to the front passenger seat. She rips the box open and screws the nipple onto the small, two-ounce plastic bottle. She covers the rubber nipple with her pointer finger, shakes the bottle, and puts it on the dashboard.

She blasts the heater, quickly takes off the old, soiled rags layer by layer. She finally sees the baby. It's a little girl. The baby is naked, covered in dried blood, has a tint of blue and purple all over her little body. The baby is not moving. She places the baby on her lap. She frantically takes off her hoodie, long sleeve shirt, bulletproof vest, and t-shirt. She puts the baby on her chest against the top part of her exposed chest and sports bra. She starts rubbing the baby's little back, legs, arms, and head with both hands.

As she rubs the baby, she says, "Hey sweetie. Sweet, little girl. Wake up, sweetie. Come on. You're okay. You're going to be okay. Sweetie, wake up. I know you're hungry, cold, exhausted, but I'm here, okay? You need to get up for me now."

She knows with all her heart the baby is alive, even though the baby has not taken a breath, moved, and not giving off any body heat, she knows she's alive and hanging on. Melissa rubs the baby up and down her little body. The tiny baby lies on her beating chest.

She takes a breath and refrains her heart from sinking. She looks down at the baby.

She says with a slightly shaky voice, "You know, I'm a mama. I promise you this will never ever happen to you again, okay? So, you get up and you live. You fight. I'm so sorry this happened to you. You're so tiny, but I know you're strong. I can feel it. Wake up, sweetie. Come on. Listen to my voice."

Melissa is not paying attention to the officer and the woman outside in front of the unit, but she hears scuffling and the woman yelling something. The baby is so tiny, light, and lifeless.

She keeps rubbing the baby up and down her cold, little body.

She says, "Don't give up. Don't give up. I'm here for you. Come on, sweetie. It's going to be okay. Listen to my heartbeat, sweetie. Do you feel it? My heart is right here for you, just for you. Warm up, my little baby. Come on."

Seconds later, the baby's head makes a slight movement, then her feet twitch, then her little hands move. She continues rubbing the little baby.

She looks at the baby, smiles, and says, "Yes! Oh my little brave girl! Look at you. You're so strong. Yes, you can do it. Listen to my heartbeat, sweetie. I have milk for you. Drink some milk for me. Oh! Look at you! You're so beautiful. I am so proud of you. Look at you!"

The baby jolts. The baby starts to make gurgling sounds as she moves around more and more. She continues rubbing her. She starts to feel the baby's little body slowly retain heat.

Moments later, the baby starts to cry. Melissa's tears start to form on her lower eyelids. She slowly and gently rolls the baby onto her little back to prepare to offer the petite, two-ounce bottle. The baby's eyes are closed. The baby's cry grows louder in pitch. She places the tip of her pinky on the side of the baby's mouth. The baby turns her little head, making the notion she's hungry. Melissa grabs the bottle. The baby slowly starts to suck the plastic nipple.

She says, "I am so proud of you, sweetie! Look at you. You're eating. Good job, sweetie. I'm so proud of you."

The baby finishes an ounce. She puts the baby back on her chest and gently pats the baby's back.

She says, "You are a strong little lady. Don't you ever forget that, okay? You will get through this. I want you to know that you don't ever give up, no matter what, okay?"

The baby coos and eventually lets out a small burp.

She laughs and says, "That's a good girl. Good girl. Well, look at you, my strong little lady. I'm not going anywhere, okay? I'm here. You're going to be okay. Listen to my voice. Listen to my heart."

The baby grunts and moves her arms and legs. From the distance, she hears sirens. She rubs the little baby that's lying on her chest. For just a few minutes there's a still silence. Then, firefighters open her door. She looks up.

The guy smiles and says, "It's okay. We will take care of her."

She slowly gives him the baby.

She says, "I fed her an ounce of newborn, premade, infant formula."

The firefighter nods his head and takes the baby to the paramedic van.

With the car door open, she stands up. She puts her shirt back on, bulletproof vest, long sleeve shirt, and hoodie.

A white ambulance shows up. Soon there's two fire trucks and more police. The firefighters get an IV on the baby and leave to the hospital with sirens blaring. The woman was tackled and placed in the back of another police unit. Melissa gets back into the unit. She turns the blasting heater off. She stares into the heater vent. She closes her door. She stays in the unit for the next twenty minutes while the officer talks with other officers.

It's daybreak—4am. The officer gets into the vehicle and tells Melissa that he is not taking any more calls for his shift and they will go back to the station so he can finish his reports. He tells her she doesn't have to stay for that this time and she can help with his reports next time. They drive back to the station listening to the scratchy voices on the police radio.

It's been twelve hours.

The officer says, "You did pretty good there, Miss Lady. Usually the ride-alongs freak out and they are done. They drop out of school or they change their internship. I can tell you will finish your hours and you would be one hell of a cop if you were to ever consider it."

Melissa stares at the yellow street lines as he drives.

She says, "I don't want to be a cop."

She wants to say something else, but she just stops herself in her tracks. She doesn't say anything more. They make it back to the station. The cop shakes her hand and tells her he will see her tomorrow evening. Melissa grabs her backpack and gets into her mother's SUV.

She drives home in silence. The sun's bright orange rays break the dawn's horizon. She makes it back. She goes inside and walks to her boys' room. She kisses them on the cheek while they lie asleep in their warm beds. She then goes to the bedroom where her aunt is. She watches her little baby girl sleep in her soft pink basinet. She bends over into the basinet. She wraps her baby's hand around her finger. Her little baby girl squeezes her finger and makes a calming sigh. She slowly puts her little girl's hand down. She kisses her little girl's soft, baby cheek. She gets into the shower and stays under the hot water for what seems like ten years.

** ** ** ** **

Her internship hours come to an end. Something different crosses her path every night during her entire internship. From grand theft auto stings to drug deal stings to domestic violence calls to DWI stops to larceny calls at the local casino, through it all, she watches. She observes and writes an intense final paper. Her paper elaborates how she witnessed first hand on how much the government, legal system, and formal and informal America has failed their youth and quite possibly the future. It's a minute bite of an analysis, but she takes her experiences from the ride-alongs as her back up and evidentiary support.

She lands an 'A', and a spot in the college newsletter, but she will never forget the first 12 hours of her internship. She learns not to treat life like it's a game.

For the next semester, she lives off of beans and rice most days, but always making sure her kids eat. She applies for food stamps, but is told she doesn't qualify because she has no income. She feels bad when it comes to the boys' school functions. From sports events to award ceremonies, she's not ever able to go because she has classes and study hours to fulfill. Any extra time is filled with studying, cleaning, and figuring out the very basic of needs of gas and food. She feels horrible. She can't even buy the boys their school photos when that time of year comes around. She keeps telling herself it's only temporary. Still, she keeps to herself. She only makes a few friends through her classes, but she severs all ties once the class is over. At this point, it is very hard for her to trust anyone.

She's been able to take several online classes for as long as she could. She avoids hiring a sitter and taking her little girl to daycare, but now is the time she has to be present on campus. She establishes daycare assistance through the state. She finds a daycare between her mother's house and campus.

Today is the day. She's anxious. She makes the six-minute drive to the daycare. The boys reassure her it is only temporary and their little sister will be okay. She takes a deep breath. She's ready for the slap in the face. She's ready to face her separation anxiety attack.

She carries her daughter whom lies peacefully asleep in her car seat. She enters the daycare. A staff member tells her the infant room is down the middle of the hallway. She takes her precious, ten-week old, baby girl out of her car seat and starts walking down the hallway. She knocks on the door. A woman smiles and greets her. The woman is older than her. The woman is pretty, tall, and she can feel the love she has for children almost immediately. Melissa holds her little baby girl as she talks with the woman.

She says, "My daughter will be here on weekdays. I'm nervous. I'm done with all of my classes by 4 and I will come as soon as I'm done for the day. Is there anyway I could get your number so I can check on her? Maybe text you?"

The woman smiles and says, "Sure. It's no problem. I'm Maddy, by the way. It's nice to meet you. I work here full-time. I promise you, your baby girl is safe with me. I only work in the baby room. We play music, sing to the babies, and make sure they are well taken care of. I will take care of her like she's my own."

They exchange numbers. She slowly gives Maddy her baby girl. Her baby girl is asleep. Maddy rocks back and forth holding her little baby girl in the rocking chair. Maddy laughs and promises she will be fine and she can text anytime. Melissa slowly backs away. Maddy looks down at Melissa's baby girl and smiles. She walks down the hallway. She stops and watches through the classroom window. She looks at her baby girl still asleep as Maddy softly sings. She looks at the time on her phone and realizes she's going to be late if she doesn't get going. She drives the boys to school and heads to the campus.

After a year and a half of her mother's bullshit, classes, studying, being a mom, she finally graduates from the community college.

On the morning of her graduation she gets into a heated argument with her mother. She felt the tension beforehand and knew it was coming. As it got closer to her graduating, her mother started acting like a grown brat, asking Melissa why she hasn't given her any money, and more repetitively, why she hasn't cleaned up for her graduation reception to be held at the house on the day of graduation. She tells her mother her attention is focused on finals and not dusting her mother's books.

Her mother's fits grow old quite quickly. Melissa repeatedly tells her mother she did, in fact, clean and she's not about to dust her books just because her mother feels like it's not her special day and the attention is not centered on her for once.

Her mother tries to threaten Melissa by telling her she will cancel the graduation reception if she doesn't dust her bookshelves. She ignores her mother. Her mother doesn't like being ignored so she pushes her threat saying she won't take her boys to the graduation ceremony. Not being in the mood any longer, she tells her mother not to worry about it. She walks past her heated and unreasonable mother and goes to her bedroom. She closes her door. She calls her dad. He confirms he's coming to pick up the boys. She already knew her mother would try to pull such a stunt so she asked her father if he could take the boys with him to the graduation ceremony.

Her father arrives and picks up the boys. She hugs and kisses her boys good-bye and leaves for the graduation ceremony. Melissa can't understand why her mother isn't proud of her. She realizes it's a waste of time to figure any of it out. She reminds herself how her mother is and that it's no surprise.

It's time. She lines up for graduation and the ceremony begins. She sees the graduating class greet friends they know and are graduating with. She looks at people in royal blue robes. She sees how happy they are. She knows someday she will have a close friend that will show up to one of her graduations. She sees family members and friends put decorations on other graduates' caps and around their neck. She smiles.

Hours later, it's official. She's awarded her associate's degree. Months before, she applied to the local university and she was accepted. All of her credits transfer and she can immediately begin her bachelor's degree journey.

She lands an internship on campus. She feels good and happy about everything. More so, she is happy Grandma and Cheíí are there to watch her get her piece of paper she vigorously worked hard for.

The graduation ceremony is over. Her mother and stepmother don't bother to show up for the graduation ceremony. Everyone that showed up at the graduation ceremony heads back to the house for the reception. Her mother apologizes via text message before she makes it back to the house. Melissa knows the only reason why she apologizes is because there is an array of people at her house. It's now time for the show horse to shine.

The party is actually nice. Different people both familiar and unfamiliar perform speeches about Melissa and how much of not only a determined Lady she is, but how much of a good mother she is.

As the party progresses, the house becomes filled with more and more strangers. Melissa is very happy to see Maddy show up. They laugh and eat.

Melissa is exhausted from lack of sleep, food, and normalcy. She just wants to take a nap with her daughter, but she doesn't. She spends time with Maddy, and Grandma and Cheíí. Those are the only three people she wants to talk to. She hugs Maddy and tells Maddy she wouldn't of been able to get where she is without her.

After Maddy leaves, she makes tea for Grandma and drives Cheíí to the bookstore across the street.

** ** ** ** **

Melissa takes a break for two weeks before she dives into her next semester at the university. Her oldest son secretly takes her phone from her and posts her graduation photos on social media. She doesn't realize it until she logs on a few days later. She's surprised of the support from her online friends.

One morning, she gets a message from an old time friend from middle school. She smiles as she reads the online message.

It reads, "Hey Lady! I see you graduated! Nice, very nice. Well good luck and I wish you the best. You're a smart lady, keep it up. I wish I could take you out to a nice place to celebrate. That's a big accomplishment so good for you. I will try to make it to the next graduation and take you somewhere to celebrate!"

She reads the message and wants to message back. She knows her friend is just being nice. She fights the urge to message back. She doesn't write back. She thinks it might be nothing but another story of drama.

She's fortunate enough to receive scholarship after scholarship. Scholarships along with student loans help pay for school every semester. She adjusts quickly to the single mom university life.

She gets up at 5am and gets her little one ready. The night before, she prepares the diaper bag, charges her laptop, packs taking-notes supplies, textbooks, a peanut butter and jelly sandwich and an boiled egg, and ensures there's enough gas for the day. Once everyone is ready to go, she piles her kids into the SUV and they trail off to start their day.

Her first stop is daycare. She drops off her, now, toddler baby girl and next oldest son. The daycare takes drops off her son at school an hour later. The second stop is a Native American focused grade charter school. She drops off her oldest son in front of the school. She makes the loop back around and heads to the university campus. The university campus is ten times bigger than the community college she transferred from. It's less personable as she doesn't run into anyone she knows.

Once in a while she runs into her mother's colleagues and her mother's students she's met before, but she doesn't stay long enough to make conversation. It's a quick smile and wave after they've called out her name or a hug at the very most and she's back on her way to a study group, tutoring, or class.

There are only two professors, her mother's colleagues, she's semi-close to. They understand her and her mother's relationship. They have an identical relationship with their own mother. They are warming and inviting to her.

One in particular often helps her out when the kids are sick. The professor is a chair of the department. The professor always tells her she's more than happy to have the kids over at her office until Melissa is ready to leave campus for the day. Melissa is always indebted to the professor. She feels like she doesn't know how to return the favor, but the professor never complains, tells Melissa she's too busy, or rejects Melissa when she needs a quiet place to study. There are often times the professor offers the study quarters in her office to Melissa to take a power nap.

Melissa appreciates the little things like that. It means so much to her. The helpful and loving professor tells Melissa that she knows what it's like being a single parent and going to school.

After all these years, this is the first time Melissa has ever heard someone say that to her. This little moment gives Melissa a lot of determination to keep going. But, unbeknownst her, she is about to lose something that's dear to her.

Chapter 13. Chop Chop

"You're my beautiful lady. Always smart and always beautiful. Awww, my Lady!"

-Frank Nez

Melissa officially enters the first world and it still has problems—White people problems, but still, problems. It's a set of easy problems, but it's the world she is now in. No more homelessness. No more struggling paycheck to paycheck. She only gets one paycheck that has to hold its' breath for four months. She is thankfully not stuck in the muck of drama anymore or so she thinks. Her problems consist of not being late for class, using the money that jingles to pay for gas, making dead President Ulysses S. Grant stretch to feed her family of four, and arguing with the professors that think she's not good enough because of the color of her brown skin. She is always occupied by reading books, memorizing textbook terms, and fortunately, working on campus.

She becomes comfortable with this person of her. She's grown into a person striving to finish college. She has no idea where she wants to go to law school, yet. For now, it's baby steps. She overcomes her stress by acing one test and one paper at a time. Her plan remains the same—finish her undergrad years, finish grad school, and then conquer law school. Strangers, fellow students, distant family members, and even college professors have told her she's not going to make it. Nevertheless, she leaves that thought there with them.

She just smiles and always tells them, "Okay, yeah. I'll quit school just for you, no problem."

She is now an urban Native and she couldn't be prouder.

She knows she's different than the other natives on the university campus.

During the beginning of her first semester, she tries to make friends with other native students on campus, but for some reason, they look at her as competition and make the friendship process a battle of drama dragged with cheap eyeliner and ignorance fit for a European king in the 1800s.

There are natives in some of her classes, but it seems as though all come from the same wit—petty, jealous, and enraged that she has brains. It was middle school all over again, except name-calling is replaced with dirty looks, hard blinking, and exaggerated sighs. She has no idea what the beef is about, but she pays no mind. She gives up on the Native urban fah-la-la distant family reunion attempt to make a new native friend and isolates herself with her sole goal in mind—finish school.

Once in a great while late at night amongst tapping of her laptop keyboard and her pepto bismol painted walls, her humanness sets in. She misses Grandma and Cheíí back at home. She knows they miss her, too. She manages to save up money to go see them every few months. The only drawback is going back to becoming a mere servant to her stepmother. A small part of her dreads it. It's always the same when she goes home.

Before her SUV's 5.0 liter engine is able to cool down from the two-hour drive, her stepmother chucks a list of errands at her. From paying interest on her stepmother's pawns to picking something up from Wal-Mart to fulfilling a mission on finding the cheapest place for velvet material, she was merely a doormat. This not only interrupts her time to study, but it makes it even more stressful come nighttime because her sole purpose for spending time with Grandma and Cheíí has to wait until every box is checked. This always leaves returning to the city with less sleep and energy. But, overall, she thinks as long as she's able to see Grandma and Cheíí, she's happy.

She takes awe when she first arrives home. She goes to Grandma and Cheíí's bedroom with the kids so they can see how big the kids have gotten since the last visit. Cheíí always holds her tight, smiles, and pats her head. Grandma always grabs onto the kids and cries.

Over the next three years, she notices Cheíí's strength is seemingly weaker. He goes from walking to shuffling slower to now using a cane. It's hard for her to see this man that she looks up to become vulnerable to earth's gravity and the trickles of the inevitable sand in the time glass. Regardless, Cheíí always hugs her tight like he doesn't want to let go. Because of Grandma and Cheíí's vulnerability to old age, they are forced to move into her stepmother's house. Melissa helped build this house back in high school, but never lived in it. She loves going home and as there is no other nostalgia like it.

Arriving home is the same routine for her and she wouldn't change it for the world.

A three-day weekend is coming up. She decides she wants to spend every second with Grandma and Cheíí, so she packs her bags the night before and makes the two hour drive home on Friday as soon as the boys get of out school.

For some reason, the two-hour Friday drive feels like forever, but it's always worth it. She makes it and drives to her stepmother's house. She parks the SUV, gets the kids out, and goes straight to Grandma and Cheíí's bedroom. Her heart beats happily as she opens their bedroom door and walks in with the kids.

Cheíí is reading, "The Book of the Dead", on his bed. Grandma softly sips her hot tea while listening to KGAK sitting on the brown, plush recliner.

Cheíí puts his book down.

He smiles, and says happily. "Ahhhhhh! The Lady is home! The Lady is here!! Ahhhhhhh! My Lady! You're still as radiant, as always. Beautiful! Just beautiful! My smart Lady! How's the city? How's the weather?"

Grandma puts her tea down and cries as her great-grandchildren surround her petite body

When Melissa had her last baby, things changed for her. Coming home changed for Melissa.

It's one particular weekend she will never forget.

It's Melissa's sophomore year at the university. Melissa and the kids return home for a weekend. She figures if she finishes her stepmother's to-do list before sundown she can work on her paper and have it completed that night so she can spend the entire day tomorrow with Grandma and Cheíí. She wants to take Cheíí to the flea market and Grandma to eat lamb stew and frybread at the local casino.

She succeeds in her goal for the day and finishes her stepmother's agonizing to-do list. Soon, day turns to night. She's working on her paper in the back room next to Grandma and Cheíí's bedroom. It's just past midnight. The house is asleep. She just manages finished her paper. She wants to take a break and make a quick midnight snack before she edits it. So, she gets up and starts walking down the hallway. She mentally tells herself she'll make something small and have some tea, too.

As she walks down the hallway leading to the kitchen, she hears voices in the dining room.

She smiles.

She is about to yell out something when she hears a voice at the end of the hallway say, "You know she'll just get pregnant again."

Another voice giggles and says, "Yeah, she won't finish school."

Another voice laughs harder and says, "She'll just be another broken mom for her kids, living off of the state, living check to check, it's pathetic, I mean… why doesn't she just give it up already? And her pretending to be happy when she comes back? Uh, can we say, 'dumb'? It's all a phony act. Nope. She won't finish school."

She leans up against the wall. Her chest sinks in. Her throat tightens. She rolls in her top and bottom lip together. She doesn't feel like crying, oh, no. Her heart cracks. It's not broken, no. It just cracks, just a little. She doesn't know if she wants to hear the rest of the conversation. Just as she is about to walk back into the back room, they end the conversation. She hears chairs lightly skid across the dining room floor.

She slowly sneaks a look around the corner. She sees her stepmother and her adult kids, one older than her and one younger than her. Two walk upstairs and one walks out the front door slamming the screen door behind them. Melissa slowly walks back into the back room and packs up her backpack. She hears the bedroom doors upstairs close. She packs her bags and puts it in the SUV.

Before she goes upstairs to get the kids, she slowly walks into Grandma and Cheíí's bedroom. Grandma is lying down on her bed still awake. Cheíí is reading David's Schultz's, "The Andromeda Galaxy and the Rise of Modern Astronomy". A reading light shines on the pages of his open book.

She walks slowly towards him. She hesitates to tell him she has to leave.

Cheíí looks up and smiles. He puts his book down, takes off his glasses, and opens his arms to her. She can feel his warmth and love across the room. She wants to tell him what she heard and how much it hurts. She wants to tell him so badly. The urge to cry is written all over her face, but she holds it in and faintly smiles back as she walks to into his arms.

While they hug, she says, "Cheíí... I.. "

She wants to say that her heart is cracked. She wants to tell him exactly what she heard and who said it, but her thought is interrupted by Cheíí's arms wrapped around her. He squeezes her just a little tighter. She feels his heart beating against her breath. He pats the top of head. He takes down her messy bun and starting putting his fingers through her hair.

Cheíí says in English, "I know, My Lady, I know."

He pushes her back with his arms and looks into her eyes.

His face becomes stern.

He says in English, "You're strong. I know why you need to leave. You keep going no matter what, okay? Don't worry about anything else. Now go. You know what you have to do. When you have poison in your life, sometimes you have to keep going and leave the poison alone. Keep going to school. Don't give up."

She walks over to Grandma's bed and hugs her.

She says in English, "I'm sorry Grandma, but I can't stay. I have to go."

Grandma smiles and says in English, "You know there are no exact words in Navajo that says, 'I'm sorry'. The Creator didn't create the saying because we are suppose to help each other live this life, not bring each other down. Me and Cheíí love you. You do what you need to do, okay? Me and Cheíí are fine. We aren't going anywhere. We are here when you are ready to come home, okay? Now go. I love you, Lady. Don't you ever forget that."

She nods her head. She takes a deep breath to hold back her tears. She quietly wakes her boys and carries her little girl down the stairs and she leaves.

She drives down the dirt road with only the sound of her tires driving on the dirt road. Her oldest son is sitting next to her, awake, and asks her if she's okay. She smiles and tells her son she's fine, just has to finish a paper, and doesn't want to make the long drive back later since she's been up late.

She stops in Gallup, puts in gas, buys coffee, and gets back onto the main street leading to the freeway.

Her chest tightens as she merges onto the freeway. She can only hear the engine of her dusty SUV. A single tear rolls down her cheek as she thinks to herself, "I'll be home again soon."

Two hours later, they make it back to her mother's house. She feels different about her family back at home now. Her stepmother would call her to check on how's she's doing. She would answer the phone ready to tell her the latest about being a mom, work, or about her classes. She thought maybe her stepmother really wanted the role of being a mom to her. Maybe she grew into a love that a stepparent yearns and values the relationship of family. Just maybe.

But that wasn't it all. Her stepmother just wanted something to add to the evil and tormenting grapevine.

The urge to talk to her stepmother is dead. She ignores her calls and text messages. The only person she talks to is her aunt because it's actually Grandma or Cheíí calling.

It's only been a few weeks since she walked upon the poisoned grapevine, but for some reason she can't concentrate. She's finds it hard to focus to do anything let alone study. An unwholesome feeling of numbness and an ugly surrealness sets in.

One morning after class, Maddy texts her. Maddy texts her asking how classes are going. Maddy continues to text saying how sweet her baby girl is and how smart she is like her mama. She faintly smiles looking at her phone's screen. She doesn't text back. She puts the phone in her back pocket. She gets out her black bean, cheese, and egg sandwich out of her backpack. She eats it walking to her next class.

When she's out of class, Maddy calls her. She answers.

Maddy says. "Hey! How's your day? I know you're stressed about something. I know you're alone, but I'm here if you ever need to vent, okay? You're a strong Lady. Okay, well I gotta get back to work. I just wanted to say that you're doing a really good job with everything, okay? See you later, Mel."

She finally feels a single ray of sunshine on her shoulder.

She says, "Okay, thanks", and hangs up.

She finishes her day at school early because her last class is canceled. Her boss texts her that he doesn't need her at work today. She realizes she doesn't need to do anything else on campus so she leaves back to her mother's house.

It's hours until she has to pick up the kids. She goes into the empty house. The house is like her spirit—hollow, empty, and cold. She grabs a towel and heads to the bathroom. She takes off her clothes slowly and stands under the water streaming from the showerhead. She starts to cry as the water streams down her face and down her body. She relives the voices in her head saying she'll just get pregnant again and won't finish school. Her tears blends in with the shower streams.

As she stands in the shower crying, she realizes her heart is so broken and that is why she can't concentrate in school. The "parents" that helped raised her were the very same parents that broke her heart and she doesn't understand why.

She knows she can't carry on like this. She finds the strength to wash her hair and scrub her numb body. For once, she doesn't rush. For once, she takes her time. She finishes washing herself, gets out of the shower, and slowly dries off her wet body and drenched, heavy, long hair. She wraps herself in a towel. She grabs another clean towel and dries her hair. She goes to the mirror above the bathroom sink. She divides her hair in half with her hands. Her hair falls down over her breasts, down her front ribs, and stopping as her hips. She grabs the royal blue, plastic, bristled brush. She slowly brushes the tangles out. It takes her five minutes to brush it down to a smooth, tangle-free consistency. She puts the brush on the sink. She slowly opens the bathroom mirror in front of her. She grabs a pair of large, sharp, blood red scissors. She washes the scissor's blades in the sink with Dial. She carefully dries each blade with the towel.

With her right hand, she puts the scissor's handle horizontal up against the left side of her neck just under her left ear lope. With the other hand she grabs a section of long, wet, shiny, smooth, black hair. She opens the scissor's blades with her right hand. She slowly puts the sectioned off hair in between the opened blades.

A single tear streams down the left side of her face. She stares at her reflection and slowly closes the scissor's blades. The scissors makes its' first smooth, straight sever.

Another tear rolls down her right cheek. She looks at herself in the mirror as she opens and closes the blades cutting her long, shiny, black, wet, beautiful hair.

As the blades open and close with each cut, she hears Cheíí's voice.

She's eight years old again.

She his voice say, "Only cut your hair when you are grieving. When it is too much to bare. This way you start over, brand new. There's nothing wrong with starting over brand new. You start over. Rid of the bad, okay? Then, you leave it alone. You leave it there."

She's done cutting. She builds a small fire in the backyard. As the small fire crackles, she places sections of hair on top of the orange and yellow flames.

When all of her hair is burned she puts out the fire and waits for the hot ash to cool. After it cools, she digs a hole in the ground and buries the ash.

She picks up the kids right after. She checks them out of school and out of daycare. She takes them to eat Phó at a local Vietnamese restaurant.

She finally did it.

She cut the poison out of her life.

Now there is more room for the good things in life.

Chapter 14. Blast from the Past

"The Moon is waiting for you. The time is coming. Very soon, indeed, very soon."

-Frank Nez

The next day, the haircut shocks her mother. Her mother actually says she likes it, in fact, her mother says she really likes it. It shocks Melissa even more that her mother has something nice to say. Her mother asks to take a photo and post it on social media. Her mother wants to see if people agree that short hair on a Native woman looks good.

Melissa says, "I don't need validation."

Her mother's attitude quickly changes.

Her mother says sternly, "I honestly don't think you should of cut your hair. What will people say?"

She responds, "I don't give a fuck what people say."

Her mother catches on to her I-don't-give-a-fuck vibe and quickly says, "Well I have some stuff to do at the office. You're on your own for dinner. I'll be back later."

She has no idea why her mother has it carved in her brain that she thinks she provides for her and her children. Her mother bolting is how her mother copes with the guilt of not ever being involved in Melissa's life. After all these years, her mother hasn't changed. Her mother still carries a sour attitude as an essential body part like a camel and its' hump. When her mother's thirst for attention goes unsatisfied, her mother relies on her camel's hump.

When her mother is upset, which is almost as often as the sunsets, her mother slams kitchen cabinet doors, violently clings pots and pans around, and even goes to the childish realm of huffing and puffing, but fortunately, not enough to blow the house down. Melissa has known this like of her and it doesn't bother her. Her mother has tried to engage into arguing time and time again when things don't go her way. Melissa is used to it.

After Melissa and her mother's the normal conversation fueled by her mother's resentment takes place her mother abruptly throws a few books in a bag and leaves slamming the front door. Melissa knows her mother enough to know her mother is a very discouraging person to be around if a person is around her long enough. Her mother's hi-ho cherry-o demeanor changes faster than a toddler changing their mind.

Still, Melissa keeps to herself. She figures if she ends up alone in a big house with a small dog to confide in when she's scared at night or lonely, she can be happy during the holidays when her kids come pouring in. She tells herself she'd rather have her goals squared away than to regret it later.

The next morning she is very thankful to run into free samples of energy drinks in the university courtyard. She knows she will need it when she goes to work. It's only the first class of the day. She still has her entire day, three more classes ahead of her. She's starting to feel the exhaustion weigh in. She sits in the back of the classroom today since the study slides were released two nights ago. She already studied and took notes on the slides.

One of her classmates notices her sitting in the back instead of the usual front and center seat and sits next to her. He quickly takes note on her exhaustion. He tells her she should take a power nap after she signs in and he will wake her up when class is over. They sign in and class begins. It doesn't take but a few minutes. She passes out. She falls asleep with pen in hand, wearing a faded black, v-neck, cotton, t-shirt, ash black yoga pants, worn lace-up Nikes, a black and green Starbucks baseball cap, and a messy ponytail sticking out of the cap's loop. She awakes up to her classmate tapping her arm. She wipes the drool from the side of her mouth and gets up.

She makes it to her next class with two minutes to spare. She sits in the front row this time. The class immediately starts. She shakes off her tiredness. She blinks her eyes hard several times. Because of her anemia, she is very sensitive to energy drinks. The professor is seemingly having a long day, too. He changes the class' daily lecture agenda to watching a movie. As soon as the movie begins, the professor falls asleep in his chair. She's tempted to fall asleep, too, but she can't. She is convinced that there will be a quiz on the movie before the class is over. So, she takes her time sipping the energy drink forcing herself to wake up. She takes notes on the movie.

Soon, the movie comes to an end and here it comes. The professor wakes up and tells the class to write a paper on the movie's message and how it relates to class. Melissa feels herself finally waking up and starts handwriting her essay in her college ruled notebook. Her BIC pen presses against the fresh, smooth, and clean paper. She starts to remember the movie chronologically. She glances at her notes off and on. She starts to feel her energy rise and soon her pen's ink splashes a tsunami across every page. She smiles. Her paper is coming together beautifully. It's five minutes until the class is going to end and she finishes. Several people fell asleep in class and they now look lost and panicked. She's glad she isn't one of them. She turns in her paper and walks out of class. She now has a long gap until her next class. So, she heads to work.

Before she heads to work she grabs her lunch out of her backpack. She likes eating on the benches under the trees just outside the student union. She eats half of her food and heads to work. Work keeps her occupied. She schedules meetings for her boss, talks with other college students through their own first world problems, and dusts her workstation. She quickly prints out her research paper before her next class. She sits through the last lecture and she's done on campus for the day.

She doesn't have time to stay on campus to study today. She has a parent-teacher conference at two different schools. Her bulging backpack bounces up and down against her back as she jogs from her last class to the parking garage. A few hours later, she picks up her little girl at daycare and heads back to the house with the kids.

Today was a handful as always, but she is grateful for the lifestyle she is handed thus far. She types her paper on her laptop as her kids play in the backyard in front of her. Her mother is back on the university campus in her office, so Melissa has some quiet time for once.

Melissa pulls away from typing her paper and logs into social media. She thinks about going M.I.A. Just as she's about to deactivate her account, her laptop screen 'dings'. She receives a message. She has no idea who would message her. She knows it couldn't be Maddy because she always texts or calls. She opens the message and is very surprised to see whom it is.

She reads the name of who the message is from.

She says to herself, "Wow, a blast from the past."

She begins to read the message.

The message reads, "Good afternoon. It snowed really good early Saturday morning then the rain came. Now the roads are muddy, pot holes, and idiots that can't drive in the mud."

She reads the message, faintly smiles, and messages back, "Hey. So, I'm about to go M.I.A. I just really need to focus on school. Also going through some fucking bullshit.. but it's okay. I just have to learn not to trust so easily. Life has its' bumps in the road, I guess. Had a really weird confusing weekend that I wish I could of fast forwarded through."

She sends the message and decides to type another message, "It also sucks for me right now I guess. My humanness is kinda kicking in. Feeling kinda sad and down a little bit…Just have to keep busy and not let it consume me…"

She adds a last separate message, "It's so hard to trust people you know. It's like the trust from people is gone poof** there it goes floating away lol. Well, I am off to go workout and do one badass workout. I'm really stressed and need to get out of it. Then it's homework."

He immediately messages back, "If you do decide to go M.I.A......don't be a stranger to call.....text.....to.talk...this is my number.....but I do have rules and regulations.... times that I am available..... hahahaha..... I'm joking... hahahaha... 8675309. My number yo. You went M.I.A. on me once......don't go again..."

Melissa's English editing pet peeves kick in. She slightly blushes thinking he must of not really known what to say since he didn't use a single period. Perhaps, he must have been in such a hurry. Or even nervous, maybe? She's not sure. She just knows he was a long time friend and wants to be friends, again. This makes her feel all warm and fuzzy inside.

The only friend she has right now is Maddy. She sees Maddy like a big sister she's never had. Maddy often asks her how she's doing and knows Maddy actually means it. Melissa appreciates this new friendship since she has given up on everyone else in her life. She feels it in her soul that Maddy knows exactly what she is going through. Maddy is a single parent, too. Maddy often deals with bullshit on a daily basis like Melissa does. Melissa feels a bond between her and Maddy that she's never had before. Melissa always been a single parent, but this time it's different.

Before, she thought her dad and her stepmother always had her back, but she found out they genuinely don't care. She used to be a single parent that had verbal and emotional support from her family every now and then. This time she has no one's support.

Her mother treats her like a stray dog that pays rent to live in her mother's house and gets kicked out when Melissa and her pups become an "annoying" problem. Her dad doesn't have the strength to step up to his wife and fight for his only daughter to help her.

She now knows her entire family is a poisonous vine of gossip, jealousy, and hatred. She doesn't want to partake in any of it. She doesn't understand why they turned out the way they did, but she decides she doesn't want to be like that. She was done trusting a pile a mannequins. So, she leaves everyone alone. This time, she has gone completely solo. She becomes M.I.A. in any news and updates and falls off the planet.

Her stress all hers and hers to keep. She finds the obvious ways to vent it and let go of it. She takes the kids for a walk, goes to the university gym and swimming pool, and offers mountain tobacco and a prayer to the Holy People.

She wishes once in a great while she could go have a nice quiet cup of coffee with a close friend or even a beer or two and just have some laughs, but she doesn't have the money or the time to do either. She wants to ask Maddy if she wants to bond over a cup of coffee, but she also doesn't want to feel like she's bothering her. So, she does what she does best. She smokes mountain tobacco and keeps going. She tells herself she doesn't have time to be wasting on feeling down and sad. She has tummies to keep happy, pages to turn, and a scorned mother to deal with.

She doesn't message her blast from the past back. She gets rid of her social media. Before she does, she saves his number in her phone. She doesn't know if she'll even text or call. She now has trust issues. The people she's known all of her life stabbed her in the foot hoping she won't possibly move forward. As hard as it was to pull the rusty blade out of her foot she knows she has to start with trust somewhere.

She finally sleeps that night and more than the usual four hours.

For the next few weeks, she feels lighter and stronger in spirit.

One morning as she's getting ready for her day and high on her happiness, she texts her blast from the past.

She doesn't want to say much.

She texts him, "Hey this is Melly Mel. Save my number. I'm probably just as busy as you are, but I will try to text when I can. Have a badass and productive day."

She puts her phone in her bag and finishes getting ready. She often wears the college mama gear—sports bra, fitted yoga pants, running shoes, t-shirt and a hoodie. Her hair is so short all she can do is use bobby pins to pin up the sides like a little girl would.

She adjusts to her new social and family circle, which isn't much of a circle of all. It's more like a few points of people she trusts. There just isn't enough people to make a circle. And she's happy with it.

Satisfied with her grades and being ahead of things, she decides to treat herself for once.

She also decides to make a new friend. She grows to know a classmate, Mai. She met Mai her religion course and confides in her. Mai carries the same vibe as her, not giving a fuck of what people think. Mai helps Melissa dye her short hair dark forest green and goes with her when Melissa pierces the bottom right side of her lip.

It always seems like Mai has a million things going on like Melissa does. Even though there are long gaps in-between communication between the two, they always pick up exactly where they left off.

Melissa doesn't bother her phone for the next few days.

During her third class, she notices her blast from the past text her back right away the day before.

His text reads, "Cool. Cool. No worries. Yeah, I work all the time. When I do get a day off I use it to sleep and chill. You know down time."

She doesn't text back. She goes about her usually mommy-student splendid day and spends the evening at the local park playing basketball with her kids.

The next morning, she gets her kids off to daycare and school. She then heads to the university.

Her phone is in her backpack behind her seat.

As she drives, she hears it 'ding'. She immediately thinks it's Maddy. She continues to drive for another ten minutes.

She grabs her phone while stopped at an empty intersection. She sees two text messages. One text is from Maddy and the other from her blast from the past.

Maddy texts her, "Fuck I got flat tire. Sucks. So that made me late. On top of that my boss is being ass about it thinking I made it up, ugh!"

Melissa texts her back, "It's all good girl. I'm glad you got to work and don't worry about your boss. Don't let it bother you. How's my baby?"

Maddy texts, "She's asleep and thanks, girl. What's up with you?"

Melissa texts, "No problem. Well, not much. I cut my hair haha."

Maddy texts, "Oh yeah? How short?"

Melissa texts back, "Short, bro. Just under my ears. Haha."

Maddy texts back, "OMFG are you serious? But your hair was so long! What made you cut your hair? I bet it cuts the getting ready time in half."

Melissa texts, "I cut my hair because I'm grieving. My entire family broken my heart. It was too much to deal with. In my culture when the grief becomes too hard, you cut your hair. Sometimes it hurts so much and we can't focus on our life. In order to get rid of the heartache we have to get rid of our memories in order to move on. I went home this weekend and found out what my family really thinks of me. I trusted them. They want me to fail. It tore me apart and I have shit to do. I don't have time to be stuck in the mud with my grief."

Maddy texts, "Damn, girl. You need to write a book about this shit. This shit is crazy AF. But I'm sorry I know what it's like to be alone. I've been there. It's hard but you're strong. I know you have a lot of shit to do, but I know you can do it."

Melissa smiles while reading the text.

Maddy sends another text. "Hey, I wanna see the haircut! Send me a pic."

Melissa smiles takes a picture of herself on the phone.

She tries to focus on the crowded streets of cars.

She puts the phone in her lap.

She sends the photo while she's driving looking back and forth from her phone and the road.

Melissa puts her phone on the passenger seat. She drives to the university parking garage. She grabs her phone, keys, and backpack. She locks the SUV and starts walking to class. She looks at the time on her phone and realizes she has to run to class or the front row in class will be taken. The class is being held in a huge auditorium occupying around five hundred fellow students.

She makes it in time. She sits down, pulls out her notebook, pen, and puts her backpack underneath her. She pulls her backpack back out to grab her phone. Just as she is about to put it on silent her phone 'dings' with a text message.

It reads, "Usually when ladies cut their hair they look ugly, but you look really good. I like it. You look like Mulan, but better."

Melissa says out loud. "What the fuck?! …what?!... Oh shit… shit, shit, shit!"

Melissa goes into her text message main screen that displays the list of people she texts.

She's frantic.

She feels stupid and utterly embarrassed.

She looks at her phone screen and says out loud. "No, no, no! Fuck!"

A guy sitting behind her asks her if she's okay.

She turns around, smiles, and says, "Yeah, I just did something very stupid, that's all, no biggie."

The guy laughs and says, "Well, you're here now, so it can't be that stupid."

Melissa smiles and replies, "Thanks."

She makes her eyes big, turns back around, and looks at her phone screen.

She selects the text between her and her blast from the past. She sent the photo of her new haircut to her blast from the past instead of Maddy. Her panic comes to a halt and is quickly forgotten as the professor starts the lecture. The first slide pops up against the white wall and she starts to take notes.

Months go by and she can't seem to be more stressed as her classes get harder and much more tedious. It's the beginning of midterms. This means not only does she have to take away Friday movie night for the kids, but she has to spend all of her five hours of sleeping at night to study.

Her blast from the past texts her every now and then, but she can't respond. She can't sacrifice ten or even five minutes to get distracted. She tells herself she can't text him back no matter how much she wants to. The texts from her blast from the past are not angry that she hasn't text back. The texts ask how she's doing, how classes are, asks about how the kids are doing, the weather, and some are even supportive expressing she needs to take a breather every once in a while or she will burn out.

One late morning, on her way to her second class she gets a phone call. It's her blast from the past. They've been texting off and on now for the past six months. The text messages are not daily, but they get along really well. Her instinct is to keep the communication to a minimum as she needs to focus on school.

After midterms there's finals and then the semester is over. As each semester floats by, Melissa and her blast from the past start to text more often and once in a while, they talk. There is no flirting in conversation. There is just honest words exchanged between two hard working people.

Her blast from the past is pretty much settled in life. He's an ironworker and he loves it. He's been working since he was 15. She thinks, based on their conversations, he sounds genuinely happy with his career choice.

They exchange texts more than voice conversation.

Their texting conversation becomes a strong base of friendship. It goes something like this:

"Hey Melly Mel, what's up? Your nose sore from being in those books yet? Haha"

"Hey! What's up? Haha For realz, it is. Yeah, I feel like I will never be done. When I'm done reading and writing they just pile more on, such is life. Haha. Hows work? I saw it rained there, maybe sprinkled? Does is smell like it does back on the rez? I'm so homesick I could puke sagebrush and frybread haha"

"Well keep it up there, lady. You'll finish. Remember to take it easy once in a while, homie. Don't burn yourself out. Go to movie or go get some good food. I usually go to Olive Garden. MMmmm, love their pasta or seafood. You should go. You need to go I should day. Need to treat yourself once in while, homie."

"Sorry, homie. I gotta go. Class is starting. Have a badass work day, okay? Hugs, homie."

"Aight. Ttyl. Remember, rest. Take some time off."

She often cuts the texting conversation.

With nothing, but time on her side, she doesn't realize that she's slowly been building a friendship with her blast from the past.

One late night just after midnight, her phone buzzes while charging next to her on the bed as she's pounding on her laptop's keyboard.

"Hey, what's up?"

She doesn't respond much less glance at her phone. She ignores the vibration. She thinks it's her phone's cue telling her it's done charging.

The phone vibrates, again.

She picks up the phone and reads the text.

A second text comes in as she's reading.

"One of these days I will take you to get some time off. Can't say when, but I know I will. You deserve it, both you and the kids. You work so hard. Let me take care of you. I think I'm starting to have feelings for you. Been having these feelings for you since we first messaged on social media. Always thought about you, how you've been, thinking to myself what you're doing. Let me take care of you so you can finish school."

She smiles, and then sadly sighs.

She sends the responding text, "I don't want to rely on anyone. It's hard for me to trust. I figure it's easier to be alone and I'm going to keep it that way. My only focus is school and the kids. Homie, I need to be falling asleep, not falling in love. I find you annoying right now."

"At least you found me, that's all that matters."

She reads his text and softly giggles. She shakes her head. She turns her phone off and goes back to typing her paper.

As the weeks pass, she starts to admire the conversations more and more. Her blast from the past doesn't judge her for being a single parent like most people do. Her blast from the past also doesn't seem like another Natives that look at her like competition. She enjoys the fact that this person actually wants to know how she is doing. She doesn't go into full detail, but she tells her blast from the past that she has to live with her mother for a while because she can't afford rent in a small apartment. She tells this curious person that she doesn't get along with her mother and the only reason she agreed to living with her is because she travels a lot. She thinks to herself that maybe this will scare this human off. She thinks that maybe her blast from the past will finally judge her for living with her mother and would paint her like a "john", living with their parent. Surprisingly, the human tells her that he admires her ambition.

At this point, Melissa is slowly starting to feel like she can trust this human being. Her blast from the past vents to her and she does just the same. She feels relieved that maybe she can trust, just maybe. Even though the conversations are just a mere ten minutes here and five minutes there of venting, it feels like a weight has been taken off her ankles. She later confesses that she feels like she's a bad mother because she is only able to provide the bare minimum for her children. This supportive human being encourages her and tells her that there are not very many people going to college much less being a single parent and working, too.

She learns that they both are on the same boat in having first world problems.

Between the text and talking conversations there are wide gaps of days and even weeks they don't communicate. It's been three weeks and Melissa has been on the go with her kids, school, and work.

One day after her first class, he calls her.

"Hello?"

"Hey, Melly Mel, what's up?"

"Nada. Just headed to my next class. What's up?"

There is silence on the other line. She hears him sigh.

She asks, "Are you okay? What's up? Tell me."

He answers, "Fuck man. I don't know. I just…I want to come home. I miss my daughter. My life feels so fucked up right now. I'm stressed and I can't fucking… I don't know… I feel like my life is fucked up, you know? My life is fucked, man! Fuck!"

Melissa listens and responds, "Come on, your life isn't that bad. You're just having a bad day, that's all. You have a lot of good things going on for you."

He says, "No. No, I don't. I feel like shit. My life is a fucking mess."

She says, "I know you miss your daughter. I know you do, you miss her a lot. But, you are blessed with a lot of good things. You have your health. You have a really good job and it's your dream job. I still have a long ways to go before I get to my dream job. You have stable income, you have food in your stomach, and you have a roof over your head. There are a lot of people that don't have half of the things you have. So, no, bro, your life is not fucked up. Just remember that you are a good person and you have more than you could ever need. I know you miss your little girl, but regardless of the bullshit that goes on with that, I know you will see her again. Try not to stress, okay? Just focus on work and being there as much as you can for your little girl."

He answers, "Yeah, shit, you're right. I shouldn't be bitching, really, about anything. I just wanted to…"

Melissa looks at the time on her phone and interrupts him, "Shit, man. I'm so sorry, but I gotta go. Class is starting. I'll talk to you later."

He says, "Oh shit, my bad. Yeah, go to class and call me after, cool?"

She quickly says, "Yeah sure, gotta go, bye."

She hangs up her phone and goes inside the building.

As she sits at her desk and takes out her notebook and pen, she thinks about him and thinks, "Oh shit! No, Mel, no, no, no! You can't be trippin' and falling over some guy. Tie your damn fucking laces and stop trippin'."

She forgets to call and text him after class and goes to work. She goes to work, then to her last classes. Her classes come to a completion for the day. She is mentally exhausted and goes back to work. She's been working as an office assistant and a college mentor since her freshman year. She mentors college minority students. Often times, the students that come into her small cubicle are having a hard time adjusting to college life. They complain they don't have a life besides reading, writing, and studying. She talks them out of dropping out and makes the harsh reality they must endure it. She asks them if they would rather struggle paycheck to paycheck, indefinitely, once they leave college or would they rather do the reading, writing, and studying temporarily and have a degree under their belt when they are ready to apply for a high paying job later on or even furthering their education. She tells them there are a lot of people that have tried getting into college and either never start or they get in and don't finish for a variety of reasons. Each student she mentors rethinks their college drop out and decide to continue their madness of white people education. Some students tell her that they have no one that supports them in any way. She now can tell them that she is in their shoes and that no matter how much they want to give up, they can't.

After a few hours of mentoring students out of scholastic suicide, she manages to get a lot of studying in. She logs off her computer, logs in her hours, and starts to walk to the university parking garage.

Just as she is about to walk up the stairs she notices someone walking with a fast pace behind her. Her paranoia kicks in and she runs to her SUV. She makes it to her SUV. Just as she gets in, she sees a man. He must of followed her from the stairs. She frantically locks her door and tries to start her SUV. It starts. She sees him walking up to the SUV. She doesn't know what to do. She thinks to herself if she should drive off hitting him with her SUV or if she should wait and sees what happens.

She's so frantic she's still wearing her backpack on her shoulders. She leans forward, takes off her backpack, and tries to look for her phone so that she can call campus police. She can't find her phone. She's trying to stay calm, but she can't find it. The guy walks up to her SUV and taps on the window. She doesn't want to look up. She's frightened stiff. The man taps the window, again. She finds the courage to look up. The man has her cell phone. Her guard is still up. She rolls down the window enough to slide the phone through. The man apologizes and tells her he didn't mean to frighten her as she dropped it by the stairs. She tells the man "thank you" and drives off. The man walks off. She takes a moment to calm down. Her heart is still racing.

Just as she is about to make another sharp turn in the parking garage, her phone rings. She screams a high-pitched scream as her phone rings. It's her blast from the past. She answers.

"Hello?"

"Hello? Hello? Hey, what's up? How was your day?"

Melissa quickly brings herself back together.

She laughs and says, "Someone just now scared the shit out of me."

He laughs and says, "Yeah, I hate that. That happens to me at work, too. I just got off work. I was going to go eat out, but nah, I think I'm just going to stay in."

She says, "You should go out."

He says, "I would, but I'm tired. You know, I never hear that you go out to eat."

She is slightly embarrassed. She tries to play it off.

She says, "Yeah, I just don't have time. I have a lot to do, you know?"

He says, "Well, you should. Go. Now."

She says, "I can't. I just can't."

He pauses and says, "Do you want pizza? I can order it for you and the kids, some pizza, if you want. I don't know what else delivers there, but let me know. You should be able to eat out once in while."

Melissa faintly smiles.

She replies, "No. I'm good. Thanks, though. I don't want to ask you for anything. I'm not like that."

He says, "I know."

She smiles.

She says, "Well, I gotta go. I'll talk to you later."

He says, "I'll call you later. Be careful while driving. Go do something with the kids, okay? Pizza, if you want it, let me know. I'm always a text away. Talk to you soon, okay?"

"Okay."

"I mean it Melly. I'm not saying it just to say it."

"Yeah, I know."

"Okay."

"Okay.."

"Bye."

"Take care."

Melissa drives out of the parking garage and without thinking about it, she thinks about him. She holds onto his voice. It's so smooth and so soothing. It was so comforting and sounded so nice. She doesn't remember when, if ever, she's ever felt like that before.

She catches herself and tells herself, "What the hell is wrong with you? No! You can't be thinking about him. You have things to do. Remember, you have to focus."

The next night, he calls her at 1am.

She answers energetically, "Chow?"

"Hey Lady, what are you doing?"

"Reading, trying to absorb the pages of my life. You?"

"Not much just getting a naked, nasty, nasty dance at the strip club."

She laughs and says, "You're stupid."

She hangs up the phone.

He calls her back.

She laughs and answers the phone, "What? What do you want? Go get your balls licked and leave me alone."

He laughs and says, "I was joking. Yeah, I'm at the club, but I just have a few drinks when I'm here and then I go back to my room and sleep. I don't come here much."

Melissa says, "Okay, well have fun and be careful. I'll talk to later."

She hangs up.

He calls back.

Melissa looks at her phone and says to her phone, "What the fuck do you want?!"

She laughs and answers the call, "What the fuck? What you do want?"

He says, "My bad, my bad, Melly Mel. You know I've been thinking about you a lot. I know I don't ever say it, but I think I like you."

Melissa hangs up her phone and frantically turns it off.

She shakes her head and says to her phone, "dumbass."

She continues reading and heads to bed with only three hours of sleep to her name. She gets up and does what she always does in the morning. For the rest of the day, she feels a little happier. Her children make her happy everyday, but this was a weird kind of happiness. She was just very honored to have two close friends, Maddy and her blast from the past. They are there for her and make her laugh.

There are days it's hard for her to get up and deal with her exhaustion, but she punches through it. Weeks pass and it's the same routine everyday still. She takes the kids to daycare and school then goes to the university campus and then to work. When she is done for the day, she picks up the kids one-by-one and goes back to the house. Then, she has to deal with the bullshit of her landlord that is related to her by umbilical cord. The mood swings and insane logic almost becomes too much. It's been a pure minute since she's been staying at her mother's house. She knows she has already worn out her welcome. Her mother indirectly signals to her she wants her out.

Oddly, it changes like the hot summer days to the cold winter autumn as her mother is suspiciously nice to her. Melissa waits to see what her mother is up to as the atmosphere always turns into a quick quid pro quo. She finds out soon enough. Melissa's mother wants to put her kids on her tax return. Melissa refuses. Her mother's hissing tongue becomes more visible and Melissa's mother tells her she is no longer welcome at her house. The heated argument ends to her mother slamming the front door leaving.

Melissa sighs and says. "Fuck!"

She packs as much as she can. She has no place to go. She can't call home as her "parents" either never answer and when they do, they give an excuse as to why she can't talk to Grandma and Cheíí. She can't put this situation on Maddy. So, she drives around the city figuring out where to go. They end up in the parking lot of a closed business and sleep in the SUV for the night.

She falls asleep thinking, "What a fucking mess! I must be one of the shittiest mothers there are on this planet, fuck!"

Morning comes and with little to no sleep, she takes the kids to the university gym where all they take a shower and get washed up for the day. She knows the kids can eat at school and daycare, but what will she do for dinner?

She takes her kids where they need to go and heads to the university campus. She goes straight to class and charges her phone. During classes and at work, she researches online where she can go with her kids. She makes several phone calls. She finds out the shelters available are for domestic violence victims, drug addicts, and are for people that are truly homeless. She learns that she is in fact not homeless. According to the city's definition of homelessness, a homeless person is a person that does not have a vehicle.

She thinks to herself, "Well ain't that some fucked up shit?!"

It's the fourth day of sleeping in the SUV.

It's just after midnight.

Her kids are fast asleep in the back of the SUV. She's sitting in the driver's seat and she is trying to sleep. She turns on her phone to set the alarm and then puts it on silent. She tries very hard not to waste battery life since she has no way of charging her phone come nighttime. For a few minutes she looks at the photos in her phone.

She smiles to herself as she looks at photos of the day she bought her SUV. She took photos of the kids happy about the SUV. She didn't expect them to be that happy about a mere vehicle and a used one.

Just as she is about to put her phone in the small, cubby hole underneath the radio, her phone vibrates.

It's her blast from the past.

He texts her, "Hey there Melly Mel. I hope you are doing good. I'm here if you need anything. Just let me know. Been thinking about you. Hugs to you, my friend. Hope to hear from you sooner than later. Going to bed. Night."

She faintly smiles, deletes the text, and puts it under the radio. She tries her hardest to fall asleep.

The next day, she tries as hard as she can to make more phone calls and see what she can do to stay in school and find a place for the night for her and her three kids. She gives in to spending money and they sleep in a hotel for three nights. She becomes more anxious because she knows she's digging into money for dinner now. She can't donate plasma. Being anemic, she could risk her future health or even worse.

After weeks of staying in crack-driven hotels and sleeping in her SUV with her kids, one of the college students she mentors quickly notices that Melissa is not her usual upbeat self. Melissa is silent when she is asked if she's okay. She soon finds herself in a situation that is about to break her. She never stopped and took a breath and now that deep breath that will erupt into crying and maybe even giving up has sneaked up on her.

She must put herself into check and not break or even crack. When asked if she's okay, she quickly changes the subject and turns her attention to the student she's mentoring and turns on a fake happy facial expression. She knows it's awful to lie, but she has to lie to herself and tell herself that she is okay. She has no choice but to lie to herself at this very moment. She has to do this because she knows if she gives in it all could come crashing down with no warning. She has to keep going, she just has to. She leaves work not proud of what just happened. She tries desperately to fill in the cracks of her cracked, emotion-filled, concrete wall before it bursts open and collapses. She heads to her next class.

Before she enters the classroom, her phone rings. It's a call from a blocked number. She doesn't want to answer it. She ignores the call. Her phone rings again two more times. She wonders who it could be. Her phone rings again from the assumed same blocked number. She decides to answers it. It's her mother. She's crying and oddly enough sounds sober. Melissa doesn't say anything. She listens as her mother pleads with her to move back in. She tells Melissa that she's sorry and didn't mean anything she said and that she wants to have a mother-daughter relationship with her. Melissa is numb at this point. Her facial expression remains stoic and she doesn't even sigh. She's exhausted and has forced her hunger at the back of the line with the rest of her other problems.

She thinks to herself, "Fuck."

She doesn't believe anything her mother says. She knows it's all a made up anecdote, a faux fox coat, a placebo. She also knows that she has to swallow her damn pride and put up with her mother's bullshit just a little bit longer just to finish school. She doesn't say anything to her mother. Her mother continues to plead with her. She hangs up on her mother and becomes even more numb. She goes into the classroom and does what white people do with their problems. She writes the pros and cons of living back with her mother.

After just a few minutes of free writing, she circles the biggest pro, "graduating college".

She looks at the words circled on her piece of college ruled, white paper and says, "Fuck it".

She rips out the piece of paper from the notebook and crushes it into a ball and throws it in the trash.

She texts her mother that she'll be back later today or tomorrow. Her mother says dinner will be waiting both days. She feels a teeny, tiny, light inside her that is happy, it's just a spark of a spark, but at least she will have a roof over her kids' heads.

It takes less than a month, but her mother is rain dropping her bullshit again. Melissa tries her best to stay out of the house until it's dinner time. Despite this semester's bullshit, she finishes with good grades and begins another semester.

She manages to get a substantially plentiful scholarship in this new semester because of her good grades. She not only buys a nice, '03 GMC Yukon in cash, she's able to registers it, get insurance, and she finally has enough money left over to treat her kids out to eat. She doesn't eat, of course. She just wants her kids to enjoy themselves. She keeps the news of her nice SUV to herself. She doesn't tell anyone. Her mother notices the new SUV faster than flicking a flea. The sun hasn't even set when her mother asks Melissa how long her friend is going to let her borrow the SUV. Melissa already knows the routine. She ignores her mother's nosey nature and keeps studying her textbook. She already knows that whatever she tells her mother her mother will just make another submission to the grapevine.

Her mother is like a politician evil behind the curtains and nice, front and center, feeding lies to the public. Melissa knows for her mother it's an unclear conclusion, and an unclear conclusion equals make something up in her crazy mother's head. So far, her mother told people back at home that Melissa is, yet again, pregnant. All because Melissa wears baggy clothes. Melissa has lost a significant amount of weight since she's had her daughter. She just doesn't see the point in buying new clothes. Her clothes may be baggy on her, but it's still of good use. She just can't be wasting grocery and gas money at this point. Melissa doesn't care about the grapevine. She knows to tend to her own beehive.

No matter what she does, her mother finds the time to send text after text talking about her. She just ignores it. She tries to save up money to move into an apartment. She badly yearns for her own space. The few times she's able to save up money for an apartment, her mother somehow smells the money and starts nagging at her about the bills and the so-called mess that her kids make in the house. She gives her mother enough money to shut her up until her next disbursement.

She tells herself over and over, "This is only temporary. This is only temporary."

Late nights are still the same—typing, reading, and highlighting. Her blast from the past is texting her and calling her more often now. He's often up late, too.

At 2am he texts her.

"Hey. What's up, Melly Mel?"

Melissa grabs her phone and texts back right away, "Studying"

"You go, Melly Mel. I need to ask you something. I've been thinking a lot about something."

Before he sends another text, she texts, "No."

"But you don't know what I'm going to say."

"The answer is 'No'."

"haha oh Melly Mel. Aren't you curious what I'm going to say?"

"I already know."

"Oh yeah?"

"I don't want a relationship. I know that's what you want to ask me. I don't want to be with anyone. No relationship. Nope. I am not about to go through some bullshit only to be left with a broken heart, broken spirit, no. I don't want to. I have children. I am okay with not being with anyone, ever. You can go find someone. I just don't want it."

"Yeah, haha that's what I was going to ask. I'm right there with you on that. I told myself that all females are the same. They ALL are. Then we started texting, talking. I started thinking that you are different than what's out there. I've never met anyone like you. Idk what you've been through but I want to be with you."

She ignores the next few incoming text messages and turns off her phone. She tells herself that she can't be distracted. That she has a job to do. A teeny, tiny, part of her says that maybe she should take a gamble. She has known him since middle school. Even though they weren't really friends growing up, she feels that he wouldn't hurt her in any way.

Then she stops this thought and tells herself, "No. You can't! You can't fall for him. No! Fuck no!"

She continues to study. It's now 4am and she decides to call it a night. She turns her phone back on and plugs the charger into her phone. She takes a brief three-hour nap. Her phone's alarm goes off and she wakes up. She can feel her energy drag. She feels the ugly weight of being sleep deprived.

This is night number four of staying up late. She decides that she will definitely get at least six hours of sleep after tonight's study session.

She goes about her day as usual and conquers it. It's now bedtime. The house is clean and the kids go to bed. She takes a quick shower to wake herself up because it's only 10pm but she is about to fall asleep. She makes herself some coffee and sits at her small desk in the room she is staying in. Her little baby girl is so tiny and fast asleep in her bed. Melissa closes her bedroom door when she stays up late. Otherwise, her mother sighs from the bedroom across every few minutes. The annoyed sighs are loud enough for the coyotes to hear from the next mesas down.

It's now after midnight and the house is fast asleep. She takes the last soft sip of her coffee. She's reading and highlighting. Her phone vibrates. It's her blast from the past. She smiles tiredly and answers the call.

"Hey, hey, Melly Mel. Getting a lot of studying done?"

"Yeah, for the most part. I'm going to be done soon. What's up?"

"So, you haven't text me back. I just wanted to make sure you're okay."

"Yeah, I'm good. Tired, but good."

"Okay. Well I still want to help you out. You deserve to be happy, Melly Mel. I know you think about me. I can feel it. I know it. What don't you like about me? I'm a good guy. All I do is work. I want to share my life with someone. Don't you? I want to be there when you graduate. I…"

Melissa hangs up the phone. Her phone rings half a minute after she hangs up. She takes a tired deep breath and answers it.

"Hello?"

"What the fuck? Why did you hang up on me?"

"Because I told you I don't want to be with anyone, ever. Not a one night stand, nothing more than a friend, no relationship, no sugar daddy bullshit, no long distant love, fuck no to all of it. I just can't. I can't be caught up in something that will only set me back or something that will leave me having a broken heart in the end. I just can't."

"But I like you. You're more than just beautiful. You're smart. You work hard and you don't play. I like that. It would just be me and you against the world. You said you don't have anyone, but here I am."

She doesn't know what to say.

After a minute, she replies, "That's a very nice fairytale you have there, but every person that said they will be there for me has lied to me. I don't want to fall in love with you only to end up broken hearted, alone, and maybe even still in love with you. I love you as a friend. Once that line is crossed I know it will be hard to get over once we break up. I'm scared as fuck, so I am just happy with it just being me. I can rely only rely on me. Why can't you find someone else? Why me? I'm sure you have other friends or people that you're attracted to. I have a past and eventually it will surface. I know you'll use that shit against me someday. I know it. Honesty is rare these days and I know it's hard for humans to be honest. It's human nature to lie and I just don't want to deal with any of it. I am not about to be hurt and go through some bullshit, no, homie. I just..I just want to be with my kids and finish school. That is all I want. I gave up on trying to trust people and I gave up on love. That shit doesn't exist."

"I wont hurt you. I wont give up on us. All I do is work. I want to be there for you, Melly Mel. I.."

Melissa hangs up her phone. She turns it off and plugs it back into the charger.

She goes back to studying after only smiling, softly giggling, and saying to herself, "Horny fuck."

In those few minutes she gets stuck in a daydream. She imagines what it would be like. He would fly in. She would pick him up at the airport. Maybe they would go see a movie with his arm around her, or maybe they'd have a picnic in the park, or maybe they would just always laugh at stupid things like they do when they talk on the phone. Then, she stops herself, sighs, and goes back to studying. She studies for three more hours and calls it quits. She turns her phone back on, sets the alarm, and goes to sleep.

It's now over a year. Her blast from the past calls her often now and they talk like close friends do. Besides Maddy, he's the only other trustworthy friend she has.

One evening, she has dinner with Maddy at the house. She finally has the courage to tell Maddy about her blast from the past. Maddy doesn't hold back her excitement.

Maddy says, "Well, you lucky son of a bitch! That's awesome! I'm so happy for you. How's it going, I mean what did he exactly say? I mean he knows you have kids, right?"

She softly laughs and answers, "Yeah, he does. He offers to help me, but I've already told him, 'fuck no!'. I mean you know how I am. I am not like that. I'm scared Maddy. I think I like him. Fuck! I know I like him, but all the 'what if's' pop into my head. I don't even know how this happened. He found me on social media. We just started messaging. I wanted to focus so I was going to get rid of my account. Before I got rid of my account, he gave me his number and told me I could vent to him whenever. Then it started from there, but lately he's been calling me telling me he wants to be with me. He says he won't hurt me and wants do whatever it takes to be with me. I just… don't know. Am I being stupid? My head and heart start arguing when he texts and when we talk. My head throws my heart in the cupboard and tells it I don't have time for this bullshit, you know?… Fuck!"

Maddy laughs and replies, "Giiiiirl, you know you better get that! There ain't no man coming after a woman with kids. Plus, you know you'll regret it later. Girl, you have no time for later! Shit! Hell, I'd say 'fuck it' and see if he's going to put with all the bullshit with your mom and school. You never know. It's crazy that shit like this happens when you don't want it to. Ooooh Giiiirl!"

She is still confused about how to feel about her blast from the past. They finish eating dinner. She walks Maddy out to her SUV and they hug. She tells Maddy that she really does appreciate their friendship. Maddy tells her she knows what it's like not to trust anyone. Maddy tells her she better get some sleep and she will see her tomorrow.

Before Maddy drives off, Maddy yells out the driver's side window. "You better get that dick, girl!"

Melissa puts her hands over her face in embarrassment and says. "What the fuck?"

Maddy laughs, honks her horn, and drives off waving to Melissa. She waves back and smiles.

She is happier as the days press on and Maddy notices.

Melissa and Maddy have a conversation as Melissa drops off her baby girl.

"Good morning, girl! Heyyyyy so did you get some or what?"

"Ha ha, Nooooooo! I'm just happy. I haven't said I was going to give in to him. I'm just happy. I'm scared as fuck, though!"

Maddy laughs and says, "Melly Mel, it's okay. You'll be okay. Give it time. You'll feel it in your heart. I know you will. He seems like a good guy. Giiiiiiirl, I'm telling you, you better get that while you can."

Melissa laughs.

She says, "I don't know. I'm not worried about it. It'll be okay either way. I know it will. It has to be."

She hugs and kisses her baby girl and son good-bye. She leaves to take her oldest son to school across town.

As soon as she's on campus, her phone 'dings'. It's a text message. She reads it while she's entering the campus building.

The text reads, "Good Morning, Melly Mel. Kick ass at school there miss lady. The weather is just right today. Usually it's hot and no clouds. Today there's a slight breeze. I'm planning to maybe come fly in this weekend. I'm going to try and get my daughter see if I can spend some time with her."

She finds a seat and gets out her notebook and a pen. She looks at her phone and reads the text message again. She smiles.

She texts him back, "Good Morning, Mr. Rico. I shall indeed. Been a busy morning as usual. I have a test today and I'm confident I studied well enough. I'm not worried about it. I just want it out of the way. You're lucky. It's hot here, dry, not as hot and dry as the Rez, but enough to make me sweat when I run to classes. A breeze would be nice. Awww! That's sweet. I hope you get to see her. Nothing compares to spending time with the sweet baby."

He texts back, "Yeah, I need to go home. You're just right there you can go home anytime you want."

She texts, "Nah. Not for me. I have to save money or wait until the beginning of the semester when my student loans and scholarships come in. If I could go home more often, I would. The only people I want to see are my grandparents. I miss them."

She sends a second text, "Okay. Putting my phone on silent. I have three more classes after this one. I'll talk you later. Class is about to start."

Before she taps the 'send' button, she adds, "hugs" with a winking emoji following. She quickly deletes it, and slowly retypes "hugs" followed by a winking emoji. She reads the entire text message, again. She stares at the words reading "hugs" with the cheesy emoji wondering if she should just send it. Now, she just wants to delete the entire text message. She deletes "hugs" and the wink emoji, but doesn't muster the courage to press that nagging 'send' button.

The professor walks into the room and tells everyone to turn their phones off and get out a pen for the exam.

She quietly says to herself, "fuck it". She retypes "hugs" with the wink emoji and quickly sends it. She panics and quickly regrets it. The embarrassment is quickly forgotten about as she puts her phone in her bag. She mentally recites all the criminal law terms she been memorizing for the past three weeks.

The class gets settled and it becomes quieter than the city morgue. The only sounds are the echoing scratches of pens against the tables and people flipping over stapled pages with their hands. The professor stands near the door and dismisses anyone that tries to come into the lecture hall. The test is eight pages long. The first half is multiple choice. The next half is fill-in-the-blank. The final part is the most grueling, an essay on three questions of her choice. She flies through the exam concentrating with her every brain cell on every word and question. With about half of the class remaining, she is finally done. She flips through the pages and checks her answers four times making sure she marked and wrote in the correct answers. She's confident about the exam, turns it in, and leaves the lecture hall.

She checks the time and realizes she finished the exam surprisingly early. She still has two hours until her next class. She decides she can get some hours in at work. So, she heads to the other side of campus.

Seven minutes later, she arrives at work. No one is checked in for her to mentor and there is nothing on the to-do checklist, so she takes out her textbook and starts taking notes for her next class. Her phone doesn't get a signal inside the building, so she turns it off and charges it.

An hour later, the office has a luncheon for employees. There is three rectangular tables of sub sandwiches, an array of chips, freshly cut vegetables, bottled Gatorade, chocolate sprinkled donuts, and freshly brewed and boxed Einstein Bagel's coffee. She doesn't want to make it seem like she's at work that day solely for the food. She doesn't get up from her cubicle.

She's been stressing lately. She's only paid for half of her tuition placing her in debt with the university. If she doesn't pay it before the end of the semester, she won't be able to register for classes leading to a wave of problems. She was awarded a substantial scholarship, but the scholarship office has yet to pay her student account. So, she's been on a vice choking budget for the last month and a half. She calculates with the scholarship she will be able to pay off her remaining tuition, fees, and be able to buy essentials in bulk.

She uses the office phone and calls the scholarship office while her coworkers dive in head first into the table of food. After fifteen minutes of an endless ringing tone, she gets through. They tell her the original scholarship check was mailed to the wrong office on the university campus. Thus in turn voiding out the original check. Fortunately, they quickly mailed another check to the correct office. They said it could a range of a month or until the end of the semester for the amount to be credited into her student account. She feels the stress rise. She knows the end of the semester is just a mere three months away.

Frustrated and have been living off of beans and rice for the past three months, she slams the office phone down, sighs, and says. "Fuck."

The money budget's vice breaks her phone bill. She has no choice but to let her phone cancel its' service. She doesn't feel anything about it. She keeps running as fast as she can in her large, metal, thin, hamster wheel. For the next week she takes every chance she gets and applies for every campus job online, but runs into no such luck.

While on campus one morning, she luckily runs into a retired judge she used to work with at the attorney's office. The conversation lands her a housesitting job for a week. She's barely able to keep her money boat from sinking. She's paid to simply occupy, clean, and water the house plants. The homeowner is aware she has kids and doesn't hesitate to tell her she's more than welcome to bring the kids to help housesit. She's more than relieved. She's finally able to have some peace and quiet with her kids for the week. Watering the green, lush, backyard lawn, playing with the small, white, Chihuahua "Princess", and eating the veganlicious food was more than enough motivation to see exactly what she's working her ass off for.

She can't imagine a house like this on the Rez. The modern, tan, adobe-like house is screaming her name. From it's exposed, clear varnished, log ceilings to its' white, marble counter tops to it's peaceful study room to its' inviting backyard barbecue made of flagstone to the shelves and shelves of books, she wants something to call her own—"home".

She soaks in the quietness of the house. For a moment, she imagines it's her house. She closes her eyes and smiles.

Soon, the week is over. The homeowners, an elderly couple, return. They're amazed how well she cleaned. They tell her "Princess" is pleased. They refer her to other housesitting and babysitting gigs. She's grateful. Even though she's paying for gas out of pocket, she takes it day by day. She doesn't spend a hair of a penny more than she should on anything.

After a month, her scholarship check comes in. Her tuition gets paid off. She buys everything she needs in bulk, fills up her gas tank, and changes her

SUV's oil. The very last thing she does is turn her phone back on.

With her phone back on, she activates her social media. She posts a meme from the movie, "Half Baked". It's a meme of the film's fast food scene. A guy is on the microphone saying, "fuck you, fuck you, you're cool, and fuck you, I'm out." She decides to keep her social media on. For some reason, she feels good to post about life's frustrations and to her luck, it's expressed in one meme. She doesn't go back onto social media until a few days later. She surprisingly, sees a post from her blast from the past. He posted a Tech N9ne concert on her profile and asked her if she wants to go. As much as she wants to go, she can't. Not only does she not have the time, she doesn't have the money, and she sure as hell doesn't want to feel guilty for doing something for herself without her kids.

Nonetheless, that doesn't stop her from imagining it for a few moments—standing in line at the concert feeling the excitement and the concert rush. Feeling a sense of relaxation and down time for once. She imagines walking next to him going inside, sitting by each other, laughing together, and just having a good time. She finds happiness in just wishing it alone in her spaced out moment. Even when she bitch slaps herself in the face with reality, she still smiles about the idea of possibly having fun with him.

She replies to the post online a few days later. She tells him she really wishes she could go, but she is slammed with school. He immediately replies and comments he got pulled back to work that weekend so it wasn't a biggie.

For the next month, they comment on each other's social media, mostly about silly stuff and laughing together about random things.

One late night after a very long day, he calls her.

"Hey homie, what's yo flay-va?"

He laughs and says, "Why hello there, lady. My flay-va? Well, I've been wanting it to be you. Whatcha doin'?"

"Reading and highlighting, you?"

"When can you read me and highlight me?"

She shakes her head, laughs, and hangs up.

He calls back. She answers, but doesn't say anything.

"What the fuck?! I get it okay, okay. But I'm serious Melly let me take care of you."

She hangs up before he says anything else. He calls back. She answers, again.

"Do you know where I am?"

"Having a drink at a bar. I'm assuming a strip club?"

He laughs and says, "Yeah. But I am not here for what you think. I just like the laid back atmosphere here, you know? It's just something I do just to do it. I don't get drunk. I just want to relax. I come to clubs off and on. I thought coming here would fill that void, you know, being lonely and shit. But, that changed since we've been talking. I like you. I mean I really, really, like you. I am here to just relax and it got me thinking. You know…I just want that for you. I want you to be able to relax. I want that for you so bad. I bet you haven't spent any time for you. Have you? Oh, and I lied. I'm not at the strip club or even a bar. I'm at Applebee's. Just having a cold one. Thinking about you. Once we started talking on the phone I stopped going to bars altogether. I don't have that lonely feeling anymore. I don't know what it is about you, but you have something special, homie. I can feel it when we talk. You're real."

"What do you really want?"

"I want you. I want you to trust me. All I do is work. I don't fuck off. I don't mess with anyone. I see the fire in you, that fire that you have, Mel's fire. I want that in my life. I promise I will never leave you, hurt you. I will be here for you. Fuck all those fucks that tried fucking you over. You're a good lady, Melly Mel. And that's what I want. All these years I've been single. Been wanting to be single and not giving a fuck about anything or anyone, that was, until I met you."

She says, "I gotta go. I have a lot of studying to do. I'll call you tomorrow. Be safe, okay? Take a cab. I'll talk to you later."

He says, "Okay, Melly Mel, I sure will. Think about what I said and I'll talk to you later."

Melissa says softly, "Okay, bye."

She hangs up the phone. She looks at her phone. She puts her phone up to her nose like she's smelling it. She holds her phone just for a few more seconds and sighs. She is no longer confused. She is starting to admire his honesty. She tells herself he's a good guy, but what else does that mean?

The next day, he calls her just as she's coming out of her second class and heading to work. She answers her phone.

"Hey Melly! So listen, uh, I am flying in tomorrow afternoon. Any chance you could come pick me up? All these fucks that I text haven't text me back. I'll put in gas. I thought maybe we could go have dinner or something. I just have some things to do in town for a day then I have to fly back out."

"Okay, yeah, sure. You can use my ride if you want. You'd just have to drop me back off on campus and pick me up at 4."

"Nah, I don't want to use your ride. I didn't expect you to say that. Thanks, though. I just need a ride from the airport then we can get something to eat after. My flight is coming in around 1130 so, I'd say around noon?"

"Okay yeah, perfect. See you tomorrow."

"Cool."

She hangs up.

She finishes her day on campus and is able to get some sleep that night.

The next morning, she goes to class. He texts her he's boarding his plane. She texts back she will head over to the airport around noon. Her second class is canceled so she heads to work and prints out some papers.

It's now time to pick up her blast from the past. She knows he's still on the plane because he hasn't text her back, yet. When she's half way to the airport he texts her.

"Hey, lady. I just landed."

"Okay, cool. I'm on my way."

She is very nervous, either because the last time she saw him was in middle school or because she's been fighting herself to admit that maybe she likes him. Either way, she knows she is fucked. She drives up to the airport arrival portal. She drives very slowly as she texts him a description of the SUV.

There he is.

He's standing on the curb with his huge, black, duffel bag. She pulls up. He opens the back door, puts his duffel bag in the back seat, and hops in the front seat. The nervousness strikes her like a lightning bolt, strong, fierce, and without warning. She's never been so nervous. The palms of her hands sweat and slip as she grips the steering wheel. She doesn't want to make eye contact. She slightly turns her head, but keeps her eyes at the slow traffic driving around her. She finds the courage to look his way. She looks at him and smiles.

He smiles and says, "Hey what's going on, Melly Mel?"

She smiles and says, "Not much, same ol' bullshit. How was your flight?"

"It was good, I slept. Been tired."

"That's good. So, where to?"

"Oh, yeah. What kind of food are you in the mood for? It's your call."

"I don't know. Doesn't matter. I have no idea what places there are to eat."

"Wanna go check out Olive Garden?"

"Sure."

The entire drive becomes less and less nerve wracking as she drives through each stoplight. She realizes that he doesn't care if she's nervous. He just wants to have a conversation and just catch up. Thinking this settles her nerves a lot. Because of her nervousness earlier, it made her jaw tense up. They get to the restaurant. She parks. He tells her she has a nice ride. She happily tells him she just recently bought it. They head inside. They get seated and order their food. The food comes quickly.

As they eat, they talk about his work, her college experience, and they both are seemingly exhausted. Her jaw really hurts now. She can no longer open her jaw to chew her pasta. She stops eating and feels embarrassed. He notices she stopped eating rather quickly.

"You can order soup, if you don't like the pasta."

She doesn't panic. She's now more embarrassed. She thinks that he thinks she's a picky eater when she's not. She is too embarrassed to say anything about her jaw. Nonetheless, he orders soup for her. She takes her time softly slurping it. He barely touches his food. He tells her he's just tired and wants to check into the hotel. They take their food to go and he surprisingly orders three more entrées to go. He tells her it's for the kids. She's shocked and wasn't expecting that.

Before they leave, she goes to the restroom to freshen up. She washes her hands. She looks at herself in the mirror. She looks exhausted. Her hair is a little bushy. She has slight bags under her eyes. She gives herself a faint smile and she exits the restroom.

They leave the restaurant. He asks her to drop him off at a nearby bar and grill. She thanks him for the food. He offers her $200, but she doesn't take it. He grabs his duffel bag and they part ways. She spaces out again for half a second and thinks it would be nice to have someone there for her for once, but she knows that will never happen. That wish will stay as is, just a thought, a wish, and not anywhere close to reality.

She drives back to the house and puts the food in the fridge, goes back to campus, and heads to work. Today at work they are having a banquet in one of the university banquet rooms. She heads over and helps set up. She finishes and waits for her coworkers to show up.

As she's waiting, he texts her, "So, the thing I was waiting on for work didn't work out. The guy I counted on bailed. I was supposed to start work here and be here in Albq."

"Shit, that sucks. I'm sorry. What are you going to do now?"

"Well, I was only here to meet up with an old coworker but he bailed. I booked a hotel room but I end up cancelling it. Then, I booked a flight back. I have to go back to work. I just wanted to see if this would work out here. But it fell through. I'm just gonna fly back. I text one of my other bros. He's supposed to take me to the airport. But no word from him. I'm going to miss my flight it leaves in 25 mins. I won't make it."

She reads it and texts back, "Damn. You should of told me. I wouldn't of had a problem taking you to the airport."

He texts, "Nah, I'm good. Fuck it. Guess I'll just get a room like I planned. I'll take a cab or something."

As soon as she's done reading it, she gets busy and has to mingle with the students she's been mentoring. She puts her phone away.

Three months pass. It's the usual, daily merry-go-round, single mom life, school, ducking the fire breathing dragon, and figuring out how she's going to survive until the next disbursement.

One afternoon while eating lunch, he texts her.

"Hey Mel. What's goin' on?"

"Nothing. Just about to head to work. What's up? How's work?"

"Same ol', same ol'. I'm planning to come home. Any chance you could help me out? I need a ride to Grants to pick up my mom's car. I'll put in gas for you."

"Don't worry about gas. Day and time, homie."

"Saturday at 1"

"Okay, sure."

"Okay, cool. Thanks. See you then."

"How's your daughter?"

"She's good. I'm going to pick her up. That's the reason I'm coming back."

"That's nice. I hope you see her and spend as much time with her as you can."

The day comes. She owns her style—yoga pants, v-neck, university t-shirt, and running shoes. She doesn't think much when she dresses like this. She just knows it's comfortable and affordable. Her aunt and uncle are in town. As the sun rises, they quickly chase her out of the house to do something for her and have some "me-time". She thinks it's funny. She doesn't know what that means to any extent. She hugs and kisses her boys and little girl before her uncle shoves her out of the house and tells her to "get". She goes to a local coffeehouse and reads until it's time for her to leave. Hours later, she leaves the coffeehouse.

She picks up her blast from the past from the airport and they drive straight to Grants. She can tell he's exhausted, so she doesn't say anything. He falls asleep in the passenger seat while she drives with the radio on. She wakes him up as she parks the SUV in front of Love's. They open their door to get out of the SUV. He gets out first and walks around the back of the SUV and starts to walk up the driver's side.

She gets out, closes her door, and steps up on the sidewalk.

He's ten feet behind her standing in front of the back door of the driver's side.

She takes a few steps and feels his eyes on her.

She turns around.

As she looks at him, she sees his eyes on her butt. He smiles and quickly looks up.

She thinks to herself, "Oh, my God."

She nervously asks him, "Did you need the keys or are you going inside?"

He makes eye contact with her, smiles, and says calmly, "Yeah, I'm going inside."

She smiles back, turns back around, and starts walking towards the entrance. She hears him walk behind her.

She thinks to herself, "Oh, my God. I hope he's still not checking me out. Oh, my god. Is he still checking me out?"

She can fill his eyes go up and down her body as she walks.

As she walks into the bathroom, she says to herself, "I can't believe he was checking out my ass."

Minutes later, they both come back out and go to the SUV. She goes to the back of the SUV and grabs his duffel bag.

He grabs it from her and says, "I got it. I got it, Melly."

She says, "You should buy an energy drink. You're tired."

He says, "Yeah, I will. Alright, well I gotta get going, Melly Mel."

They walk to the parking lot on the side of Love's where his mom's white station wagon is parked. He stops at the driver's side back tire. He puts his duffel bag on the ground and starts to bend down next to the back tire.

As he bends down reaching behind the tire, she raises one eyebrow. She checks out her blast from the past's cute butt. It's perfect in her opinion. Even with it barely noticeable under his baggy jeans, she sees it's firm.

He finds the car keys, opens, the back door, and puts his duffel bag in the backseat. He closes the door and turns around.

He smiles and says, "Thanks, homie."

He takes a step forward and reaches his arms out to hug her. His hug lasts but a mere five seconds, but to her it felt like forever. Oddly, she discreetly sneaks a whiff of his shoulder and neck. Time freezes. She closes her eyes. She thinks it would be nice to have someone like him by her side. The hug ends.

She says, "Alright, I'll see you later. Drive safe."

"Okay, Melly Mel. Yeah, I'll see you later. Thanks. Thanks for everything."

With nothing else to say and feeling a little bit awkward, she turns and starts walks back to the SUV. She can feel him watching her walk away.

She says to herself, "Is he watching me walking away?"

She quickly stops, turns around, smiles, and waves at him.

He waves back and smiles. He looks slightly embarrassed. She caught him watching her butt as she's walking away.

She turns back around and starts walking.

She smiles and says to herself, "Fuck, he's watching me walk away."

She smiles and gets into her SUV. She gets settled in the driver's seat and sits there for a minute. They both start their vehicles. They both drive in reverse and back out of the parking spot. He ends up driving behind her. They separate at the bridge getting onto the freeway. Before she goes out of his sight, he honks the horn and flashes his headlights. She smiles and laughs to herself. She returns the honks. They both merge onto the freeway and in opposite directions.

The next day, he texts her. He tells her he is not able to get his daughter. They talk about his frustration. She tries to cheer him up. He tells her he has to go back to work. He's already booked his flight and is leaving back to work next week. He asks her if they can meet back at Love's gas station in Grants. She tells him it's not a problem.

The time comes. They meet back up at Love's in Grants. He offers to drive. She obliges. He notices she's tired and tells her to take a nap. She does. She wakes up as he pulls into the departing terminal of the airport. He gets out of the SUV, grabs his duffel bag, and closes the back door. She is still standing at the passenger door trying to wake up. He comes up to her. He hugs her. She has another moment of spacing out. She imagines him kissing her. She quickly snaps out of it as they separate from the hug. She notices that he noticed she was getting an extra close during the hug. With just inches away from each other, he smiles at her. She faintly smiles back. It looks like he wants to say something.

Just as he's about to say something, she interrupts and says, "Well, you better get going. Don't want you being late and rushing for your flight."

She quickly walks around the front of the SUV, gets in the driver seat, and puts her seat belt on.

She feels him staring at her, so she looks out the passenger seat window. She rolls down the window.

He says, "Bye, Mel. Drive safe."

Without thinking, she says, "Okay, bye, I'll miss you!"

Inside her head she quickly panics.

She thinks, "Fuck! Why did I say that?! Fuck!"

Embarrassed, she smiles and waves anyway.

Through the passenger window he smiles and says, "I'll miss you, too, Melly Mel."

He starts walking along the sidewalk. From the driver's seat, she watches him walk inside the building. Just as he gets inside the building, he turns around. He smiles and waves to her. She smiles, laughs to herself, and waves back.

He turns around and starts walking.

She laughs to herself and says, "Yeah, I was watching your ass walk away."

She arrives back to the house. The house is empty. She goes to the fridge. Her aunt taped an envelope with her name on it. She opens it. Inside the envelope there's $40 and a note. The note reads:

Your Grandma and Cheíí said to go to a movie or go get something to eat. NOW!

She smiles. She takes the money and goes to the movies. She writes on the back of the note:

Thank you Grandma and Cheíí! I love you! Movies it is :)

She puts the note back into the envelope and heads to the movies. She picks a chick flick to watch. She buys herself a small popcorn, small soda, and a pickle.

For once in her entire life, she feels at peace.

She tells herself to hold onto that very moment for she doesn't want it go away, ever.

Chapter 15. A New Destination

"I cannot see you graduate college for I will no longer be in this world, but listen when I say the Moon will be there for you, always, and [the Moon] promised me you will be protected and happy."

-Frank Nez

It's nearing the end of the semester. She decided to make this semester different. She decides to take two classes that are only eight weeks at the beginning of the semester. Her two other classes are only two weeks long total and it's at the end of the semester. She wants to spend more time with the kids and it works out perfectly. She finishes the first two classes. Soon, she has to take her last two classes. Her classes are back to back. One class is one week with the second class following the next week. Both classes are Monday through Friday from 7am until 7pm. She masters her first course, an American studies course. She enjoys it. She glides through the first course and begins her second week-long class. She has never ever been more excited to go to class. Her second class is a conspiracy theories class.

One her first day of class during the lunch hour, her blast from the past texts her.

"Hey, how are classes are going?"

"It's awesome. It's only the first say and I am completely hooked haha. I wish this class was longer than a week.

They don't text anymore and they both go about their usual day.

The next day in class he texts her.

"What's up, how are you?"

"Hey. It's going well. I'm excited for class today. This is my last class of the semester. It's really interesting. It's a conspiracy theories class. The lectures are crazy as fuck. Very interesting. Intriguing. Haha. What's up with you?"

"Are you doing anything for the three-day weekend coming up?"

She looks at her calendar.

"I don't have anything planned."

"You should take a road trip with the kids or go do something with them."

"Well, my dad and stepmom are taking the kids. Family picnic in the mountains. I'm not going though. I'm just gonna chill haha."

She just realizes it's a three-day weekend. She texts her dad how long he is going to have the boys. He responds and saying he's hoping for the entire three-day weekend. He says he's been meaning to ask her if he could, in fact, have the kids over for the entire weekend since he never sees them. She thinks about Grandma and Cheíí and how happy they'd be to see the kids. She agrees. Class begins.

Her phone vibrates.

He's calling her.

She denies the phone call and texts him that she's in class.

He apologizes and asks her to call him after class.

She texts him that she will and puts her phone away.

In the next four hours, she absorbs every piece of information coming out of the conspiracy theories professor's mouth. She is floored. She knew about half of the information he elaborated on. Still, she is stunned and even more excited for tomorrow's class. The class is now over. She feels the mental exhaustion set in as she begins the drive home. The class is at branch campus, a 45 minute drive. She counts her change and puts in $11.09 in for gas. She goes home, has dinner with the boys, takes a shower, studies her notes for an hour, and goes to bed. She does most of her work in class, so she actually doesn't have homework for the very first time. She's happy as she's able to get at five hours of sleep.

At 1am, she gets a phone call. It's her brother. He got kicked out of a club and wants her to come pick him up. She wakes up her mother. She tells her she will be right back and if she could watch the kids. She tells herself if she hears her mother sneer in the darkness she will say "fuck it" and go back to sleep.

Surprisingly, her mother agrees. She puts her baby girl next to her mother. She drives into the city night life only wearing a sports bra, tank top, short shorts, and flip flops. She doesn't have time to grab anything else, but a hoodie. She arrives at the strip club and goes inside. There he is slumped over breathing heavily, drunk—black out mode. She annoyingly sighs and is grateful to get help from bystanders to get him into her SUV. Once she's in the SUV, she asks him where his wallet, phone, and house keys are. He's too drunk to even realize she's talking to him. He passes out. She checks his pocket and realizes she has to go back inside for all three.

She goes back inside and luckily, gets all three from the bartender. The bartender invites her to stay and even offers her a free drink. She laughs, takes a shot, and leaves the bar. She parks in front of the garage. She tells her brother to snap out of it because she doesn't have the strength to carry him inside. Severely sloshed, her brother is able to make it back into his bedroom in her mother's house. She goes back to her mother's room, tells her she's back, and takes her baby girl back to her room. Through the paper-thin walls, she hears her brother's wet, thick puke, spew into a something plastic. It doesn't long as she hears her mother's footsteps stomp from the bedroom to his room. She hears her brother's room door open. She hears her mother ask him if he's okay. As she lies on her bed, she looks up at the ceiling listening to them talk.

Her brother yells. "No, just leave it. Just let me be drunk. Leave it alone. Let me be!"

Her mother asks, "What happened? Are you okay? Here let me get you some water."

She sets the alarm on her phone. Her brother barfs for two hours. It sounds like his throat was drier than dirt being poured down a plastic pipe. It sounds like he's throwing up on an empty stomach. He made a, "huuuuuuuuuuuuh!" gagging sound, but nothing came out. She imagines his face turning red, ears moving, and neck muscles extract with vengeance as he gags himself. She sighs and blows a soft raspberry. She turns to her side and forces herself to fall asleep.

Just as she's falling asleep, she starts an aroma of a sour liquor stench seeps under her door. Irritated, she opens her window and manages to fall asleep.

With two hours of sleep, she gets the kids ready, drops them off, and then heads to her class across the county. The professor is kind today and provides donuts, coffee, muffins, and breakfast burritos with green chile for the class. He somehow miscounted his students ordering three times as much food. He forces students to take more food and coffee. She drinks enough cups of coffee to wake up her soul.

It's a little after 9 o' clock now. Just as the coffee kicks in and the guinea pigs in their wheels start to spin faster, he texts her. She grabs her phone out of the front pocket of her backpack.

"Good morning, Melly Mel."

"Good morning, Mr. Rico."

"What's up?"

"In class, learning some tripped out shit and it's very interesting. And yourself?"

"Well, I've been thinking. I think I'm going to check out Vegas this weekend."

"Vegas, NM. Why would you want to go there?"

"Haha. Very funny, Melly. But yeah, I have some bros there that I haven't seen in a while."

She puts her phone on her lap and starts taking notes. Her phone vibrates and vibrates with incoming text messages, but she ignores it. The professor clutches her hearing and seeing senses as he talks about the Roswell, New Mexico conspiracy theory. Her eyes and ears become obsessed on the lecture as if it was her new religion. Her right hand starts to hurt from pressing her BIC pen against the college rule paper. She becomes so intrigued by the information that she hardly blinks. She doesn't move anything other than her pen and her head to look at what she's writing and to look back up at the slides.

Besides learning about different aspects of the law, this is another fascination of hers—aliens, bigfoot, conspiracy theories, and all the information suppressed from her reach. Listening to the, now exposed, secret ingredients makes her feel high and giddy like she just won a million dollars. She opens her eyes more as she dives deeper into the euphoria of undocumented and documented alien life. She feels a rush of blood waking up her nerves with excitement. It's a tidal wave of utter bliss and a weird satisfaction.

The professor concludes the class indicating it's now lunch time. Her heart all the way to her soul is content. She feels revived with an intangible enlightenment. The class is a breath of fresh air. The last time she felt this way was when she first wanted to go to school to be a marine biologist. She feels like she's been given shots of endorphins and it runs deep in her veins reaching all the way to her soul.

Smiling, she stands up. Her phone on her lap falls onto the floor. She fell so much into a trance she forgot her phone was on her lap. She picks it up. She decides she wants to eat lunch outside on the grass. She usually just eats on the tables just outside of the classroom or in her SUV, but today, she wants to breathe in fresh air molecules. She thinks maybe she'll see an UFO. She grabs her brown paper bag out of her backpack and sits in the grass under the shade next to a tree.

As she gets comfortable, takes out her turkey sandwich out, two women come and sit facing her. They introduce themselves and talk about class. They, too, have been given shots of endorphins. As she talks with them, she can hear it in her voice. She's genuinely happy. Despite all the bullshit she has to deal with on a daily basis, life's not as bad as she thinks it is. She feels like she's on the right path. Her spirit feels refreshed. The two women are just beginning the college experience. They are much older than her. Lunch is over and they head back to class. Her phone was buzzing, but she too stuck in another galaxy to notice.

She gets to her seat. She has two missed calls and sixteen text messages, all from her mother. She makes a quick call to see what's going on. Her mother asks her what she's doing this weekend, as if she has a family vacation planned or something. She tells her she has nothing planned. Her mother rants on saying she's inviting people over. Which, translates to, "I'm having people over and I don't want you or the kids there". She tells her mother she has to go and they'll her phone starts to vibrate. She overlooks her crazy mother's texts and looks at what her blast from the past texts her.

"Hey. How's class going? It's about to rain so I think I'm getting off early."

She decides to text him back.

"Nice. Now you can go have a beer and get some down time."

"Nah. I'm tired. I'm just going to take my food to go and go back to my room."

"You better get some rest."

"Come to Vegas with me."

"Vegas?"

"Yeah, Vegas."

"I can't."

"Why can't you?"

"I don't have any money and I just don't want to put you out like that."

"I'm offering. Bring the kids. You guys can leave Friday as soon as you're done with class. I'll take care of it don't worry. You deserve a break, Melly Mel. Do this for you. Let me help you dammit. Haha."

She softly giggles as she reads the text. She puts her phone down. She doesn't mean to, but once again she spaces out. She thinks about how it would be, getting on plane with the kids, the kids being excited, checking in to the hotel room, going sightseeing, and most of all, being there with one of the best friends she's ever had. Someone that didn't judge her for any reason at all. She tells herself it sounds so damn cheesy, but it sounds like a dream and sadly, it will probably just stay as so. A minute of imagining made her extremely high, high enough to smile and softly sigh, and smile again.

The discussion of aliens quickly forces its' attention on her and she dives right back into listening to the untold truth of life on another planet. She starts to take notes. Without any regard, something weird happens. The professor pauses. He looks around the room. Then, he looks at her. Then, he scans the room, again. The professor breaks the unforeseen silence.

The unpredictable fairy of fate makes the professor say, "I'm glad you've decided to take this course. This course will change your life because you can't find out the truth if you choose to stay blind to it."

At this very moment, she takes this as a huge sign of destiny pimp slapping her in the face.

She texts him back, "Homie, you win. I'd be honored to go."

She smiles, does this weird thing of putting her phone up to her nose, and closes her eyes. She opens her eyes and puts her phone back in her backpack.

She centers her high towards the rest of the alien lecture. Soon, the class is over. She picks up the kids and asks them if they would like to go Vegas instead of Tohatchi. They immediately tell her they don't want to go to Vegas. They tell her they've been looking forward to going back to Tohatchi. She tries to convince how fun Vegas it's going to be. Her kids remain adamant and they come up with a clear solution. They tell her she can go to Vegas and they can go to Tohatchi— everybody wins. She's stumped. She wonders why they don't want to see Vegas. Later that evening, they tell her they miss Tohatchi and want to see the new puppies her uncle has. Her kids tell her they choose Tohatchi over a scorching, blazing, city full of strangers and bad luck.

After dinner, she breaks the news to her blast from the past. He tells her he doesn't mind. The conversation is short as she still has to write a final paper. She works on her paper as her kids play monopoly on the floor in front of her in the living room.

Just as she finishes up her paper, they text back and forth. He's booking the plane ticket. After a few minutes, he tells her it's official—she's coming to Vegas. Since she's done with her paper and it's still fairly early before bedtime, she wants to take the kids to the park.

The boys get into the SUV. As she's buckling in her little girl, her dad pulls up in his truck and parks behind her SUV. She smiles, tilts her head, and makes a puzzled facial expression. Her dad gets out of the truck. He comes up and hugs her. She tells him she thought she was meeting him in Grants tomorrow. He tells her something came up and he has to take the kids now. She turns to her boys and asks them if they want to go now. They get excited and race inside the house and start packing.

She laughs to herself and says under her breath, "Well ain't that some shit?"

She invites her dad inside, but he refuses. She tells him she's going inside the house and will be right out. Her dad gets the toddler's car seat and puts it in his truck.

Ten minutes later, Melissa and the boys come out of her mother's house. The boys run to the truck and get in. She holds her baby girl reluctant to let her go. Her little girl starts to cry and push herself off of Melissa. Melissa laughs. She puts her little girl on the ground. Her little girl runs to the truck screaming happily. She picks her daughter back up when she reaches the truck.

She looks at her daughter and says, "Do you want to go, sweety?"

Her little daughter yells. "Mama, I wanna go! Please, I wanna go!"

She looks into her little baby's eyes and says, "Are you sure? You won't cry for me?"

Her little princess says, "No mama. I won't cry. I want to go see old gramma! Old Cheíí!"

She kisses her cheek and says, "Okay, gimme a kiss and you can go."

She quickly shoves Melissa's face away and points to her car seat.

Melissa laughs.

She puts her daughter in the car seat. The boys get out of the truck and hug her. Melissa's dad gets in and says they have to get on the road. She tells her boys they better help Old Grandma and Cheíí. They smile and say they will. She closes the truck door. Her boys and little girl wave as the truck slowly drives off. She stands and watches the truck disappear around the corner. She sighs. She stands there and looks at the other houses in front of her. A slight breeze starts to blow through the leaves of the tall trees she sees in backyards.

Her phone 'dings'. She takes her phone out of her back pocket and reads the text from her blast from the past.

"What do you really want?"

He sends another text, "What do YOU want? Really want?"

She opens the text message. She looks at the digital keyboard and the flashing texting cursor on her phone screen.

She texts, "Be a good mom, finish law school, my own firm, a house back at home on the land my grandma gave me, take a few family vacations, see the beach, listen to the waves, I've always wanted to see UCLA, the law school there, walk on a pier with the ocean beneath my feet, and most of all, just make my Grandma and Cheíí proud of me."

Moments later he texts back, "Okay. I promise it'll happen."

She smiles and looks at her phone and puts it in her back pocket. She decides she wants to go for a run. She changes her clothes and visits the local law school campus. Next to the law school is a dirt trail. She runs three miles. She feels better after her run. She goes back to the house and takes a shower. When she gets out of the shower, he texts her. Her body is damp. Her short hair is soaking wet and dripping down her back. She grabs her phone, and reads it.

"I wired you some money."

She texts back, "But I thought you already paid for the plane ticket."

He responds, "I sure did. Go buy yourself something nice to wear. I wanna show you some cool spots. So yeah, just something nice, you know, for you. I would get it for you, but I won't be able to because I get off work late. So, buy a few nice sets of clothes for the trip, some nice shoes, and the rest is for the hotel. Book it now."

She gets on the internet and books a room at the Stratosphere since that's the only hotel with the lowest price and seemingly the only room available. It takes her only a few minutes to book the room.

She texts him, "The room is reserved. I will pay it when I get there."

He texts, "Okay. Now go pick up the money and go shopping since you have time."

She texts, "Okay. Leaving now."

She sends a second texts, "I haven't the slightest clue as to what to get."

He texts, "Something nice. It's Vegas. You know a nice dress, if that's what you want to wear and a nice pair of heels or sandals, idk. And another set, something nice, dressy. Something. Take your time, don't rush. I'm sure you're pretty in anything you pick out."

She texts, "Okay."

She indeed doesn't have the first clue where to go for something like that. The only place she can think of is the mall. She drives there and goes to two different stores. She asks one of the sales associates to help her. She picks out three, long, casual, maxi dresses. She tries it on and shows the sales associate her picks. The sales associate asks her where she is going and what the occasion is. She tells the sales associate she's headed to Vegas. The sales associate tells her she doesn't need to say anything more. The sales associates rushes Melissa back into the dressing room and tells her to wait as she has the perfect dresses. She was afraid of that. She has never dressed provocative and knows she's about to go way out of her comfort zone. The sales associates comes back in exactly five minutes and she is much more cheery than before.

The sales associate puts the dresses over the door and says, "With your sexy curves, girl, these are perfect. Try these."

She looks at the first dress. It's a black strapless dress. It looks like something she would maybe wear into a club if she were to seeking to get laid and if not laid, then a lot of attention to the very least.

She looks at the dress and says, "There is no way this tiny sleeve will fit me. No fucking way."

The sales associate overhears Melissa and says, "Girl, you gotta trust yourself. It'll fit you. Just try something new for once, go outside yourself, and see how gorgeous you are. Try it on and come on out. Come on, miss Lady. You going somewhere you have never been and it being Vegas, is not the reason why I picked out those dresses. I picked it because I know you either never trust yourself that you're gorgeous or maybe you're just too busy for you. Once in a great while you gotta wear something out of your comfort zone that makes you feel confident, you know? Something dressy, yet classy, and that's what I chose for you."

She tries it on. She can't believe it. It fits perfectly. She's stunning.

As she looks at herself in the mirror with the dress on, she says, "Oh my God!"

The sales associate asks her to come out. She hesitates. She slowly opens the door. She steps out of the fitting room wearing the little sexy black dress. The sales associate does not say a word. She walks barefoot over to the body mirror against the wall on the other side of the dressing room. She looks at herself up and down. She can't believe what she sees. Her shoulders are exposed.

The dress hugs her body like a wrapped burrito.

The dress proves its' transformation as another sales associate walks by and says, "Ooooh girl! You slammin'! Work it, sexy!"

The dress is midnight black. There are a few sequins on the hem. It gives her breasts a slight sexy lift out from the sweetheart neckline. She can't figure out if that's her boobs enjoying the fresh air or if it's the dress pulling her girls up and out. The dress is short barely covering her curvy and plump butt. Her butt and leg muscles show just how much she works out.

For the first time she sees her hard work of losing all that weight and it's all over her body. Her collar bone is exposed, arms are legs toned, and her butt is a perfect painting of what a butt dreams to look like, round and toned. She was afraid that the dress was too much for her eyes, too much skin to bare, but it turns out she forgot how beautiful she is even when she changes her style. She's overwhelmed by how beautiful she looks in a sexy dress.

The sales associate comes up behind her and says, "Absolutely stunning."

She smiles. She turns and looks at the side of her body.

The sales associate says, "I can see you take good care of your assets."

Melissa remains in awe and utter shock, from the time she tries on the rest of her destined shenanigan gear to when she pays for it, and it becomes hers, she feels so happy.

It takes her a mere thirty minutes to finally leave with her virgin Vegas gear. She doesn't leave with just a pile of material, she leaves with a reminder that no matter what she wears, she's always gorgeous.

She grabs her shopping bags and drives back to the house. She drives with a huge smile on her face. Not even a tsunami could wipe out the smiles and happiness she has. It goes straight to her soul. She's so excited. She's never been so nervous and anxious before, well, at least not like this.

She goes to her bedroom and starts packing. As she's packing something happens.

She falls into a daze. It feels like she can't grasp onto reality. She starts to think, "what if this isn't really happening?"

She pauses.

She says out loud, "Shit, this is really happening."

She thinks to herself, "Oh my god, am I really going to go to the airport? Am I really going to get on a plane? This is so fucking crazy."

She packs her new sets of clothes and shoes—new sandals, a few new dresses, and a sexy, plunging v-neck of a neckline, short shorts of a romper.

She finishes packing.

That night, she is so excited she dreams the most wonderful dream she has every dreamt, but strangely she doesn't remember it when she fully wakes up the next morning and gets ready for the last day of class.

In the dream, she remembers someone laughing with her and a guy buying her a diamond ring, but the dream slowly starts to feel fuzzy. Soon and just as quickly as she dreamt it, it becomes fuzzy and floats away in her bucket of dream memories.

She finishes taking a shower and gets ready. She calls the kids back home, but there is no answer. She calls her aunt, but it goes to her voicemail. She leaves a voicemail asking her aunt to tell her babies she misses them, hopes they're having fun, and to tell Grandma and Cheíí she is doing well. She gets in her SUV and takes the long drive to class.

She feels refreshed and is hyped knowing she'll get her refill of endorphin shots today. She is saddened as it's the last day of class. She is half way to class when her phone rings.

She answers it, "Hey, what's going on? You're not at work?"

"Yeah, I'm at work I just wanted to see how your morning is going."

"It's going really well. My final paper is done and the kids are having so much fun they won't even call me back."

He laughs and says, "That's good. I'm happy the kids are having fun. So I heard you're going to Vegas? So, this guy you're going with? Do you like him? Are you gonna give him some booty?"

She laughs, "No, no booty. And I don't know. I think he thinks he knows the answer to that question. I just can't believe he's doing this. I don't know how to tell him 'thank you'".

He says, "Well, me being a guy, all I can say is you can give him some booty to say 'thank you'."

She laughs and says, "You're stupid. What time are you getting off work?"

He laughs and says, "Probably late, but I gotta go. I just wanted to call and see how your morning is going and don't forget to get yourself something to eat. I gotta go. Talk to you later, bye."

She hangs up the phone and smiles.

She shakes her head, laughs to herself, and says, "Booty, yeah right."

She goes to class and absorbs the last of the secret evidence of alien existence. The butterflies in her tummy settle down.

She gets a coffee and a croissant from the café during the ten minute morning break.

The class concludes early. She is so excited. She can't believe she will be at the airport within just a few hours.

Soon, it's time for her to go to the airport. Her heartbeat becomes frantic. She drives and parks her SUV at the airport parking lot. She grabs her small duffel bag and small backpack and walks inside the airport. She goes through airport security. She walks to her assigned departing gate. She finds a seat. She still has an hour until her plane departs. She walks to one of the steakhouse restaurants and sits at the bar. She can't seem to calm down, so she decides to call her boys and little girl. She finally reaches them. They are so excited they briefly talk to her and quickly hang up the phone on her. She laughs. She gets a beer to calm her nerves. It's not enough to calm her down so she orders another one. Now she can feel herself relaxing, finally.

She goes back to the gate. Soon, its time to board the plane. She lines up with the rest of the airport strangers like sheep going inside the corral and boards the plane.

She walks onto the plane. She decides to sit next to an elderly couple. Everyone boards the plane. She texts her blast from the past. She tells him she is on the plane. He texts her to have a good flight and to text him back when she changes planes. She tells him she will.

Just as she is about to turn her phone on airplane mode, her phone rings. It's her aunt. She answers her phone. She's is so happy. She immediately recognizes the voice on the phone.

The voice says in English. "Hey Lady! How's Albuquerque? How's the weather?"

She laughs and says, "It's nice. Nice weather and Albuquerque is good. How are you Cheíí. Are you having fun with your great-grandkids?"

Cheíí laughs and says in English, "Yes, tons of fun. The house is alive again. I know you're busy, I just wanted to call you and tell you that when it's dark out, you can't see, and when it feels like you can't find your way, the brightness of the moon will shine your way. So, you don't forget that, okay? The moon will take care of you. Through the storm you be might be scared, but at the end of the storm the moon will always be waiting for you. So, don't worry. The moon will always be there for you. Okay, Lady. I gotta go. I love you. Go have fun. Do things to relax and get some good sleep. I'm going to hang up now."

"Okay, Cheíí. I love you."

She smiles and listens to Cheíí hang up the phone. She smiles and turns her phone on airplane mode. She sits in her seat and soon her human body is flying up in the air headed to her destined destination.

Her plane switches in Phoenix. She is still very nervous. She texts her blast from the past her plane landed. The layover is forty-five minutes. He tells her to go get something to eat because by the time he gets to Vegas it will be late. She gets a beer at the local restaurant to help ease her nerves once more. She feels better and boards the next plane.

She decides to sit next to an older couple, again. The couple notices her happiness and excitement and they ask her if she would like to sit next to the window. She happily agrees and tries to take a nap. She is exhausted and tired, but she just can't. She glances beyond the airplane window. She watches the sun set. Soon, the open sky is dark.

The husband says, "Is your last stop Vegas?"

She smiles and answers, "Yes. I'm so excited. I've never been to Vegas."

The wife laughs and says, "Well, it's a three-day weekend, so I'm sure there will be plenty to do. Any shenanigans planned?"

She laughs, "I don't think so. A really good friend of mine invited me. This is the first time I'm actually going to take his advice and do something for myself, I guess."

The husband says, "Yeah, that's always a good thing. Taking time off for you. There's nothing wrong with it."

The wife asks, "What do you do?"

She answers, "I'm in school."

The wife says, "That's nice. What are you going to school for?"

She says, "Criminology."

The Husband says, "That's a good field. What degree are you getting?"

She answers, "Bachelor's, but I really want to go to law school."

The old couple smiles. The husband grabs his wife's hand.

The wife smiles and asks her, "So, this good friend of yours, is he just a friend?"

She smiles, "Yeah, a really good friend. He's really the only friend I have besides Maddy. They've both been there for me. I'm not close to anyone else besides my grandparents. He's always been there for me. I'm glad I have him as a friend. I feel like he's my best friend."

The husband smiles and looks at his wife and says, "That's how it always starts."

She laughs.

The wife looks at her, waves her hand in the air, and says, "Nah, you guys will be more than friends before the weekend is over. Believe me, a woman, knows."

Melissa and the woman's husband laugh.

Seconds later, the plane starts to shake going up and down. The pilot makes an announcement on the intercom they are going through an unexpected storm resulting in high turbulence and no one is allowed to be up and about in the plane.

She feels the anxiety come on as the plane yanks her up and down and the rest of the passengers. Just as she checks her seat belt and tightens it, the cabin lights go out in the entire plane's cabin.

Acknowledgements

This book has developed as a series of important events in the author's life, both positive and negative. As the author, I am eternally grateful to have had the wisdom and humbleness of my Cheíí, Frank Nez. He was the most humble human being I have ever known. Thank you Cheíí for giving me the gift of holding onto my passion to write. I cannot thank you enough and I hope I make you proud. Love always, The Lady.

I would like to include a special note of thanks to all of the little loves in my life—Tyler Denetdale, Nathaniel Denetdale, Daniel Denetdale, Nayeli Rico, Nora Denetdale, and Kaliko Rico. All of you have given me nothing but joy and love in my life. I am so blessed. You always make me laugh. We always have fun. Some of you helped me with parts of the book. Thank you for the moments of enlightenment. I love you.

Thanks to all the wonderful people I have met and are mentioned in this book. In some way, you touched my life enough to play a part in this work. So, thank you.

Finally, I cannot thank my husband enough for the preparation of the manuscript. I am honored and blessed to have someone that loves me so much to believe in my works. Words cannot possibly describe what you have shown me.

Thank you, Elmondo Rico.

With All My Love,

Melissa Marie Denetdale
"The Lady"

Coming Soon

Other works by the author is, of course, the second part of this work. It's going to be just as heart wrenching. The purpose of these works is to reach someone that may be going through the same thing as the author once did. The author wants to tell her readers there is hope. There is the desire to find what you want in life regardless of what obstacles come in the way.

The author is currently working on a book about a young Navajo adult experiencing the transition of becoming an Urban Native entitled, "Surviving College With Your Rez Car". The author has three other books coming and scheduled to be out within 2020/2021 year.

A few entitled, "Yádah-fucking-lá", "College, Kids, and Single AF" and "Boom Wife Boom Life."

The author wants to reach out to younger readers so she's also working on a collection of scary stories, short stories. She is hoping to have 12 volumes of, "Yíi Yáh! Scary Stories of the Rez" written and readily available on Amazon by the end of the 2021 year. The author's goal is to hit mainstream readers so they know a taste of what living on the reservation is like.

So come check it out and add the author on Facebook, Melly Mel Rico. The author greatly appreciates your support and wants you to know that you purchasing book is a great deal to her as you now are officially a fan. So, thank you and stay in touch for her new coming works.

Made in the USA
Coppell, TX
28 May 2023